D1738770

Trotsky, Stalin,
and Socialism

Trotsky, Stalin, and Socialism

Robert V. Daniels

Westview Press

BOULDER • SAN FRANCISCO • OXFORD

Copyright © 1991 by Westview Press, Inc.

Published in 1991 in the United States of America by Westview Press, Inc., 5500 Central Avenue, Boulder, Colorado 80301, and in the United Kingdom by Westview Press, 36 Lonsdale Road, Summertown, Oxford OX2 7EW

Library of Congress Cataloging-in-Publication Data
Daniels, Robert Vincent.
  Trotsky, Stalin, and socialism / Robert V. Daniels.
    p.   cm.
  Includes index.
  ISBN 0-8133-1223-X
  1. Trotsky, Leon, 1879–1940.   2. Stalin, Joseph, 1879–1953.
3. Communism—Soviet Union—History—20th century.   4. Soviet Union—
Politics and government—1917- . I. Title.
HX313.8.T76D36   1991
335.43′0947—dc20   91-17831
                                                                          CIP

Printed and bound in the United States of America

The paper used in this publication meets the requirements
of the American National Standard for Permanence of Paper
for Printed Library Materials Z39.48-1984.

10   9   8   7   6   5   4   3   2   1

Contents

Preface

This book brings together ten of my recent and not-so-recent articles and conference papers bearing on the direction taken early in its history by the Communist regime in Russia. Apart from slight editing to avoid overlapping, change tenses, supply a few missing sources, and improve readability, all items are presented as they were originally written. The individual pieces appear not in the chronological sequence of their writing but according to the dates of their subject matter, so as to underscore the evolution of the Soviet system and its guiding ideas. I have preferred not to attempt any substantive updating of the earlier articles, because the conclusions therein are still valid and because they illustrate the insights that could be arrived at from the sources available at the time of writing.

Explicitly or implicitly the central question among the Communist leaders in the first twenty years of the Soviet system was the meaning of socialism and the proper path to achieve it under Russian conditions. Two leaders stand out as protagonists in this context: one, Leon Trotsky, a virtuoso in matters of theory; the other, Joseph Stalin, a master of political intrigue. The arguments of the former and the actions of the latter go far toward defining the kind of socialism ultimately arrived at in the Soviet Union, the socialism that was the point of departure in the 1980s for reform in the USSR and for revolution in the former satellite countries of Eastern Europe.

The work opens in Chapter 1 with a newly written overview, "Socialism and the Course of Revolution," that explores the interaction in Russia of these two historical categories. Chapter 2, "Trotsky's Conception of the Revolutionary Process," considers the course and conclusions of his thinking about these fundamental questions. This paper was prepared for the conference "Trotsky After Fifty Years," organized by Professors Paul Dukes and Terry Brotherstone at The University of Aberdeen, Scotland, in August 1990. Chapter 3, "The Left Opposition and the Evolution of Soviet Communism," outlines the long series of controversies within the Communist Party of the Soviet Union as Trotsky and the more genuine ideologues struggled for influence and then for survival, during the first Soviet decade, against the relentless counterpoint of postrevolutionary changes in Soviet society. This piece was published in German in the volume *Sozialismusdebatte,* edited by Ulf Wolter (1978). My original English text appears here for the first time. Chapter 4, "Socialist Alternatives in the Trade-Union Controversy," was a paper presented at the international conference on "Russia in the Twentieth Century," held in Moscow, April 1990, by the USSR Academy of Sciences. The chapter details the conceptions of socialism and of Russia's future implied by the proposals of the three factions—Left (Trotsky and Bukharin), Ultra-Left (the Workers' Opposition and the Democratic Centralists), and Right (Lenin, Zinoviev, and Stalin)—in the debate that racked the Communist Party in the winter of 1920–1921.

From the broad perspective of the revolutionary process in Chapters 1 through 4, the focus in the next four chapters moves in toward closer empirical examination of political change in the early Soviet years, starting with the formation of Stalin's machinery of personal power. Chapter 5, "Forging the Apparatus: The Secretariat and the Local Organizations in the Russian Communist Party, 1921–1923," appeared in *American Slavic and East European Review,* vol. 16, no. 1 (February 1957); it was an offshoot of my doctoral dissertation written at the Russian Research Center, Harvard University. Chapter 6, "Evolution of Leadership Selection in the Central Committee, 1917–1927," was my contribution to *Russian Officialdom,* edited by Walter Pintner and Don Rowney (1980). Chapter 7, "Trotsky on Proletarian Democracy and Party Bureaucracy, 1923–1937," details Trotsky's cumulative response to the form that the Communist Party was taking under Stalin's leadership. This study was prepared for the International Trotsky Symposium held in Wuppertal, Germany, in March 1990, under the leadership of Professor Theodor Bergmann.

With Chapter 8, I return to the effort to define in broader terms the emergent Stalinist system. "Soviet Socialism: From Redistribution to Production" was originally published as "Toward a Definition of Soviet Socialism," in *New Politics,* vol. 1, no. 4 (1962). In Chapter 9, "Stalinism as Postrevolutionary Dictatorship," I look again at the question of the revolutionary process, this time to put forth my own analysis of Stalinism in those terms. I presented this paper at the international conference on "The Age of Stalinism," sponsored by the Gramsci Institute and the University of Urbino, Italy, in May 1989. It appeared as "Lo stalinismo come dittatura postrivoluzionaria" in the proceedings of the conference— Aldo Natoli and Silvio Pons, eds., *L'età dello stalinismo* (1991). Chapter 10, "Soviet Thought in the 1930s: The Cultural Counterrevolution," was based on work I did at the Russian Research Center and appeared in *Indiana Slavic Studies,* vol. 1 (1956). It details the antirevolutionary aspects of the Stalinist system as it was consolidated in the mid-1930s. The final chapter, "Stalinist Ideology as False Consciousness," was presented as a paper at the Fourth International Colloquium of the Feltrinelli Foundation on "The Myth of the Soviet Union in Western Culture," held at Cortona, Italy, April 1989, and was published in the proceedings of the colloquium—Marcello Flores and Francesca Gori, eds., *Il mito dell'Urss: La cultura occidentale e l'Unione Sovietica* (1990). This essay spells out the development of the notion of "false consciousness" and its applicability in understanding the contradiction of theory and practice in postrevolutionary Russia.

* * *

The challenges now faced by the peoples of the Soviet Union and Eastern Europe in reconstructing their institutions and redefining their social values are far too complex and challenging to be appreciably eased by mere academic reflections. Yet there are certain self-imposed impediments to the accomplishment of these tasks that might be alleviated by appropriate reconsideration of the past and above all of the problem of the meaning of socialism.

Socialism now is obviously anything but the panacea that it was seen to be in many quarters in the early years of this century. But neither is it the vehicle of all evil that blanket revulsion against the language of the Communist Old Regime makes it appear to be. Everything depends on which of the many possible varieties of socialism one has in mind and on the particular political conditions that accompany it. The burden of past sufferings and disillusionments cannot be exorcised by stamping out one verbal formula in favor of another. If the essays in this work should have any utility in clarifying the nature of the Communist past and in clearing the way for a more humane and pragmatic future, the hopes that went into their preparation will be more than fulfilled.

NOTE ON TRANSLITERATION

In the transliteration of Russian names and terms I use a modified Library of Congress system, using the letter *y* wherever English phonetics require it and retaining conventional spelling of familiar names such as "Trotsky." The term *soviet* (as substantive or attributive) is lowercased when it refers to the governmental bodies rather than the country. Similarly, *communism* and *communist* are lowercased when they refer to the utopian ideal rather than the party and the movement.

Robert V. Daniels

Acknowledgments

I am indebted to many people for ideas, expressed in person or in print, that have contributed to the formulations about the history of the Soviet Union that I put forth in these pages. Even more, I owe a debt of gratitude to the individuals and organizations who originally invited the preparation of the papers and articles included in this work. I also wish to thank Diann Varricchione for a fine job of wordprocessing a difficult manuscript and Susan McEachern of Westview Press for her enthusiastic support and indispensable counsel.

R.V.D.

1

Socialism and
the Course of Revolution

Socialism and revolution are the two commanding themes in the twentieth century history of Russia and the Soviet Union. Together they encompass virtually the entire Russian historical experience of this era. Socialism, in one form or another, embraces the goals and justifications of Russia's rulers and the system of institutions under which the peoples of the Soviet Union have lived. Revolution designates the dynamics of change and conflict that have driven those rulers, institutions, and peoples through decades of terror and hope. The two concepts are inextricably intertwined. Socialism gave the Russian Revolution a faith and intensity unprecedented in past epochs. In turn, the unfolding revolutionary process shaped the Russian practice of socialism into a political and social system unprecedented in its coerciveness and brutality.

In a sense, the Russian Revolution is not over yet. The reforms attempted under Mikhail Gorbachev and their tribulations in a country still far from civil peace all represent facets of the revolution's legacy and efforts to come to terms with it. The same is true of the democratic revolutions in East Central Europe that startled the world in the amazing year 1989, even though these countries knew the Russian Revolution only as an expansive imperialism that forced them into its own rigid mold.

It is natural that people both in the Soviet Union and in the countries of Eastern Europe, breaking with an oppressive and mendacious past, should, no less than the nations of the West who had seen in the Soviet bloc a grave threat to their own way of life, reject that experience as an undifferentiated evil, fortunately irrelevant to their own new hopes. Yet no human group can exist totally disconnected from its history. The Gorbachev Revolution and its galloping extension in Eastern Europe make it all the more compelling to understand the social systems within which these changes were incubated and against which they were directed.

This need is underscored by the mixture of myth and reality in these reactions. Only a critical historical analysis of the Communist regimes, their structure, their development, their ideology, can show what kind of a political and social system has actually arisen, prevailed, and failed in this part of the world. Surface perceptions of that discredited system—among the people concerned as well as outsiders—must be measured against the historical reality. Central to this task of understanding is the term by which the old Communist regimes described themselves, and under which their former subjects now include everything they repudiate—namely, socialism.

Socialism is a concept encompassing a great range of forms, both in theory and in practice, that vary widely in degree and method. All that is essential to the idea was long ago summed up by Emile Durkheim: "We denote as socialism every doctrine which demands the connection of all economic functions, or of certain among them . . . to the directing and conscious centers of society."[1] Only one very important thing is missing from this formulation—the sense of the just cause in pursuit of a better society that has animated (or justified) all socialist movements since their first appearance a century and a half ago. Put differently, socialism is the conventional term for various forms of the urge to overcome the domination of the many by the few on the basis of the economic power of private property, and for the conviction that such a transformation would realize a new moral order.

This understanding of socialism does not attempt to set up a certain standard type to the exclusion of all others. Both in theory and in practice socialism may be either partial or complete; gradual or sudden; peaceful or violent; democratic or dictatorial. The common identification of socialism with Marxism and usually with Soviet practice should not be permitted to exclude from the category of socialism other possibilities, both in the past and in the future, that do not take either Marxism or the Soviet experience as their guide.

It was not particularly inevitable or even logical for Marxism to become the ideology of victorious socialism in Russia. The Marxist belief in the industrial proletariat did not fit Russia, with its overwhelming mass of backward peasants, nearly as well as did the philosophy of Russian populism that inspired the Party of Socialist Revolutionaries. Marxism was either vague or utopian about the future socialist society. It never came to terms with its own inconsistency as regards the determining role of capitalist industrialization versus the voluntaristic role of inspired revolutionaries in the making of a socialist revolution. Under the Soviet regime Marxism proved to be a difficult framework on which to hang the justification of revolutionary politics and postrevolutionary rule.

The meaning of socialism, both theoretical and applied, was deeply affected in Russia by the experience of revolution. Revolution, as a far-reaching and violent upheaval in the political and social order, was a well-known phenomenon in the history of the West long before its manifestation in Russia. Indeed, the revolutionary experience was familiar before the idea of socialism was ever formulated except in the most ethereal philosophical speculations. Russia in the twentieth century was the setting for the fusion of revolution and socialism, socialism posing the goal for revolution, revolution offering the vehicle for the realization of socialism. In this combination, revolution profoundly affected the understanding of socialism, the form of its implementation, and the peculiar relation between Marxist theory and Soviet practice. As far as the original ideal of socialism is concerned, its identification with the Russian Revolution may be the worst thing that could have happened to it.

To grasp this point, it must be realized—as Trotsky, virtually alone among Marxists, came to see—that revolution is not a momentary event but a long process. It is not just an act of insurrectionary will, but a deeply rooted crisis in a given society's history. The Emperor Napoleon observed, in his reflections in exile, "A revolution can be neither made nor stopped."[2] Revolution hardly ever works out as those who initially lead it intend. As Friedrich Engels wrote, "People who boasted that they had *made* a revolution have always seen the next day that they had no idea what they were doing, that the revolution *made* did not in the least resemble the one they would have liked to make."[3]

Revolutions typically begin with high hopes for social justice without violence, and most articulate Russians in 1917 were socialists in this sense. But the early liberal ideals of the revolution are quickly undercut by counterrevolutionary resistance on the one hand and radical impetuousness on the other. In Russia the radicals—the Bolsheviks—with their fanatical commitment to a still unrefined vision of socialism, with their "revolutionary illusions and revolutionary impatience," as a Soviet historian recently described them,[4] prevailed in one of history's nastiest examples of civil war. Only then was their revolutionary enthusiasm tempered by realization of the circumstances of their venture. Russia's backwardness, "the absence of developed democratic traditions, the low level of political culture of the people," according to another Soviet writer,[5] confronted the Bolsheviks with the need for a very long-term effort to hold power while sustaining their revolutionary faith and advancing toward some form of the future that they might still call socialist. All this required major adjustments in the relationship between theory and practice, modifying practice to accommodate the needs of the postrevolutionary regime, and adapting theory so as to maintain the legitimacy of this regime while its goals were being postponed or reformulated.

*   *   *

In the attempt to fit the spirit of Marxian socialism to the evolving reality of the revolutionary regime in Russia, two figures stand out. These were, of course, Trotsky and Stalin, the one distinguishing himself as the theorist of socialism under revolutionary Russian conditions, the other as the power-wielding shaper of the particular form of socialism that was to prevail for more than half a century in postrevolutionary Russia. Brought together, Stalin's political practice and Trotsky's theoretical critique of it afford an unequalled angle of vision for understanding the point of departure for the Gorbachev reforms and the East European revolutions of the later 1980s.

The Stalinist system against which the reformers of the 1980s were reacting was certainly a form of socialism within the limits defined by Durkheim, but it was a peculiar and unanticipated form. Furthermore it had been dressed up with a version of socialist theory that diverged radically from the old socialist tradition, though the divergence could never be acknowledged. Consequently the real nature of the Stalinist system is very difficult to get at except by following its historical development during the first two decades of the Soviet state. To this end, the works of Trotsky intellectually and the accomplishments of Stalin politically are keys to the postrevolutionary regime that, as the dialectic ran its course, eventually became the *ancien régime* of a new upheaval.

*   *   *

A framework for a developmental approach to revolutionary systems and ideas emerges from Trotsky's own works. Trotsky was unusual as a practitioner of revolution who managed to work out in the heat of combat a creative view of the actions in which he himself was an outstanding participant. He tried to understand the forces that were carrying the Russian Revolution in an unexpected direction, even though his attachment to the inappropriate doctrines of Marxism made this an elusive objective. Nevertheless, in the course of his career, from fiery challenger of the Old Regime, to bold and ruthless leader in a revolutionary government, to floundering oppositionist and exiled Enemy of the People, Trotsky's cumulative attempts at the analysis of events brought him to a comprehensive grasp of the nature and ironies of the revolutionary process.

A critical point in the relationship between socialism and revolution came during the Russian Civil War, when the Bolsheviks' drive to establish a socialist society by military methods reached the point of exhaustion and imminent defeat. This crisis was reflected in the bitter debate that broke out within the Communist leadership late in 1920, ostensibly over the role of the trade unions in the revolutionary system, but implicitly over the whole strategy of achieving socialism.

In most revolutions, at the point of maximum radical fervor, the leadership divides between those who are sustained more by utopian vision, and those whose eyes are mainly on victory and power. In Russia the utopians were represented by the idealists of the Workers' Opposition and the "Group of Democratic Centralists" (actually anticentralists). Reacting against the centralized and coercive system of War Communism that had been embraced by the Communist Party in the struggle for revolutionary survival, this left wing of the Party proposed to put the entire administration of the Russian economy in the hands of the trade unions. Thereby the country would advance immediately and democratically toward the socialist ideal as the Ultra-Left conceived it. Trotsky and his supporters rejected this position as utopian, and urged the opposite tactical approach: militarization of labor and the "governmentalizing" of the unions to press the drive toward socialism by an intensification of command and discipline. Lenin, however, feeling his way toward an exit from the premature and discredited aspirations of War Communism, encouraged his more compliant lieutenants such as Zinoviev and Stalin to stake out a third position, assigning the unions a role of workers' defense like their function under capitalism. Consistent with this approach he prepared a "strategic retreat" from the revolutionary rigors of War Communism to the semi-capitalist measures of the New Economic policy. He could not acknowledge that this retrenchment would amount to the "Thermidor" of the revolutionary process in Russia, but nevertheless he accepted the fact that the goal of socialism would require a long preparatory period.

The long bout of accusations and counteraccusations that broke out among the Communist leadership following the onset of Lenin's terminal illness in 1922 has usually been understood as a simple struggle for power between the chief protagonists, Trotsky and Stalin. In fact, Trotsky hopelessly lost his hold on the levers of power at the very beginning of the contest. The primary significance of the Left Opposition of 1923–1927 is not as a politically viable alternative to Stalinism, but as a record, expressed through its escalating protests, of the actual evolution of the powers and policies of the Soviet regime during the years when Stalin was rising to a position of personal dominance.

Decisive in Stalin's rise and in his defeat first of the Trotskyists and then of the Bukharinists was the use that he made of the organizational machinery of the Communist Party. Working from his position as General

Secretary of the Party after 1922, Stalin used the powers of the Secretariat to make the party structure more thoroughly hierarchical and bureaucratic, and then to manipulate the Party's nominally democratic committees and conferences at all levels, culminating in the nationwide party congresses that met annually (up to 1924) and elected the party leadership. In this manner Stalin created what I have termed a "circular flow of power," down through the party secretaries at each level, over to the committees and conferences, and up to the congress where Stalin dictated the membership of the Central Committee that confirmed him in his own job. From a team of well-known revolutionary publicists and agitators he turned the Central Committee into the sort of top-level bureaucratic status body that had long existed in one form or another under the Tsarist regime. All this illustrates how Stalin transformed the Communist regime from a revolutionary dictatorship into a postrevolutionary despotism.

Meanwhile, political adversity had a direct effect on Trotsky's thinking, not only about the process of revolution in general but about the ways and means of constructing socialism. His position of coercive authoritarianism during the Civil War naturally led many outside observers and more recently some in the Soviet Union itself to regard him as a Stalinist before Stalin and a forerunner of Stalin's industrialization and collectivization program. Stalin's recent biographer General Dmitri Volkogonov writes of his "methods of compulsion, violence, orders, which in his own time Trotsky shared."[6] But after 1921, Trotsky turned by stages into a champion of democracy (only within the Communist Party, to be sure, until near the end) and became an ardent foe of the progressive bureaucratization that he saw eating at the foundations of the workers' state.

Unfortunately, these reconsiderations were too little and too late. Hiding behind Nikolai Bukharin and the proponents of the gradualist approach to socialism that Lenin intended by the NEP, Stalin isolated and humbled his opponents on the Left, first the Trotskyists, then the Zinovievists, then the two groups together. These victories put him in a position to turn against the gradualists and, freed from the constraints of opponents who could challenge his redrawing of the revolutionary road map, to launch his own "revolution from above." In terms of the revolutionary process, this was "Soviet Bonapartism," the postrevolutionary synthesis of revolutionary forms and rhetoric with traditional, authoritarian values and methods of coercive rule. In terms of socialism, it was an experiment that gave the term an altogether new meaning.

Until the onset of the "Stalin Revolution" in 1929, all schools of socialist thought, however different in approach, had the same purpose in mind: namely, the achievement of distributive justice in society. Stalin's purposes, infused into the Five-Year Plans of intensive industrialization and the forcible collectivization of the peasants, were quite different: the use of the planning and administrative power of the socialist state to build national productive capacity and bolster the great-power status of the Soviet Union. In other words, he set out to pursue the tasks of industrialization that Marxists up to then had accorded to the capitalist system as it prepared the preconditions for its own revolutionary demise. In short, classical distributive socialism was replaced by what may simply be called "production socialism." In place of individual justice, national and personal power became the ultimate values to be served by socialism. To be sure, this was not the only way for the nation to advance, not even the most effective, and certainly not the most humane, but there was a certain perverse logic to it: to attack Russia's backwardness with the blunt instrument of totalitarianism.

Following his implementation of a new model of socialism, Stalin undertook systematically to revise or replace the entire array of social goals and cultural norms that had accompanied the Soviet experiment until the 1930s. This cultural counterrevolution is a relatively neglected aspect of Stalinism, but it is of major importance in understanding the nature of the postrevolutionary dictatorship in the USSR against which the reactions of the 1980s were directed. The net effect of the Stalin Revolution, reversing old orthodoxies and purging their authors while guarding the revolutionary vocabulary as the vehicle for all public discourse, went far toward bringing the trajectory of the Russian Revolution into line with the French model of revolutionary degeneration into Bonapartism and even with the precedent of monarchist restoration, provided we understand latter-day Stalinism as its functional rather than literal equivalent.

A totally hypothetical but intriguing question is the outcome that might have come about if the late Stalinist model of bureaucratic socialism in economics plus conservative social and cultural policies could have been operated without the secrecy, mendacity, and terror associated politically with Stalin. Institutionally the system would have thrown a bridge between old Russian political culture and the Weberian bureaucratic trend of modern industrial society, both looking to organized hierarchies to manage society's public functions. But no faction in the early Soviet years understood the alternatives this way. The Left Opposition to 1927, and the Right Opposition in 1928–1929, condemned the bureaucratic monster wherever they saw it, as the enemy of any independent thinking or democratic procedure. Stalin, for his part, embracing the bureaucratic trend without fully acknowledging it, could not tolerate any such freedom or honesty about his system. He gladly accepted the burden of thought control to square everything he did with Marxism.

The form and purpose that socialism was finally given under Stalin bring us back to the problematic of the base line for the revolutions of the late 1980s. We can see now that the system Stalin bequeathed to his neo-Stalinist successors was a form of militarized socialism under a postrevolutionary dictatorship, trying to address the unfinished agenda of modernization with methods that combined old Russian autocracy and revolutionary expediency. There is a simple formula, familiar in Marxist writings though actually drawn from just a single letter by Engels, that illuminates the meaning of Communist ideology and the conception of socialism in this system. Marxism-Leninism is the ideological "false consciousness" of a system of developmental, production socialism dominated by the bureaucratic "New Class" and ruled in the characteristic modern form of postrevolutionary dictatorship, i.e., totalitarianism.

*   *   *

In many respects the era of reform under Gorbachev was a time of return to revolutionary origins, though there was no unanimity among the reformers as to the proper model to be found there. Everyone seemed to be seeking some point where history took a wrong turn, in hopes that the country could somehow return to the past and start over again on a better path.

The earlier spokesmen for reform, including Gorbachev himself, found their inspiration in the NEP as an experiment in decentralized, market-based socialism. Gorbachev proclaimed at the Central Committee's "ideological plenum" in February 1988, "We are seeking to revive the Leninist look of the new system . . . , to free it of everything that has fettered society and prevented it from fully realizing the potential of socialism."[7] Nikolai Shmelev and Vladimir Popov write in this vein, "*Perestroika* is a return to the Leninist norms of economic management that were the basis of the economic system in the 1920s. . . . NEP is an extremely rich source that can guide the implementation of today's reforms."[8]

In July 1989 a conference of top social scientists observed, "The concept of socialism as a social system presupposes the existence of a number of 'models' (variants) of development," and attributed to Lenin the recognition that "the country could be bound together into a whole either through a bureaucratic mechanism of noneconomic compulsion or through the market." Unfortunately, "Lenin's hopes for truly profound changes in the economic and political system were not realized. . . . The 'war communism' option for development was revived in the form of the "Stalinist model of socialism."[9] Gorbachev picked up the theme of "multiple variants" and asserted, "The founders of Marxism and the theory they created cannot bear responsibility for the perversion of socialism during the years of the personality cult and of stagnation, for the erroneous actions of various political leaders." Instead, he maintained, "Restructuring translates the original principles of the revolution into reality, for in the past they were for the most part merely proclaimed," with the interesting proviso, "these principles themselves and the criteria for determining *degrees of socialism* that are based on them must be spelled out in concrete terms."[10]

Gorbachev and his conservative opponents within the Soviet leadership had one point in common, namely their refusal to give up their attachment to something they could call socialism, however differently they defined it. More recent and more radical reform advocates rejected socialism altogether, though they did not take issue with the role of the state in the protection of individuals from untoward excesses in the operation of the free market. "Socialism," writes the political scientist Aleksandr Tsipko,

> is precisely that historically unique society that is consciously built, on the basis of a theoretical plan. . . . The defects in the structure are not just due to Stalin's departures from the original blueprint for socialism . . . , they also represent departures of theoretical thinking from life, its inability to fully anticipate the future. . . . Stalin's thinking and his idea of socialism were typical for Marxists of that time.

Tsipko cites thinkers as diverse as Bukharin and Dostoevsky on "the danger that awaits a society that attempts to subordinate its entire life to the dictates of an abstract theory. . . . Stalinism . . . is bound up with the deepest motives of political activism and of the revolutionary socialist intelligentsia's beliefs."[11]

Unfortunately, the effort to fashion a new model of socialism during the first half-dozen years of perestroika was not successful from any point of view. Weakening of the Stalinist planning and control mechanisms led not to a burst of initiative from below, but instead to economic anarchy. Reform thus came up against the realities of political and economic culture that Stalinism had accommodated in its own way. However much they might long subjectively for freedom, Russians in the mass seem disinclined to work efficiently and responsibly without commands from on high.

Nevertheless, the path has been opened for the Soviet peoples to reconsider all the alternatives as well as the obstacles that history has presented them with at various points in their past. This includes reassessment of the socialist heritage, freed finally both from the radical utopianism of the revolutionary years and from the deceitful doctrinal manipulations of the Stalin era.

Notes

1. Emile Durkheim, *Socialism and Saint-Simon* (1928; London: Routledge & Kegan Paul, 1959), p. 9.

2. J. Christopher Herold, ed., *The Mind of Napoleon: A Selection from His Written and Spoken Words* (New York: Columbia University Press, 1956), p. 64.

3. Engels to Vera Zasulich, 23 April 1885, Karl Marx and Friedrich Engels, *Selected Correspondence, 1846–1895* (New York: International Publishers, 1942), pp. 437–438.

4. V. Sirotkin, "Uroki NEPa" (Lessons of the NEP), *Izvestiya*, 9 March 1989, *Current Digest of the Soviet Press*, XLI:10 (5 April 1989), p. 6.

5. V. S. Lipitsky, "Sotsializm obetovannyi" (The Socialism of the Promised Land), *Voprosy Istorii KPSS*, no. 12, 1990, p. 69.

6. Dmitri Volkogonov, *Triumf i tragediya: Politicheskii portret I. V. Stalina* (2 vols. in 4 books, Moscow: Novosti, 1989), vol. I, book 2, p. 23.

7. M. S. Gorbachev, Speech at the Plenary Session of the CPSU Central Committee, 18 February 1988, *Pravda*, 19 February 1988, *Current Digest of the Soviet Press*, XL:7 (16 March 1988), p. 4.

8. Nikolai Shmelev and Vladimir Popov, *The Turning Point: Revitalizing the Soviet Economy* (New York: Doubleday, 1989), pp. 3, 21.

9. Summary, "K sovremennoi kontseptsii sotsializma" (Toward a Contemporary Conception of Socialism), in *Pravda*, 14 July 1989, *Current Digest of the Soviet Press*, XLI:31 (30 August 1989), p. 4. Cf. Yu. Olshevich, "Most k dvadtsat' pervomu veku" (Bridge to the Twenty-first Century), *Pravda*, 12 October 1989, *Current Digest of the Soviet Press*, XLI:41 (8 November 1989), pp. 4–6.

10. Gorbachev, "Sotsialisticheskaya ideya i revoliutsionnaya perestroika" (The Socialist Idea and Revolutionary Restructuring), *Pravda*, 26 November 1989, *Current Digest of the Soviet Press*, XLI:48 (27 December 1989), p. 19. Italics mine.

11. Aleksandr Tsipko, "Korni stalinizma" (The Roots of Stalinism), *Nauka i Zhizn'*, no. 11 and 12, 1988, *Current Digest of the Soviet Press*, XLI:10 (5 April 1989), pp. 3–4, no. 11 (12 April 1989), pp. 13, 15.

2

Trotsky's Conception
of the Revolutionary Process

Half a century after Trotsky's death, with the idea of Communism in full retreat everywhere, it is difficult to consider revolutionary leaders as anything but misguided fanatics. Yet Trotsky stands out uniquely among major revolutionaries in articulating a broad theory of the nature of revolution, *pari passu* with his own political career. Obviously much of what he had to say, especially after the Soviet regime was established, was for purposes of polemics or self-justification. Nevertheless he was making a serious effort to understand the events in which he was involved and by which he was ultimately destroyed.

Was there any merit in that effort? How valid were Trotsky's insights into the course of the Russian Revolution, measured against the nature of the revolutionary process as it is more broadly known to history? I believe that in endeavoring to come to terms with the peculiarities of revolution in Russia, Trotsky transcended the limitations of his Marxist faith, and approached, step by step, the conception of revolution as a long but interconnected process of political and social struggle.

The understanding of revolution as a process was widely developed by numerous Western writers during the first two decades following the Russian Revolution, after the upheaval in Russia impressed upon them its parallels with the French Revolution. Robert Lansing, American Secretary of State under President Woodrow Wilson, foresaw for Russia, "First, moderation; second, terrorism; third, revolt against the new tyranny and restoration of order by arbitrary military power."[1] The notion of revolution as a natural sequence of distinct stages, punctuated by violence, was given academic form by the American church historian Lyford P. Edwards.[2] Following Edwards, the well-known historian Crane Brinton proposed a medical image of the phenomenon: "We shall regard revolutions . . . as a kind of fever. . . . This works up, not regularly but with advances and retreats, to a crisis, frequently accompanied by delirium. . . . Finally the fever is over, and the patient is himself again, perhaps in some respects actually strengthened by the experience, immunized at least for a while from a similar attack, but certainly not wholly made over into a new man."[3]

In the perspective of the process theory, revolution is not an event but a complex chain of causes and effects, as one state of affairs leads to another over a period of years.[4] In contrast to a mere coup, a true revolution involves a general political breakdown and a progression of violent action through discernible stages, from the moderate to the extreme, followed by retreat and consolidation. A revolution of this sort is a profound structural crisis in the development of a country, typically brought on by a pace of social change—i.e., modernization—that a rigid traditionalist government cannot accommodate. Contrary to what revolutionaries have usually assumed, revolution is not a planable, elective political tactic available whenever they choose to resort to it, nor do its ultimate results necessarily or even usually conform to the intentions of those who endorse it.

By the test of the process model, the Marxist theory of revolution, which the Russian Social Democrats including Trotsky took as their starting point, is entirely inadequate. Marxism makes much of revolution as the transfer of power from one class to another, but devotes little theoretical attention to the way revolutions actually unfold.[5] Revolution as the simple displacement of classes is belied by the mix of social elements, interests, and ideas in every actual revolution. More importantly, classical Marxism misses the essential nature of revolution as a complex and extended process. It offers no conception of the natural sequence of stages in the revolution. Further, Marxism misstates the causal conditions for revolution, seeing them as the full development of the old social system. In Marx's famous words, "No social order ever disappears before all the productive forces for which there is room in it have been developed."[6] Thus the flowering of capitalism is believed to be the precondition for the next revolution (which is assumed without proof to be "proletarian"). Actually history shows revolution to be most likely at an intermediate point in the modernization process as it affects a given country, when the tempo of change is at its maximum and expectations have risen beyond the particular country's capacity to satisfy them. It is not true, as Marx believed, that "mankind always takes up only such problems as it can solve."[7] Revolutions invariably overreach, beyond what the material conditions and psychological development of the given society will support, and hence must inevitably, sooner or later, go into retreat.

*   *   *

It is a familiar paradox that Russian radicals were attracted to Marxism at the turn of the century by its quasi-scientific laws of progress toward utopia, despite the difficulty in applying the doctrine to a country deemed unready for proletarian revolution and socialism. The attraction of Marxism was not logical but psychological, and psychology governed as well the ways in which different Russian Marxists addressed the problem of the waiting period between the still unachieved bourgeois revolution and the ultimate proletarian revolution. The Mensheviks, including most of the older leaders of the Social-Democratic movement, were prepared to play the loyal opposition while Russia accomplished the requisite capitalist development—a position of correct Marxism but of fatal politics, as matters turned out. Lenin and his Bolsheviks, determined to lead the workers to power without delay, bent their Marxism to fit their own psychic requirements, by asserting that the proletariat would have an immediate role in taking over the bourgeois revolution from its weak middle-class sponsors and then in presiding over the country while economic development caught up with political.

Lenin was never one to acknowledge his revisions of Marx. But he foresaw in 1905 that the workers would take over the bourgeois-democratic revolution, "when the bourgeoisie recoils from it and when the masses of the peasantry come out as active revolutionaries side by side with the proletariat," to create the "revolutionary-democratic dictatorship of the proletariat and the peasantry."[8] He was in fact beginning to recognize revolution as a complex, multi-stage process, a process, moreover, which could carry the political regime to a point beyond what the socio-economic development of the country would normally sustain.

It fell to Trotsky to carry this modification of the Marxian concept of revolution to a bold new statement of the complex revolutionary process in Russia. This was his famous "theory of permanent revolution," or "uninterrupted revolution," as he himself originally styled it, that he worked out, first as a participant-observer in the Revolution of 1905, and then during the leisure of imprisonment following those events.[9] Prompted by his friend of those years, the German Social-Democrat Alexander Helphand, alias "Parvus," Trotsky undertook to assess the social forces which had manifested themselves in Russia in that abortive upheaval, and to justify an immediate radical role for the workers.[10]

The terms of the theory are familiar to all students of twentieth-century Russian history. In brief, "permanent revolution" held that in Russia, because of the "law of uneven development" or "combined development," the workers had become a revolutionary force while the middle class still vacillated and the peasant mass waited for leadership. Consequently, a bourgeois revolution would lead in an uninterrupted development to intervention by the workers to secure their socialist demands. "Within the limits of a revolution at the beginning of the twentieth century, which is also a bourgeois revolution in its immediate objective aims, there looms up a prospect of an inevitable, or at least possible, supremacy of the working class in the near future."[11] Inadvertently, in a compound class theory designed for Russia alone, Trotsky had grasped the nature of revolution as an unfolding process leading through various stages. His bourgeois revolution corresponded to the moderate phase in the Brintonian model of revolution, and the proletarian takeover corresponded to the extremist phase. "Above all," writes John Molyneux, Trotsky "perceived that the revolution was an historical process which, once unleashed, could not be stopped half way."[12]

Trotsky furthermore sensed, in the Russian case at least, that the process would temporarily carry extremist politics to a point more advanced than the nation would indefinitely sustain. Actually this was not a peculiarly Russian problem but a phenomenon of any revolution, since all societies caught up in a revolutionary crisis have manifested "uneven development." Therefore, barring external factors, the revolution would inevitably be set back in a step Trotsky was later to equate with the Thermidorean reaction. However, he hoped that defeat for the workers in Russia would be averted by a *deus ex machina*, the international proletarian revolution that he believed would be triggered in the mature industrial countries by the Russian example. This prognosis gave the uninterrupted or permanent revolution an international dimension as well: "The political emancipation of Russia led by the working class will raise that class to a height as yet unknown in history . . . , will make it the initiator of the liquidation of world capitalism."[13]

This argument was not Marxism but Russian messianism. Nevertheless, it eventually gave the Bolsheviks of 1917 their theoretical rationale for seizing power. When the forecast proved wrong, they were left in the sensitive position where their political legitimacy depended on revolutionary events abroad. According to Trotsky's theory, the failure to win revolutionary support abroad portended the inevitable decay of the workers' regime in Russia. Coming to terms with this implication was the central problem in Trotsky's later thinking about revolution.

*   *   *

Trotsky's theory of permanent or uninterrupted revolution in its internal, Russian sense was borne out with amazing precision by the sequence of revolutionary events in 1917. This was one of the rare historical instances where reality validated theory and was in turn steered by the adherents of the theory. A moderate revolution ascribed to the bourgeoisie unleashed a revolutionary mobilization of the worker and peasant masses and ended in an extremist take-over, which its beneficiaries chose to style a proletarian revolution. In line with his theory, Trotsky was able to predict in March 1917, "The Russian Revolution will not stop. . . . The Revolution will make a clean sweep of the bourgeois liberals blocking its way, as it is now making a clean sweep of the Tsarist reaction."[14]

The October Revolution was accomplished by a party explicitly or implicitly sharing the premises of "permanent revolution." Lenin's embrace of this viewpoint was what shocked his followers when he returned to Russia in April 1917: "The present situation in Russia . . . represents a *transition* from the first stage of the revolution—which . . . placed the power in the hands of the bourgeoisie—*to the second* stage, which must place the power in the hands of the proletariat and the poorest strata of the peasantry."[15] Nikolai Bukharin told the clandestine Bolshevik congress in August 1917, "We are going to have a great new upsurge of the revolutionary wave . . . , the declaration of a revolutionary war. . . . By such a revolutionary war we will light the fire of world socialist revolution."[16] Disbelief in such Russian messianism was what lay behind the opposition of Grigory Zinoviev and Lev Kamenev to the armed seizure of power in the October Revolution.[17]

No modesty inhibited Trotsky from proclaiming his prescience when he wrote shortly afterwards, "The standpoint he [the author, Trotsky, in 1906] then supported can be outlined as follows: The Revolution, having begun as a bourgeois revolution as regards its first tasks, will soon call forth powerful class conflicts and will gain final victory only by transferring power to the only class capable of standing at the head of the oppressed masses, namely, to the proletariat."[18] As the mechanism of this shift he saw a suddenly accelerated process of social psychology, going beyond the classic Marxist framework: "The significance of the revolution lies in the rapid changing of the judgment of the masses, in the fact that new and ever new strata of population acquire experience, verify [i.e. test] their views of the day before, sweep them aside, work out new ones, desert old leaders and follow new ones in the forward march."[19] He now recognized the same process of a grand "sweep" or "ascending line" at work in the French Revolution, worked out through the politics of "dual power": "By the steps of the dual power the French Revolution rises in the course of four years to its culmination."[20] In the Russian case, Trotsky affirmed the crucial role of the Bolshevik Party and its leadership (including himself) in consummating the extremist victory, but he conceded later on, "The most favorable conditions for an insurrection exist, obviously, when the maximum shift in our favor has occurred in the relation of forces . . . in the domain of consciousness." The party had to seize the crucial moment, because "during revolution all these processes take place with lightning speed."[21]

Throughout the violent period of civil war, terror, and utopian experiment from 1918 to 1921, known appropriately as War Communism, Trotsky continued to view the struggle as a validation of his theory, and the theory as a justification of the revolutionary dictatorship. "The events in which we are now participating," he wrote in 1919, "and even our methods of participating in them, were foreseen in their fundamental lines some fifteen years ago."[22] Critics of Bolshevik extremism—notably the Mensheviks and Western Social Democrats like Karl Kautsky—were, as far as Trotsky was concerned, traitors to the working class. In his theoretical scheme of revolution there was no distinction between the sequence of class stages—from bourgeois to proletarian—and the sequence of revolutionary methods—from moderate to extremist: "The question as to who is to rule the country, i.e., of the life or death of the bourgeoisie, will be decided on either side, not by references to the paragraphs of the constitution, but by the employment of all forms of violence."[23] Trotsky was convinced that everything the Bolshevik regime did was necessitated by the circumstance of a workers' government in Russia struggling to hold out against all the forces of bourgeois reaction until the world revolution would itself be touched off by that struggle.

With the failure of world revolution to materialize after the high hopes of 1919, and the crystallization of powerful opposition—especially peasant—to the regime of War Communism, the Bolshevik leadership had to reconsider not only their tactics but the whole theoretical rationale of their regime. Up to this point messianic notions about the international impact of their revolutionary example had spared them from hard thoughts about the later course of the revolution. But Trotsky had given a clear warning back in 1906 of what would happen to the workers' government if the world revolution should somehow fail them. As he recognized in retrospect, "War Communism had exhausted itself. Agriculture and with it everything else had arrived in a blind alley. . . . It was a crisis of the whole system of War Communism."[24] The outcome, of course, was the New Economic Policy, which Lenin introduced in 1921 with the concurrence of the entire party leadership including Trotsky.

The introduction of the NEP made immediate the question of where the revolutionary process would lead to in Russia after its phase of Jacobin-Bolshevik extremism. To certain outside observers the trend was clear: "With the New Economic Policy of 1921 began Russia's Thermidor," Brinton wrote.[25] The main anomaly was that this "strategic retreat" (as Lenin called it) from the pinnacle of revolutionary zeal was self-executed, not imposed by a coup d'état. The Mensheviks, including Yulii Martov, immediately recognized the Thermidorean parallel.[26] Kautsky, whose writings as a publicist seem more insightful than his theorizing, even predicted such a self-initiated shift. He wrote as early as 1919, "Lenin's government is threatened by another 9th Thermidor . . . in some other way. . . . It is not impossible that the collapse of the communist experiment in Russia may equally transform the Bolsheviks, and save them as a governing party. . . . The Bolsheviks have developed the art of adaptation to circumstances in the course of their rule to a remarkable degree."[27]

*   *   *

The most peculiar aspect of the Soviet Thermidor was the inability of the Soviet leadership to recognize their own move for what it was, despite—or perhaps because of—their own identification with the Jacobins. Trotsky did admit at the time that the party had made concessions to "the Thermidor moods and tendencies of the petty-bourgeois," though he could not imagine a real Thermidor except as the violent overthrow of the radical party by outright counterrevolutionaries, with the restoration of capitalism.[28] He insisted, "Historical analogies with the Great French Revolution (the fall of the Jacobins) made by liberalism and Menshevism for their own nourishment and consolation, are superficial and inconsistent."[29] Only when he found himself slipping out of the inner circle as the succession struggle began in 1923, did Trotsky awaken, and then not to a Thermidor already accomplished, but only to the possibility of "Thermidorean influences."[30] In his slashing attack on the party leadership in late 1923, particularly in his "New Course" articles, Trotsky called for a campaign to preserve the revolutionary spirit against the encroachments of "bureaucratism," and warned, "The internal social contradictions of the revolution which were automatically compressed under War Communism . . . under the NEP unfold unfailingly and seek to find political expression." Replying to Menshevik predictions of an anti-Bolshevik coup comparable to the overthrow of Robespierre, he insisted that the Russian Revolution still had its strong proletarian base with peasant support, and would be sustained by an "inevitable extension of the revolution" throughout Europe. Nevertheless, he warned that a recrudescence of capitalistic elements under the NEP could lead to "either the direct overthrowal of the workers' party or its progressive degeneration."[31]

Trotsky's hints of a possible Thermidorean tendency within the Communist regime were particularly galling to the leadership, who sought some way of countering him in the arena of theory as well as by direct political pressure. One result was Stalin's celebrated "theory of socialism in one country," designed to argue with appropriately culled quotations from Lenin that the Soviet regime was in no danger of losing its proletarian purity, because it did not after all need the world revolution in order to hold out in Russia as a genuine workers' state.[32] Another tactic was to turn French revolutionary analogy against Trotsky by accusing him, as commissar of war, of representing a threat of Bonapartism. This charge served to justify his removal from that strategic post in 1925.

In 1926 and 1927, after he had allied himself with Zinoviev and Kamenev for the last-ditch fight against Stalin and Bukharin, Trotsky responded to the growing repression of opposition with more and more shrill charges against the party leadership. At the same time, he expressed a new pessimism about the revolutionary process. In a diary entry of November 1926 he noted, "Revolutions have always in history been followed by counterrevolutions. Counterrevolutions have always thrown society back, but never as far back as the starting point of the revolution." Accordingly, "In a sense the hopes engendered by the revolution are always exaggerated. This is due to the mechanics of class society. . . . The conquests gained in the struggle do not correspond, and in the nature of things cannot *directly* correspond, with the expectations of the broad backward masses." Here was the extraordinary admission by Trotsky that all revolutions are naturally premature in relation to the availability of resources to carry out their promises. Revolution could outrun its base thanks to temporary political momentum: "The awakening of the broad backward masses upsets the ruling classes from their accustomed equilibrium, deprives them of direct support as well as confidence, and thus enables the revolution to seize a great deal more than it is later able to hold." But the backswing was sooner or later hard to escape: "The disillusionment of these masses, their return to routine and futility is . . . an integral part of the postrevolutionary period."[33]

This new fatalistic sense of the revolutionary process Trotsky tried to throw in the teeth of the party leadership during his last stand before expulsion and exile. Defending himself before the pro-Stalin Central Control Commission in the summer of 1927, he invoked the full cycle of the French revolutionary model:

In the Great French Revolution there were two great chapters, of which one went like this [points upward] and the other like that [points downward]. . . . When the chapter headed like this—upwards—the French Jacobins, the Bolsheviks of that time, guillotined the Royalists and the Girondists. We, too, have had a similar great chapter when we . . . shot the White Guards and exiled the Girondists [i.e., the Mensheviks and SRs]. And then there began another chapter in France, when the French Ustrialovs[34] and semi-Ustrialovs—the Thermidoreans and Bonapartists from among the Right-wing Jacobins—began exiling and shooting the Left Jacobins—the Bolsheviks of the time.

Reshaping his notion of Thermidor as a mere retreat, not a rout, Trotsky observed, "It is thought that the Thermidoreans were arrant counter-revolutionaries, conscious supporters of the monarchic rule, and so on. Nothing of the kind: the Thermidoreans were Jacobins, with this difference, that they had moved to the Right."[35] In Marxist terms, for Trotsky, the situation in Russia was simple: "Thermidor . . . is a departure from the rails of the proletarian revolution to the petty-bourgeois rails," opportunistically condoned by the revolutionary leadership themselves.[36]

* * *

Trotsky was a theorist who did his most creative work under the immediate impact of events around him. When he first formulated "permanent revolution," and on through his initial perception of the revolution in decline, he made no effort to extend his theory to countries other than Russia. It was the abortive Communist bid for power in China in 1927, first in alliance with Chiang Kai-Shek's Nationalists and then against them, that prompted him to universalize his process concept. He wrote in April 1927, just before Chiang turned against the Chinese Communists, of "an alliance of workers and peasants, under the leadership of the proletariat," and foresaw a "possibility of the democratic revolution growing over into the socialist revolution," while the Soviet Union would play the role of outside ally envisaged for the Western proletariat in the original, Russian version of permanent revolution.[37] By extension, this situation made permanent revolution the general model for under-developed and colonial countries.[38] The Italian scholar Pier Paolo Poggio comments, "For Trotsky, in Russia and in general in backward countries, the seizure of power by the consciously organized proletariat . . . will be easier and quicker than in the advanced capitalist countries."[39] Incorporating this perspective into his polemical reformulation of "permanent revolution" in 1928, Trotsky presented what Les Evans and Russell Block term "the theory of permanent revolution as we know it today—as a general theory of the necessity of socialist revolution in the colonial world."[40]

* * *

The radical new departures undertaken by Stalin after Trotsky's defeat, including his break with the Communist right wing and the initiation of intensive industrialization and collectivization, threw his critics into a new theoretical quandary. At first Trotsky was inclined to describe the Stalin Revolution as a "prolonged zigzag to the left," compelled somehow by pressure from the workers and the Left Opposition but still under the pull of the "Thermidorean" bureaucracy.[41] "Stalinism is inverted Kerenskyism," he suggested, "on the road to Thermidor, the *last* form of the rule of the proletariat."[42] By now the trend of the NEP years was clear to him: "A period of reaction can occur not only after a bourgeois revolution but after a proletarian one as well. For six years we have been living in the USSR under conditions of mounting reaction against October, paving the way for Thermidor."[43] To his supporters in Italy Trotsky wrote, "When we speak of Thermidor, we have in mind the creeping counterrevolution which is being prepared in a masked way and which is being accomplished in several stages."[44]

With the perspective of an additional half-decade Trotsky was more certain about the retrograde course of the Russian Revolution: "Stalin . . . is the living embodiment of a bureaucratic Thermidor."[45] Looking back from the year 1935, he concluded, "Today it is impossible to overlook [the fact] that in the Soviet revolution also a shift to the right took place a long time ago, a shift entirely analogous to Thermidor, although much slower in tempo, and more masked in form. . . . The year 1924—that was the beginning of the Soviet Thermidor."[46] Thus Trotsky finally recognized that a Thermidor had in fact occurred, not as an overt bourgeois coup, but as a more subtle political shift within the ruling party. His only trouble was that he persisted, for reasons of his own self-justification, in placing the shift three years after the real turning point of 1921.

Simultaneously with his recognition of the Russian Thermidor, Trotsky was compelled to admit the possibility of a further postrevolutionary phase, distinct from Thermidor, which was still not clearly a counter-revolution. In the French model this was the era of Bonapartism. Thermidor, in this context, was "a transitory phase between Jacobinism and Bonapartism."[47] Stalin naturally embodied this last, Bonapartist stage of the revolutionary process. Russia was thereby observing the laws demonstrated in "the consecutive stages of the great French Revolution, during its rise and fall alike," though Trotsky still endeavored to describe these stages as a sequence of distinct class elements: "In the successive supremacy of Mirabeau, Brissot, Robespierre, Barras, and Bonaparte, there is an obedience to objective law incomparably more effective than the special traits of the historic protagonists themselves."[48]

*   *   *

For a Marxist, Trotsky had an unusually supple understanding of history in general and of revolution in particular. While wedded to the usual class categories for explaining political events, he was able to grasp the complexities of a phenomenon such as revolution that in fact transcended the Marxian mode of analysis. He attempted a running explanation of unfolding developments in Russia by applying a process conception and extending it as new stages appeared: "There are certain features common to all revolutions. . . . The *tendency* toward Thermidor, Bonapartism, and Restoration [is] to be found in every victorious revolution worthy of the name."[49] This was more than a mere analogy, though it was expressed in French revolutionary terminology; it was "an obedience to objective law."[50]

Constantly attempting to use his understanding of the revolutionary process as a political weapon, Trotsky did not always react at once to a new stage, and he was slow to recognize Thermidor and the rise of postrevolutionary dictatorship. In time, however, he was able to set the realities of these phenomena in Russia into the framework of his model. "Revolution itself is neither a single nor a harmonious process," he wrote in 1931. "Revolution is full of contradictions. It unfolds only by taking one step back after taking two steps forward. Revolution in its own turn sweeps into a power a new ruling stratum which strives to secure its privileged position." Here was a hint of the New Class theory. Finally, Trotsky called the whole Marxian logic into question: "The epochs of ideological reaction which, more than once in history, have run parallel with economic successes, engender the need for revising revolutionary ideas and methods; and create their own conventional lie."[51]

Notes

1. Robert F. Lansing, *War Memoirs* (Indianapolis: Bobbs-Merrill, 1935), pp. 337–338.

2. Lyford P. Edwards, *The Natural History of Revolution* (Chicago: University of Chicago Press, 1927).

3. Crane Brinton, *The Anatomy of Revolution* (New York: Prentice-Hall, 1938, 1952), pp. 16–17.

4. I have developed this approach more fully elsewhere. See Robert V. Daniels, "Whatever Happened to the Russian Revolution," *Commentary*, LXVI:5 (November 1978).

5. A good negative example is Karl Kautsky, *The Materialist Conception of History* (abridged edition, New Haven: Yale University Press, 1988), where revolution is mentioned often but only in passing, and never analyzed.

6. Karl Marx, *A Contribution to the Critique of Political Economy* (New York: International Library Publishing Co., 1904), p. 13.

7. Ibid.

8. V. I. Lenin, "Two Tactics of Social Democracy in the Democratic Revolution" (July 1905), *Selected Works* (Moscow: Foreign Languages Publishing House, 1950–52), vol. I, book 2, pp. 87, 107.

9. Published as "Itogi i perspektivy" (Results and Prospects) in *Nasha revoliutsiya* (St. Petersburg: N. Glagolev, 1906; English translation in Leon Trotsky, *Our Revolution*, New York: Holt, 1918). The more confusing term "permanent"

revolution was applied to the theory by later commentators, but it stuck and Trotsky accepted it. See Trotsky, *The Permanent Revolution* (New York: Pioneer Publishers, 1931), p. 12; Baruch Knei-Paz, *The Social and Political Thought of Leon Trotsky* (Oxford: Oxford University Press, 1978), pp. 152–153. On Trotsky's earlier steps in formulating the theory, see Michael Löwy, "The Theory of Permanent Revolution," in Francesca Gori, ed., *Pensiero e Azione di Lev Trockij* (Firenze: Olschki, 1982), pp. 149–154.

10. See Z.A.B. Zeman and W. B. Scharhau, *Merchant of Revolution: The Life of Alexander Helphand (Parvus), 1867–1924* (London: Oxford University Press, 1965), pp. 66–68, 110–111.

11. Trotsky, *Our Revolution*, p. 92.

12. John Molyneux, *Leon Trotsky's Theory of Revolution* (New York: St. Martin's, 1981), p. 59.

13. Trotsky, Foreword to Ferdinand Lasalle's *Address to the Jury* (June 1905), quoted in "Results and Prospects," in Trotsky, *The Permanent Revolution and Results and Prospects* (London: New Park Publications, 1962), vol. I, p. 240. Cf. Löwy in Gori, *Pensiero e azione di Lev Trockij*, p. 154.

14. Trotsky, "Dva litsa: vnutrennie sily russkoi revoliutsii" (Two Faces: The Inner Forces of the Russian Revolution), *Novyi Mir* (New York), 17 March 1917, quoted in Knei-Paz, *Social and Political Thought*, p. 240. See also Trotsky, *The History of the Russian Revolution* (Ann Arbor: University of Michigan Press, 1932, 1957), vol. I, appendix 2.

15. Lenin, "On the Tasks of the Proletariat in the Present Revolution" (The "April Theses," 7 [20] April 1917), *Selected Works*, vol. II, book 2, p. 14. Heinz Schurer writes, "After February 1917 Lenin accepted the bold perspectives of the permanent revolution for Russia which would throw the lighted torch into the powder barrel of Western Europe" ("The Permanent Revolution: Leon Trotsky," in Leopold Labedz, ed., *Revisionism: Essays on the History of Marxist Ideas*, New York: Praeger, 1962, p. 75). Cf. Robert Wistrich, *Trotsky: Fate of a Revolutionary* (London: Robson Books, 1979), pp. 78–80.

16. *Shestoi s"ezd RSDRP (bolshevikov), avgust 1917 goda: Protokoly* (Moscow: Marx-Engels-Lenin Institute, 1934), p. 101.

17. See Zinoviev and Kamenev, Statement to the Principal Bolshevik Party Organizations, 11 [24] October 1917, in Lenin, *Collected Works* (New York: International Publishers, 1929), vol. XXI, book 2, appendix, pp. 328–331.

18. Trotsky, preface to "Results and Prospects," in *The Permanent Revolution and Results and Prospects*, pp. 162–163.

19. Trotsky, *From October to Brest-Litovsk* (New York: Socialist Publication Society, 1919), p. 28.

20. Trotsky, Introduction to *Results and Prospects* (New York, 1919), pp. 185–187; *The History of the Russian Revolution*, vol. I, p. 211.

21. Trotsky, *Uroki oktiabria* (Moscow: Priboi, 1924; translated as *Lessons of October*, New York: Pioneer Publishers, 1937), pp. 70–71.

22. Trotsky, Introduction to *Results and Prospects*, pp. 163–164.

23. Trotsky, *Terrorizm i kommunizm* (Moscow: Gosizdat, 1920; English edition, *Dictatorship vs. Democracy: A Reply to Karl Kautsky*, New York: Workers' Party of America, 1922), p. 54.

24. Trotsky, "Letter to the Bureau of Party History Concerning the Falsification of the History of the October Revolution, the History of the Revolution and the History of the Party," 21 October 1927, in *The Stalin School of Falsification* (New York: Pioneer Publishers, 1937), p. 29.

25. Brinton, *Anatomy of Revolution*, p. 228.

26. See Simon Wolin, "The Mensheviks under the NEP and in Emigration," in Leopold Haimson, ed., *The Mensheviks: From the Revolution of 1917 to the Second World War* (Chicago: University of Chicago Press, 1974), p. 248; Jay Bergman, "The Perils of Historical Analogy: Leon Trotsky on the French Revolution," *Journal of the History of Ideas*, XLVIII:1 (January–March 1987), p. 82 and n. 40.

27. Karl Kautsky, *Terrorism and Communism: A Contribution to the Natural History of Revolution* (London: G. Allen & Unwin, 1920), pp. 214–215.

28. Trotsky, *Mezhdu imperializmom i revoliutsiei*, translated as *Social Democracy and The Wars of Intervention in Russia 1918–1921 (Between Red and White)* (London: New Park Publications, 1975), p. 83. See David S. Law, "Trotckij and Thermidor," in Gori, *Pensiero e azione di Lev Trockij*, vol. 2, p. 437.

29. Trotsky, *The New Course* (New York: New International Publishing Co., 1943), p. 40.

30. First expressed by Trotsky, as far as can be determined, in a pamphlet of early 1923: "Mysli o partii" (Thoughts on the Party), in Trotsky, *Zadachi XII s"ezda RKP* (The Tasks of the Twelfth Congress of the Russian Communist Party) (Moscow: Izdatel'stvo Deviatogo Yanvaria, 1923), appendix, pp. 54–55.

31. Trotsky, *The New Course*, pp. 39–41.

32. See Robert V. Daniels, *The Conscience of the Revolution: Communist Opposition in Soviet Russia* (Cambridge, Mass.: Harvard University Press, 1960), pp. 248–252.

33. Trotsky, "Theses on Revolution and Counterrevolution," first published in *The Fourth International*, October 1941; reprinted in Isaac Deutscher, *The Age of Permanent Revolution: A Trotsky Anthology* (New York: Dell, 1964), p. 142.

34. A reference to N. V. Ustrialov, the emigré Russian economist who had hailed the NEP as a return to capitalism.

35. Trotsky, Speech to the Central Control Commission, June 1927, *Stalin School of Falsification*, p. 143.

36. "The Real Situation in Russia and the Tasks of the Communist Party" (Opposition Platform of September 1927), in Trotsky, *The Real Situation in Russia* (New York: Harcourt, Brace, 1928), p. 187.

37. Trotsky, "Class Relations in the Chinese Revolution" (3 April 1927), *The New International*, March 1938, p. 89.

38. See Curtis Stokes, *The Evolution of Trotsky's Theory of Revolution* (Washington: University Press of America, 1982), pp. 133ff.

39. Pier Paolo Poggio, "Le peculiarità storiche della Russia nell'analisi e nella prospettiva di Trockij" (The Historical Peculiarities of Russia in Trotsky's Analysis and Perspective), in Gori, *Pensiero e azione di Lev Trockij*, p. 108.

40. Trotsky, *Permanentnaya Revoliutsiya* (Berlin: Granat, 1930; translated as *The Permanent Revolution*, New York: Pioneer Publishers, 1931); Les Evans and

Russell Block, eds., *Leon Trotsky on China* (New York: Monad Press, 1976), editors' preface, p. 19.

41. Trotsky, "The Defense of the Soviet Republic and the Opposition" (7 September 1929; *The Militant,* 21 December 1929 and 25 January 1930); in *Writings of Leon Trotsky* (New York: Pathfinder Press, 1978), vol. I, pp. 280–284.

42. Ibid., p. 287.

43. Trotsky, *Chto i kak proizoshlo* (What Happened and How, Paris: De Nevarre, 1929) translated in *The New York Times,* 1 March 1929, as "Trotsky Reveals Origins of His Fall"; in *Writings of Leon Trotsky,* vol. I, p. 26.

44. Trotsky, Letter to the Italian Left Communists, 25 September 1929, *Writings of Leon Trotsky,* vol. I, p. 323.

45. Trotsky, "The Terror of Bureaucratic Self-Preservation" (2 November 1935), *Writings of Leon Trotsky,* vol. VIII, p. 119.

46. Trotsky, "The Workers' State and the Question of Thermidor and Bonapartism" (1 February 1935; *The New International,* July 1935); in Trotsky, *The Class Nature of the Soviet State* (London: New Park Publications, 1968), p. 49.

47. Trotsky, "On the Question of Thermidor and Bonapartism" (November 1930), *Writings of Leon Trotsky,* vol. II, p. 71.

48. Trotsky, *The Revolution Betrayed: What Is the Soviet Union and Where Is It Going?* (New York: Doubleday, Doran & Co., 1937), pp. 86ff.

49. Trotsky, *Chto i kak proizoshlo?* in *Writings of Leon Trotsky,* vol. I, p. 51.

50. Trotsky, *The Revolution Betrayed,* p. 87.

51. Trotsky, *Stalin School of Falsification,* foreword to the 1931 Russian edition, p. xxxviii.

3

The Left Opposition and the Evolution of Soviet Communism

The series of dramatic protest movements carried on in the Soviet Union between the years 1923 and 1927 under the heading of the Left Opposition is a subject of great historical and theoretical significance, not merely as a signal manifestation of the politics of the Soviet regime in the second half-decade of its existence, but as an avenue to the understanding of the basic evolution of Stalinist Communism and of the contradictions that characterized the Communist movement for the next six decades. The period of the New Economic Policy, and in particular the period when the Left Opposition was still able to function, was a key time in the development of the Soviet system and of the fundamental issues which still mark the discussion of Soviet society. With the destruction of the Left Opposition, basic alternatives were closed and the peculiar Soviet system of rule under the Communist Party bureaucracy and Marxist-Leninist ideology was firmly entrenched.

It must be recognized at the outset in any consideration of the Left Opposition in the Soviet Union that the Soviet social and political system did not emerge fully developed from the 1917 revolution. Rather, it evolved during a decisive formative period of a decade and a half or more. This evolution, furthermore, was not merely a matter of quantitative growth in the powers of the state and in the indices of production, such as the simplistic formula of "building socialism" would suggest. Nor was it simply the working out of the society of the future predicted by Marxism and supposedly foreordained by the laws of history. It was an independent development, assuming unforeseeable and uncontrollable forms in response to situational and personal factors of which Marxist theory took little or no account. Ultimately it created a form of government

This chapter was originally published in German in Ulf Wolter, ed., *Sozialismusdebatte* (Berlin: Olle und Wolter, 1978), pp. 131–159. Reprinted with permission.

and society which, ideological pretenses aside, bore little or no relation to the hopes and prognostications of the makers of the Russian Revolution.

The record of the Left Opposition is the record of a desperate struggle to control this evolution during some of its most crucial years and to hold it as nearly as possible in the direction toward which the revolution had originally pointed. This struggle by the Left Opposition failed, as it was perhaps doomed to fail, because of historical circumstances and laws of social development of which the Oppositionists had only a dim understanding, or misunderstanding. But in going down to defeat, the Oppositionists left a remarkable record of theoretical analysis and practical protest that documents in the most unmistakable terms the transformation that was taking place in Soviet Russia during these years from a revolutionary dictatorship to a bureaucratic despotism. The Opposition had little idea of why this was happening, and less of how to combat it, but they did recognize the outlines of the dismal totalitarianism that was falling heir to the revolution. For too long much of the outside world, anti-Communist as well as pro-Communist, failed to grasp the vital meaning of this issue of the 1920s that lay at the heart of the Stalinist system. It is the great and lasting significance of the saga of the Left Opposition, and of their eloquent documents of protest and analysis, to have recorded for their posterity the world over the nature of the Stalinist transformation and the perversion it represented, whether avoidable or not, of the spirit of 1917.

*   *   *

The language of the Left Opposition, of course, was the language of Marxism, and the categories of logic and perception which they employed were wholly suffused with Marxian presuppositions. This was an ironic circumstance considering their eventual condemnation as an anti-Marxist deviation. In fact, one of the elements contributing to the failure of the Opposition was their excessively literal devotion to the premises of Marxism and their failure to work their way out of the contradictions inherent in a Marxist movement attempting to hold power in an under-developed country such as Russia.

As good Marxists, the Oppositionists viewed themselves as mere agents of the laws of history, which naturally were believed to be working inevitably toward those goals which Marxists at the same time desired. They did not begin to resolve the paradoxical contradiction between determinism and voluntarism in Marxism, but struggled heroically to establish the dictatorship of the proletariat which at the same time they believed to be inevitable. They had no theoretical equipment to deal with the possibility (which during their time became a reality) that the laws or at least the tendencies of history might be working the wrong way—that, as the neo-Kantian Revisionists had warned some years before, moral goal and objective social development might not coincide—and that objective social development might be destroying their goal of workers' democracy.[1]

Even in the Marxian perspective it is difficult to find sustenance for the hopes entertained by the Left Opposition. Russia was, as Marxists of all hues acknowledged up until 1917, unready for socialism even though special circumstances might temporarily thrust the proletariat into power. Trotsky had foreseen this as the "permanent revolution," when the bourgeois revolution would lead directly into the proletarian revolution in urban Russia, and the latter would evoke world socialist revolution and international solidarity with the Russian workers. For Lenin, before 1917, the prospect was for the workers' party to carry through the bourgeois revolution with its natural allies in the form of the "democratic dictatorship of the proletariat and the peasantry." But no Bolshevik expected, until the party found itself in power, that Russia could aspire in isolation to create a socialist society in one generation. The Mensheviks, mostly writing in exile, continued to insist that it could not be done.

This quandary set the scene for the famous controversy over "socialism in one country," beginning in 1924 when Stalin suggested on the basis of some quotation-lifting from Lenin that Russia's backwardness and isolation were no impediment to the immediate construction of socialism. The Opposition made a major effort, logically compelling but politically futile, to demonstrate the inconsistency between this proposition and the understanding of Marxism expounded by all its leading lights in Russia up to that time. Gropingly and hesitantly the Oppositionists were beginning to show, until they were silenced, that the party leadership under Stalin was converting Marxism into an ideological rationale for something other than the proletarian society, for the kind of society instead which Russian conditions of underdevelopment limited the government to fostering—in other words, a despotic managerialism.

The Marxist assumption, shared as I have indicated by both pro-October and anti-October Marxists, was that the proletarian revolution in Russia was "premature" in relation to the maturation of capitalism, which was expected both to bring revolutionary tensions to a head and to provide the material prerequisites for a program of socialism after the working class took power. Why the revolution nevertheless occurred before capitalism had matured was explainable for the Bolsheviks in terms of the war and special Russian conditions. Unlike the Mensheviks, they were willing to try to hold the power thrust upon them in these circumstances, if necessary as a minority dictatorship. They accepted this role in the hope that they could temporarily advance the cause of proletarian socialism even in the absence of the material preconditions, while waiting for the international revolution to bail them out. "There is no force on earth," wrote Lenin in one of his missives to his hesitant lieutenants on the eve of the October Revolution, "which can prevent the Bolsheviks, *if only they do not allow themselves to be cowed* and are able to seize power, from retaining it until the final victory of the world socialist revolution."[2]

Broader study of the history of revolution in the modern world suggests that the notion of a peculiar "prematurity" in the Russian Revolution is unfounded. In fact there is good reason to argue that the revolution interrupting Russia's capitalist development in mid-course came at a very natural point. The Marxian prognosis of socialist revolution as the consequence of capitalist industrial maturity, not scheduled to erupt until capitalism had exhausted all further possibilities of development and established the material basis for socialist abundance, proved to be wrong. Recent history shows that the experience of modernization and industrialization is most likely to involve revolution not at the end of the process but mid-way, when the strains of transition are at their most severe.[3] Conversely, and confounding the most dramatic predictions of Marxism, a society which weathers the transition of modernization without revolution, like Scandinavia, or which has experienced its revolution early in the process, like England, is unlikely to encounter a revolutionary situation when capitalism has matured. Typically, gradual evolution toward democratic semi-socialism is the tendency at that point. Viewed in these terms, revolution is not so much a function of the rise and exhaustion of particular classes as it is of a structural crisis in the social and political system, in the course of which whatever dynamic and frustrated social elements that are available will assert themselves. From this standpoint there is no theoretical difficulty in the fact that revolutionary situations may be distinguished by various coalitions of disparate class elements, depending on when the crisis comes: aristocrats, bourgeoisie, and artisans in seventeenth-century England; bourgeoisie, artisans, and peasant proprietors in France; intellectuals, proletariat, and peasantry in Russia.

Marxism also falls short of accommodating the law of the progression of revolution from a moderate phase to an extremist dictatorship and then to a Thermidorean reaction synthesizing elements both of the revolution and of the Old Regime. The structural crisis of the Old Regime leads to a general breakdown of organization and authority, in the course of which diverse social elements may mobilize to articulate their demands, regardless of the material incapacity of the social system to satisfy them. Thanks to this effect every great revolution is in a sense "premature" in thrusting into power extremists who attempt to answer to the most advanced demands of the most demonstrative segment of the population. Therefore, we must consider it neither surprising nor anomalous but a natural historical phenomenon that the representatives of the proletariat had a chance to rule in Russia without the economic foundation that would make their program attainable. Engels' famous warning comes to mind about revolutionaries who are ahead of their times:

> The worst thing that can befall a leader of an extreme party is to be compelled to take over a government in an epoch when the movement is not yet ripe for the domination of the class which he represents. . . . He is compelled to represent not his party or his class, but the class for whose domination the movement is then ripe. In the interests of the movement he is compelled to advance the interests of an alien class, and to feed his own class with phrases and promises.[4]

What we must now recognize is that Engels' remarkable insight applies not merely to the tragic possibility of an exceptional case of premature revolution, but becomes a general law of revolutionary irony.

A further point, not discussed by Engels, is that the requirements of falsifying their representation of the popular interest, and of relying more and more heavily on administrative force and tactical compromises rather than popular emotion in order to stay in power, inevitably cause the revolutionary extremists to split. The more utopian or idealistic elements will refuse to make these sacrifices and will break away as an ultra-left opposition. However, such a group will by its very existence become an intolerable challenge to those who choose to rule by "phrases, and promises," and hence it becomes a prime target for suppression along with genuinely counterrevolutionary elements. (This is precisely what happened in 1921 to the Democratic Centralist and Workers' Opposition groups within the Communist Party and to the Kronstadt rebels outside it.) Meanwhile, those revolutionaries who have chosen to try to stay in power through stealth and coercion find, with the defection of the Ultra-Left and the exhaustion and disaffection of the by now conservatively oriented majority of the population, that there is little active social base left to sustain their extremist program. This is the circumstance that makes the Thermidorean Reaction unavoidable, whether it is accomplished by the extremist leadership themselves, as in Russia in 1921, or whether it is done for them by a palace coup, as in France in 1794.

The Left Opposition not only misapplied the notion of Thermidor when they went into action against the party leadership in the mid-1920s. They had little chance of halting the basic trend of Thermidor, certainly not through the line of workers' democracy. In the aftermath of the Russian Revolution, success was destined to go to those who could effectively wield the instruments of power and reconcile the resources of traditional authority with the needs of a society deep in the crisis of modernization.

Intellectually no Russian Marxist was equipped to do this. In fact, the more any individual was sincerely and intelligently devoted to the method and premises of Marxism, the less was he able to make this readjustment. Only one presumptive Marxist in the Soviet leadership— namely, Joseph Stalin—had the intuition to rise above principle and respond to the challenge and the opportunity that history presented to him.

*   *   *

Who were the Left Opposition and why did they attempt the impossible in quixotically rallying to the spirit of the revolution when the times called for much more pragmatic attitudes? The answer is a complex one, involving history, personalities, and basic philosophical values. Historically the lines of cleavage that opened up in the Communist Party in 1923 can be traced back to the very beginnings of Bolshevism in the Social Democratic split of 1903, when Lenin broke away over the issue of conspiratorial party discipline, and left numerous radical but anti-authoritarian individuals in the Menshevik camp. These people, including such revolutionary luminaries as Trotsky, Anatol Lunacharsky, Karl Radek, Alexandra Kollontai, Khristian Rakovsky, Adolf Ioffe, and Vladimir Antonov-Ovseyenko, joined the Bolsheviks between 1915 and 1917 because of their anti-war sentiments and the attractiveness of proletarian revolution against the Provisional Government. They were never truly reconciled to Lenin's so-called principle of democratic centralism (i.e., democratic in words, centralism in fact). Another left-wing current, psychologically kindred in its radicalism, arose within the Bolshevik faction to merge with this ex-Menshevik contingent. It originated in the controversies after 1905 over the boycott of the Duma and continued through the war years over the theory of imperialism and national self-determination. From these "Left Bolsheviks," essentially revolutionary romantics, came Nikolai Bukharin, Grigory Piatakov, Felix Dzerzhinsky, Valerian Osinsky-Obolensky, and Vladimir Smirnov.

For ten years before the revolution and ten years afterwards, the radical Marxist movement in Russia and in the emigration was deeply and consistently divided. On the one hand were the ideological purists, continually generating one left opposition movement after another. On the other were the people around Lenin, prepared to accept his discipline wherever it might lead in the quest to win and exercise power, and only wavering, as Zinoviev and Kamenev did in 1917, when the gamble seemed too risky.

Many writers have suggested that the social basis of the struggle between the Left Opposition and the Stalinists was the disparity of outlook between theoretical intellectuals and pragmatic worker-undergrounders. This distinction was in fact only partly true—a number of oppositionists had worker backgrounds, and many Communist intellectuals lined up with Stalin. A much clearer alignment is the connection of prerevolutionary experience as an emigré in the West with later opposition activity and the converse correlation of the exclusively Russian undergrounder experience with the later Stalinist faction.[5] (Stalin himself, who never attended a university and never spent a significant length of time outside Russia, typified his own closest followers.) Between prerevolutionary expressions of deviation, whether Menshevik or Left-Bolshevik, and subsequent records of opposition to Lenin and then to Stalin within the ruling Communist Party, there was a highly consistent personal continuity. Obviously the circumstances of the emigration attracted intellectuals and gave non-intellectuals an intellectual veneer, while at the same time facilitating the expression and recording of ideological controversies and commitments. In many, though not all, cases the emigré experience evidently imbued future Communist leaders with some of the Western democratic spirit, whereas the undergrounder back in Russia was naturally more prone to accept pragmatically Lenin's strictures on party discipline and democratic centralism in order to keep the party intact and get on with the job of revolution. Finally, there was a striking psychological distinction between the oppositional type and the died-in-the-wool Leninist, in the individualism and theoretical hair-splitting characteristic of the former, and the authoritarian acceptance by the latter of Lenin, and later the Party, as a father-figure capable of committing no wrong. Lenin's death evoked tremendous insecurity among those who had depended on his paternalistic leadership—Lenin was, incidentally, at least ten years older than any of his prominent followers—and it contributed to the frenzied pursuit of "party unity" in the ensuing years.

Soon after the revolution two distinct tendencies emerged within the broad current of left opposition attitudes described here. Their outlines first became apparent in the controversy over the Brest-Litovsk peace, when Lenin found himself opposed by his most enthusiastic supporters of the revolutionary months, and supported by those, like Zinoviev and Kamenev, who had dragged their feet during 1917 out of the fear of not being able to hold power. Those most fervent in resisting the peace and advocating revolutionary war followed Bukharin in the so-called group of Left Communists. Others, uncomfortable with Lenin's line but unwilling to defy him to the end, followed Trotsky's slogan of "no war, no peace"; theirs was the group that abstained in the Central Committee and allowed Lenin to win the vote for the peace treaty.

The Brest-Litovsk question was just the first in a long series of issues that divided the Leninists and what we might best designate as the moderate Left Opposition and the Ultra-Left Opposition. Organized as the Left Communists, the Ultra-Left stood up immediately to protest Lenin's abandonment of workers' control in industry and the restoration of conventional managerial authority. In 1919, as the "Military Opposition," they protested the return to conventional military organization and discipline in the Red Army under Trotsky. In 1920, as the "Group of Democratic Centralists," they protested the growing centralization of the party and the violation of the rights of local soviets. In the fall and winter of 1920–1921, represented by the Democratic Centralists and the Workers' Opposition, they protested the bureaucratization of the economic system and the failure to achieve workers' democracy through the trade unions. Repeatedly the Ultra-Left endeavored to play a role that has appeared in every great revolution, of the principled representatives of the popular interest, corresponding to the Levellers and Diggers in the English Revolution, and to the Enragés, the Hébertistes, and the Babeuvists in the French Revolution. They were just the type of people, as we have noted, whose honesty becomes intolerable to the revolutionary leadership when the crisis point is reached in the extremist dictatorship and the time for "phrases and promises" arrives.

Meanwhile, the moderate left current around Trotsky, closely identified with the party leadership during the height of the Civil War and War Communism, took issue with the Leninists on the same matter of the trade unions. Their solution, however, was one of radical centralism through the "governmentalizing" of the unions, whereas the Leninists wanted to relegate them to the more modest role of protecting the workers under a system of state capitalism. The Trotskyist approach on the trade union question reflected a readiness to combine ambitious revolutionary hopes—more than the cautious Leninists could sustain—with the pragmatic means of coercion rejected by the ultra-left purists, a combination of attitudes that foreshadowed Stalin's "revolution from above" almost a decade later. Ideologically and temperamentally Trotsky was the Robespierre of Russian revolutionary extremism, Lenin the more flexible Danton.

The resolution of the Trade Union Controversy and the initiation of the New Economic Policy at the Tenth Party Congress in March 1921 established the context of Thermidorean reaction in which the political struggles of the 1920s were waged. Economically the Communist Party retreated from the immediate goal of socialism to a transitional form of mixed economy, in which the peasants were free agents and industry was managed in a capitalist fashion, corresponding to the Leninist concept of the trade unions. Politically the lines were hardened, with the outright condemnation of the Ultra-Left, i.e., the Democratic Centralists and the Workers' Opposition, as a "petty-bourgeois anarcho-syndicalist deviation."[6] This move was reinforced by the adoption of an official ban on any further organized factions within the Party, as an activity incompatible with the united defense of the interests of the working class.[7] All these steps, constituting the real Thermidor of the Russian Revolution, were endorsed by the Trotskyist moderate left. However, the Trotskyists' loyalty to Lenin against the Ultra-Left did not suffice to ward off his reprisals for their recent opposition; the three Trotskyists controlling the party Secretariat (Nikolai Krestinsky, Yevgeny Preobrazhensky, and Leonid Serebriakov) were ousted and replaced by clients of Stalin's, including Viacheslav Molotov, with Stalin himself, of course, assuming direct control of the Secretariat the following year. The result of the Tenth Congress was that the issue (Thermidor) and the opportunity (free factionalism) for a successful stand by the Left Opposition against the bureaucratization of the Communist Party and Russian society were severely compromised. This happened because the moderate Left chose at that moment to see their main enemies in the Ultras rather than in the apparatus that Stalin was already building. This was the sort of mistake that one opposition group after another proceeded stubbornly to commit, with tragic consequences.

*   *   *

The immediate origins of the struggle by the Left Opposition in the 1920s lie in the tangled interrelationships of the leading Communist personalities in the uncertain months of Lenin's illness, extending from May 1922 to his death in January 1924. Nominally the Politburo constituted a collective leadership; in actuality Zinoviev, serving at the time as chairman of the Comintern as well as boss of the Leningrad Province, aspired to fill Lenin's shoes. To achieve this objective he had to neutralize Trotsky, the obvious heir in terms of his revolutionary and Civil War record and his public prestige. "We were strongly of the opinion that one man, and one man only, had a right to that position, because he was head and shoulders superior to his fellow-claimants and could depend upon our unswerving loyalty," a party member recalled. "That one was Trotsky."[8] Much has been written about the personal enmity of Trotsky and Stalin, but this is in part an ex post facto projection. A much more decisive circumstance at the time was the recurring personal clash between Trotsky, the flamboyant individualist, and Zinoviev, the constant shadow of Lenin, a rivalry that began before the revolution and escalated from the time when Trotsky upstaged Zinoviev as the number-two Bolshevik in 1917.

To isolate Trotsky within the Politburo, Zinoviev arranged the so-called "troika," an informal leadership of himself, his alter ego Kamenev, and General Secretary Stalin, backed by the remaining members Aleksei Rykov and Mikhail Tomsky, plus Bukharin as a candidate member. Throughout the intrigue-ridden winter of 1922–1923, despite the opportunities presented by issues of industrial development, foreign trade, grain prices, the national minorities, and above all Lenin's personal break with Stalin expressed in his "Testament" and other documents, Trotsky was unable to find a satisfactory political opening to move against the troika. He held aloof even when, at the Twelfth Party Congress in April 1923, his friends were openly criticizing Stalin on his role in coercing the Communists in Soviet Georgia. Possibly Trotsky contemplated seeking an alliance with Stalin against Zinoviev—hence his failure to develop the anti-Stalin campaign that Lenin entrusted to him,[9] though he had a sharp personal clash with Stalin on the eve of the Twelfth Congress over the handling of Lenin's criticisms of the party leadership.[10]

Trotsky's hand was finally forced when the deepening contradictions of the NEP in both the economic and political realms brought about a major realignment of potential opposition elements in the Communist Party. Now at long last the Ultra-Left and the moderate Left coalesced, as the former members of the old Democratic Centralist group and some of the Workers' Opposition joined forces with the now eclipsed Trotskyists to mount a major challenge within the party organization against the policies of the interim leadership. Known as the "New Course" controversy, from Trotsky's pamphlet of that name,[11] the struggle culminated in December 1923 and January 1924, just before Lenin's death, in the total defeat of the Opposition. This episode marked the real beginning of the struggle for power between the Left and the Stalinists. In practical organizational terms, as regards any possibility of political success, it marked the effective end of that struggle as well.

Trotsky touched off the controversy early in October 1923 by dispatching a letter to the Central Committee attacking the bureaucratization of the party, "much farther from workers' democracy than the regime of the fiercest period of War Communism."[12] This jab was quickly seconded by the "Declaration of the Forty-Six," one of the most cogent warnings against short-sighted error and repressive cover-up to be produced in the whole history of the Opposition.[13] Its signatories, including both Trotskyists such as Preobrazhensky and Piatakov and Democratic Centralists such as Osinsky and Timofei Sapronov, were obviously inspired by Trotsky's action if not actually guided by him.

These protests prompted a heavy-handed though behind-the-scenes rejoinder from the leadership denouncing the criticism as factionalism that might violate the rule of the Tenth Party Congress.[14] Meanwhile, historical precedent from other countries gave the anti-Trotsky combination some grounds to fear that Trotsky might attempt to make use of his position of control over the Red Army to effect a coup.[15] To forestall this contingency they eliminated Trotsky's supporters from the military-political administration (including the hero of October, Antonov-Ovseyenko) and turned it into an instrument to hamstring oppositionist influence in the armed forces.

For the public the party leadership professed to endorse a sweeping reform effort embodied in the "New Course" resolution adopted by the Politburo on 5 December.[16] This action gave Trotsky his opportunity to try to bind the leadership to their reform promises, which he undertook to do in his open letter, "The New Course," of 8 December.[17] Though Trotsky had fallen ill of the undiagnosed fever that took him out of Moscow at the time of Lenin's death, Preobrazhensky endeavored to follow the letter up by leading a campaign for democratization in the Moscow party organization.

This challenge finally provoked the party leadership to launch a public counterattack against the Opposition, with a campaign of denunciations in the press and in party meetings, lasting up to the convening of the Thirteenth Party Conference early in January 1924. This was the first party conclave where Stalin's apparatus systematically excluded the Opposition: only three opposition delegates, including Preobrazhensky, managed to get elected. The conference pronounced the judgment that was to echo in every subsequent condemnation of the Opposition—the Opposition was a faction, in violation of the Tenth Congress rule, and as such it necessarily represented interests contrary to the working class, since (as it was claimed) only the Communist Party, by definition, could speak for the proletariat. Accordingly, the Opposition was condemned as "not only an attempt at the revision of Bolshevism, not only a direct departure from Leninism, but also a clearly-expressed *petty-bourgeois deviation*."[18]

* * *

Politically, the entire four-year struggle of the Left Opposition after the Thirteenth Party Conference (and the death of Lenin, which followed in a matter of days) was a long drawn-out anti-climax, distinguished by divisive bickering and tactical blunders on the part of people whose chances to curb the potential postrevolutionary dictatorship represented by Stalin were slim at best. Theoretically and ideologically, the history of this struggle is rich in argument documenting the evolution of the

Soviet regime and the alternatives facing it as the various protagonists saw them. Economic issues commanded the largest share of attention in the debates, followed by questions of foreign policy and the Comintern. Sounded throughout the period was the Opposition's theme of party democracy, countered by charges of factionalism and the violation of party unity. Finally, certain fundamental questions of the nature of the Soviet system as interpreted by Marxist theory arose intermittently, including the issues of Thermidor, state capitalism, and socialism in one country. Virtually every significant question that has since arisen in the evaluation of the Soviet system was anticipated in these final years of open factional struggle.

Initially the basic issues of economic policy were posed by the NEP and the question of where it was to lead, as a long-term "evolution" or as a short-term, transitional "tactic." Further development of the NEP implied further concessions to the peasantry and to petty bourgeois enterprise, in terms of taxes, prices, and legal scope, at the expense, the Opposition alleged, of the industrial workers. The contrary emphasis was constantly pressed by the Opposition—to favor actively the economic interests of the proletariat as the true social foundation of the regime, which did indeed describe itself as a workers' state. The Opposition was concerned on Marxist grounds for the security of the regime because its social base was relatively weak. It therefore took up the cause of state-planned industrial development to draw more people into the proletarian foundation of the state.

There is a double irony in this idea. First, it was logically incongruous for Marxists, believing in the determination of the political superstructure by the social-economic base, to suppose (1) that their government could be a workers' state without a sufficient existing working-class base, and (2) that political action by the *soi-disant* workers' state could build up that base beneath itself. The whole Marxian sociology starts to collapse here in a chaos of untenable analogies. Secondly, it was equally or more ironic that the major economic challenge then faced by the Soviet state and addressed single-mindedly ever since, the challenge of noncapitalist industrialization, had never been dealt with either in the Marxian scriptures or in the early policy pronouncements of the Soviet regime. It was only for the political and sociological reasons advanced by the Opposition that discussion of this momentous task got underway.

The great industrialization controversy dominated the economic side of the intra-party struggle in its last years. The Opposition, represented in this area particularly by Preobrazhensky, came down strongly on the side of a vigorous, centrally planned industrialization drive, financed by forced savings through the tax system ("primary socialist accumulation") in lieu of capitalist saving or foreign investment. For the party leadership Bukharin was the chief spokesman; he had made a virtue of necessity by shifting from the Left to the Right in response to the NEP, and succeeded to Lenin's Politburo seat. Bukharin exemplified the method—"market socialism," Trotsky later called it[19]—of more gradual and less stressful development through the accumulation of profits by state-owned enterprises as they served the consuming public and indirectly stimulated heavy industry by spending these funds to expand their plants. The obvious parallel of this approach with conventional capitalistic expansion invited Opposition complaints against "state capitalism," a development they associated with Thermidor as a long-term abandonment of the cause of the workers.

The question, broadly hinted at by the Opposition soon after the struggle began, of whether the Soviet government under the Stalin-Bukharin leadership was in danger of losing its quality as a workers' state, led directly to the most significant controversy in the entire ideological side of the factional struggle, that is, the debate over socialism in one country. This was not, as is often assumed, a dispute between the advocates of a world revolutionary offensive and those who would retreat behind the walls of Fortress Russia. Both the leadership and the Opposition held to the doctrine of world revolution in theory, while after the final collapse of Communist revolutionary hopes in Germany in October 1923 they supported in practice any expedient efforts to normalize Soviet foreign relations and find allies and trade partners. Arguments swirled repeatedly around alleged leadership blunders in the pursuit of this line, notably the alliance with the British Labor Party from 1924 to 1926 and the alliance with the Kuomintang in China from 1922 to 1927. But the fundamental unresolved question, pressed more and more strongly by the Opposition, referred back to the doctrinal dilemma of the proletarian state isolated in a backward society. What were the implications of the long prospective delay in the world revolution for the survival and the purity of the dictatorship of the proletariat in Russia?

At this juncture the premises of Trotsky's theory of permanent revolution came into play as a contentious political issue. Accepted tacitly or explicitly by most of the Bolshevik Party as their guiding belief in 1917, and borne out by events in its prediction of a proletarian victory piggy-backing on the bourgeois revolution, permanent revolution left the victorious Bolsheviks in a state of acute uncertainty as long as the international revolution did not materialize to bring them support from the outside. The Treaty of Brest-Litovsk, resisted by the more theory-conscious Bolsheviks as the abandonment of a crucial opportunity to stimulate international revolution, implied a basic priority—observed in practice ever since—for the survival of the Soviet state in Russia. In the practical sense, socialism in one country had been a fact of life ever since 1918. Survival in isolation then posed the theoretical question, in terms of permanent revolution, whether the Soviet government could really maintain its character as a workers' state or whether it might have to transform itself subtly into another form of regime as the price of survival in a country with an overwhelming peasant and petty-bourgeois majority. The Left Opposition could not resist the temptation to insinuate just this sort of degeneration as an actual or potential threat under the pro-NEP, pro-peasant, and potentially Thermidorean leadership of Stalin and Bukharin.

It was in this situation, to defend himself and the party leadership against an embarrassing ideological attack by his cornered factional adversaries, that Stalin contrived his alternative theory, first broached in November 1924.[20] Its essence was that neither backwardness nor the forces of capitalist encirclement could prevent the construction of socialism in Russia alone. As his authority for this highly original contention Stalin cited a passage that Lenin wrote in 1915 to the effect that "the victory of socialism is possible first in several or even in one capitalist country, taken singly."[21] This, Stalin claimed, supported his contention that Trotsky's theory of permanent revolution reflected an "underestimation of the peasantry" and a "lack of faith" in Russia's potential for revolution, and hence amounted to a Menshevik heresy. However, as Kamenev pointed out in open party forum in 1926, the context of Lenin's statement clearly shows that he had in mind not Russia but one of the most advanced capitalist countries that might be prepared to lead the way to socialism.[22] Stalin had in fact snatched the Lenin statement out of context and distorted its meaning to make it serve his own purposes by alleging that it proved the feasibility of Russia's building socialism alone.

The significance of this seemingly scholastic dispute is almost incalculable, though not for any factual insights it might offer into Russian social and political reality. First of all, it established Stalin's method— to be followed for the rest of his life—of seeking political justification by doctrinal manipulation, with no honest regard for what the original texts actually meant. It illustrated, furthermore, his inclination, "scholastic" in the most literal sense, to seek such justification in textual authority rather than in empirical data.[23] But for steps of this sort to serve their purpose, it was necessary for Stalin to impose a complete ban on any independent discussion of the texts and concepts of Marxism. The measures he took to ward off criticism made him more vulnerable to criticism, and required him to take still more stringent measures to suppress oppositionist views. Ever since, it has been the possibility of criticism from within the movement and from a Marxist standpoint that has been most intolerable to the Soviet regime.

Once the system of doctrinal authority and control implied by Stalin's proposition of socialism in one country was established, and the possibility of critical reference to the original meaning of Marx or even of Lenin was ruled out, it became easy for Stalin to modify his policies at will while reinterpreting Marxist doctrine to make it appear to justify each new policy as the only correct application of the true faith. This Stalin commenced to do across the board—in economics, in law, in cultural policy, in foreign policy, in the liquidation of his enemies—once he had made himself the unquestioned master of the party in 1928–1929. Two good examples are his rejection of equalitarianism as "leveling" (to each according to his needs, but individual needs differ) and his revision of the "withering away of the state" (not to come as long as there was a capitalist encirclement outside the country and an economic development need inside).[24] As these manipulations proceeded, it became impossible within the Stalinist system to judge policy against any theoretical guidelines, since the interpretation of theory was constantly subject to change at the whim of political authority, to square with changes in policy and circumstances. It became impossible to speak of an ideological motivation of Soviet policy, domestic or foreign, since ideology was made to conform to policy instead of governing it. The Stalinist frame of mind, begun with socialism in one country and maintained to the end of the Brezhnev era, was not the ideological motivation of policy but the policy motivation of ideology.

While Stalin's manipulation of ideology, colored by a mixture of cynicism and self-justification, was breaking free of all logical and political restrictions, the Left Opposition was not above the political use of ideological arguments itself. The Oppositionists' efforts to score theoretical points against the Stalinists in fact led them into some difficult inconsistencies. They always averred their Leninist orthodoxy, for one thing, never challenging the one-party system nor even the antifactional rule, but only protesting that their own critical efforts, based presumably on a sincere appreciation of the interests of the workers, could not possibly be factional. They endeavored to make political capital out of the leadership's foreign policy embarrassments, while denying that they meant to undermine the tactical success of this policy. Above all, they were profoundly inconsistent in their appraisal of the economic potential of the isolated Russian state. On the one hand, they vehemently attacked the theory of socialism in one country and the possibility of building socialism in Russia alone as an artificial, un-Marxist, and impossible concept. On the other, they called for a far more vigorous and rapid effort by the Soviet government to expand the industrial foundations of socialism in Russia. In other words, their answer to the shortage of resources for the effort to build socialism was to attempt the building even faster, before the shortage might become socially and politically too debilitating.

This contradiction in the economic argument raised by the Left Opposition was, to be sure, honestly faced by some of its members, notably by Preobrazhensky. The "Preobrazhensky dilemma" for Russian socialism, in the words of the economist Alexander Erlich, was "a choice between mortal sickness and virtually certain death on the operating table."[25] This impasse once again underscored the truth that socialism, as its principles were understood up to 1917, would not work in an underdeveloped country such as Russia, at least not in isolation. Preobrazhensky himself could only hark back to the premises of permanent revolution and "leaning for support in the future on the material resources of other socialist countries."[26]

Under the pressure of the controversy, Stalin and Bukharin adjusted their economic line in the direction of a synthesis of the market and planning approaches. The same Fifteenth Congress that saw the Left Opposition expelled from the party voted for the principle of a five-year plan of industrial development. But Stalin and Bukharin soon parted company, each clinging to one horn of the Preobrazhensky dilemma. While Bukharin held out for a gradualist and nonviolent approach within the outlines of the plan, Stalin opted for a crash program of industrialization. In his startling "left turn" of 1928, he adopted every argument advanced by the Left Opposition in industrialization policy, peasant policy, and foreign policy—though not in the question of party democracy or the ideology of socialism in one country—and put them into practice in an almost unrecognizably extreme form. Such was the ironic policy contribution of the Left after their political destruction.

*   *   *

The political and ideological struggle between the Left Opposition and the party leadership of Stalin and Bukharin escalated in a series of steps from 1924 to 1927, with different combinations of political actors and ideological argument at each stage. Following the decisive defeat of the Trotskyists in January 1924, no serious attempt was made for several months to resist the official chorus extolling unity and denouncing the Opposition heresy. Within the party leadership there were some indications of personal and political strains between Stalin and Bukharin on the one hand and Zinoviev and Kamenev on the other. Some of Stalin's organizational appointments appear to have been aimed at undermining Zinoviev's influence. But in October 1924, Trotsky reopened the controversy with the publication of his essay, "Lessons of

October," linking the Communist failure in Germany in 1923 to the faint-heartedness of Zinoviev and Kamenev in 1917.[27] This sally drove these two temporarily back into the arms of Stalin and Bukharin, who joined them in a frenetic denunciation of the evils of Trotskyism and permanent revolution, now established as arch-heresy. Trotsky ended by being shorn of his last influential office, that of Commissar of Defense, in January 1925.

In the light of this experience it was no surprise that Trotsky would choose to bide his time when the tension between Stalin–Bukharin and Zinoviev–Kamenev resumed clearly and unbridgeably in mid-1925. Recognizing that Stalin had outmaneuvered them in the course of consolidating his own control over the party apparatus, Zinoviev and Kamenev now appropriated some of the arguments of the Left Opposition and directed them against Stalin—the charge of conciliating the peasants too much and neglecting the workers, the matter of party democracy, and the theoretical issues of state capitalism and socialism in one country. It is difficult not to regard this phase of the controversy as a purely opportunistic political maneuver. Zinoviev and Kamenev had heretofore never been associated with the Left Opposition, and their main basis for resisting Stalin was their control of the party organization in the Leningrad province through bureaucratic manipulation just as systematic as Stalin's in the rest of the country. In any case, the effort was in vain, and the Leningrad Opposition went down to ignominious defeat at the Fourteenth Party Congress—the last until the 1980s at which any open expression of opposition was allowed to take place. The Trotskyists, despite the fact that many of their own arguments were being called into question, made no effort to speak up to support the Zinovievists. They perhaps nourished once again the thought that they might enlist the services of Stalin in the pursuit of their longer-standing vendetta with Zinoviev.[28]

Immediately after the Fourteenth Congress the top party leadership moved into Leningrad and easily removed the Zinovievists from their fiefdom in the city of the revolution. Zinoviev was so shaken by this debacle that he decided on a radical new political departure, namely an alliance with his old enemy Trotsky, whom he had so effectively helped to condemn in 1923 and 1924. Such a dramatic shift in political alignments meant overcoming years of personal and ideological struggle between these two prima donnas, and the fact that Zinoviev could bring himself even to consider the alliance shows how seriously he now saw his own future threatened by Stalin.

After some hesitation, the Trotskyists accepted Zinoviev's overtures in the spring of 1926, on the basis of his admission that the whole campaign against "Trotskyism" had been a political concoction and that the Left had correctly warned about the bureaucratization of the party. Trotsky for his part toned down the theory of permanent revolution. "A mutual amnesty," Stalin called the agreement.[29]

Events were to show that the amnesty did not entirely heal the personal and ideological fissures remaining within the new opposition coalition. For the moment, the United Opposition bloc represented a formidable political combination, including as it did most of Lenin's leading associates of the revolutionary period, of whatever faction, Right, Left, and Ultra-Left, and even his widow Nadezhda Krupskaya. Over the next year and a half the bloc mounted a sustained and vehement ideological struggle against the party leadership, making this the most intense period of factional controversy in the entire history of the Communist movement. No area of theory or policy was spared; the leadership's record in party organization, industrialization, the peasants, foreign policy, socialism in one country, and the ideological definition of the Soviet state all came under scathing attack by the Opposition. By late 1927 Stalin's critics were close to accusing him of betraying the dictatorship of the proletariat, and were about to create de facto a new party to fight for the interests of the workers and international socialism.

After a period of initial ideological sparring over the economy and foreign policy in the spring of 1926 (particularly the failure of cooperation with the British Labor Party), relations between the United Opposition and the leadership were brought to an early crisis point by accusations of conspiratorial tactics on the part of the Opposition and the presentation by the latter of its first systematic statement of principles since 1923, the so-called "Declaration of the Thirteen."[30] In broad terms the Declaration of the Thirteen denounced the trend to bureaucratism and attributed it to the neglect of proletarian and poor-peasant concerns. The leadership responded at the July 1926 plenum of the Central Committee with the first of a series of organizational sanctions: Zinoviev was ousted from the Politburo, and Kamenev was removed from his Commissariat of Trade. Pointedly the leadership refrained from penalizing Trotsky, suggesting a hope of dividing the new-formed Opposition bloc. Nevertheless, the Opposition resumed a vigorous campaign of criticism in party meetings in the fall. For this they were condemned for factional splitting and compelled to renounce further oppositional activity.[31] Retribution came anyway: Trotsky and Kamenev were removed from the Politburo, leaving it totally in the hands of the leadership, while Zinoviev was formally replaced as Comintern Chairman by Bukharin.

Vehement debates still followed, even though the Opposition tried to maintain, in compliance with their October agreement, that their criticisms did not constitute factional activity. The Fifteenth Party Conference in November was noteworthy for the climactic debate on socialism in one country. Shortly afterwards, at the Seventh Plenum of the Executive Committee of the Communist International in December, the Opposition tried to bring their case to a world audience, but to little avail. To a remarkable degree the Russian leadership was able to maintain control over the foreign Communist parties and isolate the supporters of Trotsky in their respective organizations. The Opposition was now identified with the Second International and labelled by Stalin a "Social-Democratic deviation."[32] Under this sort of pressure the first signs of disintegration appeared in the Opposition bloc when the old Workers' Oppositionists, as well as Krupskaya, abjured the Opposition and made their peace with Stalin.

Events abroad again touched off a wave of activity by the Left Opposition in the spring of 1927. This time the fortunes of the revolutionary process in China took center stage in the factional controversy in Russia. China, where the Nationalist Party with Communist support had succeeded in reviving the revolutionary movement of 1911, had become as exciting to the Russians as Germany had been from 1918 to 1923, as the potential site of an international revolutionary breakthrough against imperialism. When Chiang Kai-shek turned against his Communist allies with a bloody purge in April 1927, the Oppositionists hastened to cite the setback as an inevitable consequence of the opportunism engendered by socialism in one country.[33] They followed with another broad statement of position, the "Declaration of the Eighty-Four," addressed to the Politburo but intended for a wide audience, though Opposition documents no longer had any chance of publication. Once again the Opposition linked the foreign and domestic errors of the party leadership with ideological failings of a petty bourgeois nature (the mirror image of the sins for which they were themselves denounced), and renewed their protest against the suppression of spontaneous political life in the Party.

The impact of this criticism was sharpened by the war scare with Great Britain, adduced by the Opposition as proof of the need for a change in leadership, and by Stalin and Bukharin as reason for suppressing the Opposition's potentially treasonable threat to party unity and national security. At the Central Committee plenum of late July and early August, amid rumors that the Opposition would soon be excluded from the Party altogether, Trotsky proclaimed his "Clemanceau thesis"—that he would, like Georges Clemanceau in France during the recent war, pursue his demands for a correct line until he won the leadership himself.[34] For this he was denounced simultaneously for defeatism and insurrectionism, and forced to retract his views about opposition and Thermidor under the threat of expulsion from the Central Committee. Meanwhile the Opposition lost another contingent from its left wing, the former members of the Democratic Centralist group still led by Sapronov, who proclaimed their own, more uncompromising rejection of the Communist leadership and prepared, despite their miniscule numbers, to go their own way as a separate party.[35]

When the party leadership belatedly scheduled the Fifteenth Party Congress, the remainder of the United Opposition arose once again to take advantage of what had traditionally been a free discussion period prior to each congress. They drew up yet another platform, destined to be their last, a book-length indictment detailing again the failure of the leadership to pursue workers' democracy and international socialism.[36] To have the document printed in the face of a ban by the Politburo, the Opposition had to go underground, and when their press was discovered by the police the operators were expelled from the party. Now denied any regular forum, the Opposition leaders tried to organize their own impromptu meetings, culminating in an alternative demonstration on the tenth anniversary of the revolution in November. But none of these efforts could break through the ever-tightening network of bureaucratic controls in the Party, the media, and the police. At the October Central Committee plenum, even though he was himself forced to acknowledge the criticisms in Lenin's "Testament,"[37] Stalin secured the expulsion of Trotsky and Zinoviev from the Central Committee. In answer to their demonstrations on 7 November he finally had them expelled from the Party, and at the same time he eliminated the last of their associates from the Central Committee and the Central Control Commission. In the selection of delegates to the Congress that convened early in December, not a single Oppositionist was permitted to be elected.

As the Fifteenth Party Congress prepared to denounce and expel the entire Left Opposition, the bonds of expediency that had held the Trotskyist and Zinovievist wings of the Opposition bloc together finally broke. With Kamenev as their spokesman, the Zinovievists abjured the heresy of a second party as the only alternative to monolithic unity, and threw themselves on the mercy of the leadership, whereas the Trotskyists refused to give in. For the moment both groups were treated the same, with expulsion from the Party, though harsher measures awaited the Trotskyists in the form of deportation and forced residence in Siberia or Central Asia. With these steps, the last legal opportunity for political individuality in Soviet Russia came to an end.

*   *   *

The last act in the struggle to hold back Stalin's Bonapartist transformation of Soviet politics was played out largely behind the official façade of party unity, as Stalin parted company with his ideological comrades of the NEP, Bukharin, Rykov, and Tomsky, and the latter, the so-called "Right Opposition," took their turn at futile resistance. The Left Opposition, crushed and scattered, responded in utter disunity to these new developments of Stalin's "left turn" and his struggle with the Right. Some of Trotsky's followers, led by Piatakov and Krestinsky, saw Stalin's hard line on the peasants and industrialization as a vindication of the arguments of the Left Opposition, and "capitulated" one after another to return to the party and the government in various administrative capacities. Radek and Preobrazhensky took this step in 1929, just when Trotsky, holding to his condemnation of the personal rule of Stalin, was physically expelled from the Soviet Union in the most unusual move yet taken against the Opposition. Other Trotskyists continued to hold out in their places of exile, notably Rakovsky, who began a highly distinctive effort to work out a neo-Marxist explanation of the Stalin regime in terms of the rise of the bureaucracy as a new ruling class. Meanwhile the Zinovievists, still residing in Moscow, were approached directly by the Right Opposition in the person of Bukharin, mainly for the purpose of commiseration, it seems, since no action resulted from their discussions save additional embarrassment for the Right when the contacts were revealed a few months later.

In terms of economic policy the Right Opposition may well have represented a more realistic alternative to Stalinism than the Left. They held to the NEP and a gradualist approach to socialism, industrialization, and cultural modernization. Thanks to this outlook they did not have to rely intellectually on illusions about the international revolution. On the other hand, as regards the political issues of party democracy and bureaucratization the leaders of the Right erred fatally in backing Stalin's apparatus against the Left until all chance of defending any line of criticism, including their own, had been obliterated. Bukharin was as fanatic as any in his diatribes against the Left's alleged factional menace to the Communist regime, until he realized, too late, as he confided to Kamenev, "The differences between us and Stalin are many times more serious than all our former differences with you."[38] A year later Bukharin and his associates were being removed one by one from all their leading political positions, and the Stalin Revolution was under way. All that happened afterward to both Left and Right Oppositionists was anticlimactic: denunciation, expulsion, arrest, trial, liquidation, oblivion.

* * *

The tragic demise of all the Communist oppositions, Right, Left, and Ultra-Left, would appear in the first instance to be readily explainable in simple political terms: disunity, indecision, tactical errors, confusion of purpose. In particular, the record of attack and retreat, of capitulations to party discipline followed by renewed attacks on the leadership, was disconcerting and demoralizing to any potential following of the Opposition. These mistakes, however, stemmed from one essential faulty premise, namely, acceptance of the Leninist myth of the single united party exercising the dictatorship of the proletariat. None of the oppositions were prepared to follow the logic of their position *qua* opposition and to question the one-party monopoly, however much they might try to stretch the opportunities for factional struggle within the Party to the utmost. To set up an independent organization and argue for multiparty democracy would be a Menshevik heresy from which they all recoiled, though they were nonetheless repeatedly accused of this very sin. In fact the virtue of the Opposition, particularly the Trotskyist Left, was that it was really so close to the Mensheviks in this regard, and in the end it would have had nothing to lose and perhaps a good deal to gain by frankly avowing that position. It would have been substantially in character with the basic political orientation of the Left Opposition since prerevolutionary days. As events turned out, the Opposition was defeated as much by its own acceptance of the one-party concept as it was by the bureaucracy of that one party which it rightly rejected.

Of deeper concern is the question whether the programs represented by the oppositions could have succeeded under any conceivable conjuncture of political circumstances. The hopes of the Left to curb the peasant proprietary economy and push industrialization while simultaneously reviving the 1917 spirit of workers' democracy were impossible to reconcile, as the "Preobrazhensky dilemma" demonstrated. The history of all revolutions shows how difficult it is to sustain the original spirit of self-sacrificing idealism. In Russia, particularly after the militarizing effect of the Civil War on all the country's political institutions, the notion of workers' democracy was altogether chimerical. The proletariat in whose name the dictatorship was being exercised was in large measure a raw new class recruited from the peasantry after the revolutionary proletariat of 1917 had been killed off or promoted into the bureaucracy or dissipated during the economic collapse of War Communism. For all the Opposition's appeals, the industrial workers of the 1920s remained firmly in the grip of the party apparatus; the "Lenin enrollment," diluting the Party with hundreds of thousands of new worker-members in 1924, actually spelled the end of any opposition chance to win over a significant segment of the rank and file.

The plain fact is that the Left Opposition's crusade for socialism based on an industrializing workers' democracy was fundamentally quixotic under Russian conditions. This brings us back to the basic dilemma posed by the ideals of the Russian Revolution and their contrast with Russian reality. Socialism in the old sense of the just distribution of abundant goods was impossible without more economic development, but economic development was impossible without a ruling class—bureaucrats if not capitalists—who could put the necessary pressure on the masses and direct the energies of the nation into the enhancement of production. It was the merit of the Right Opposition to be realistic enough to scale down their ambitions both for socialism and for production, in order to avoid the implications of totalitarian bureaucracy toward which this combination of goals pointed. It was the genius of Stalin, on the other hand, to recognize that the problem of production could be successfully attacked through the means of socialism in the sense of central state planning and control, while abandoning (except as to "phases and promises") the old ideal of just distribution. Stalin's solution, then, was a new implicit doctrine of "production socialism," contrasting with every school of socialism theretofore enunciated, but legitimized with Marxism as ideology in the sense of "false consciousness." Production socialism embodied the needs he perceived for the development of Russia's national strength and for the enhancement of his own personal power.

What difference would it have made if the Left Opposition under Trotsky's leadership had, by some fortunate turn of fate, gotten control of the party apparatus and ousted Stalin? Could they, in power, escape the constraints of a revolution in retreat and the discouraging logic of socialism in backward and isolated circumstances which they blamed for Stalin's backsliding from the revolutionary ideal? Or could the factor of personality in history, Marxism to the contrary notwithstanding, enter the picture decisively enough to rescue the Marxist revolution from the contradictions in which unanticipated circumstances had enmeshed it? As regards the basic organization of economic and political life it is hard to see how the Opposition could substantially reverse the trend toward bureaucratization and production socialism; a measure of relaxation in this respect would have been afforded only by the gradualist adherence to the NEP represented by Bukharin and the Right Opposition, a viewpoint that was never acceptable to the Left. Where a Trotsky leadership would have made the most difference was not in the economic and political realm they stressed the most, not in the achievement of a meaningful workers' democracy, but in the cultural and ideological area and probably in foreign policy. It is impossible to imagine under a putative Trotsky regime anything like Stalin's philistine xenophobia and egomaniacal meddling in cultural life. In foreign policy Russia might have played a more consistent and successful anti-Fascist role, while the Communist International would never have been reduced to such mindless subservience to Moscow as actually occurred under Stalin. Finally, though Trotsky could be harsh with the real enemies of the regime, it is hard to conceive of any analogue under him to Stalin's incredible purge of all factions of Communists including his own.

Whatever the alternative actually represented by the Opposition, its existence and even its memory became increasingly intolerable to the Stalinist leadership as they proceeded to redefine the goals of Soviet socialism. Any recurrence of the sort of criticism mounted by the Opposition would undermine the ideological self-justification of the new bureaucracy represented by Stalin, and expose their pragmatic policies to constant embarrassment. In consequence, beginning in the last months of the struggle against the United Opposition, the Stalinist leadership undertook to recast the entire history of the Party in order to represent the Opposition spokesmen as diabolical agents of counterrevolution. By deporting Trotsky, Stalin set up an external target for hatred and denunciation that could help discredit all questioning of the regime in power. (The analogous deportation of Alexander Solzhenitsyn in much more recent times served a similar purpose.) So extreme in the 1930s was the twisting of fact about the record of the Opposition, culminating in the preposterous charges at the show trials of 1936, 1937, and 1938, that the Soviet regime could be said to have developed a systematic national neurosis on this score. Like the neurotic individual, the Stalinized Communist Party had created obsessive myths about its own past in order to defend the contradictions of its present, and reacted with the most violent anxiety toward any attempt from within or without to get back to the historical truth. This peculiar, deep-seated characteristic of the Soviet regime stemmed directly from the history of the struggle with the Opposition, and (until the Gorbachev reforms) the Opposition remained a subject about which there could be no objective discussion whatsoever. Khrushchev's de-Stalinization and rehabilitation campaign of 1956, restoring to history the Stalinists and the military men who had perished in the purges, stopped short of reconsidering the role of the Opposition and their critique of Stalin, though Khrushchev did concede that the death penalties of 1936–1938 were excessive. Everything Stalin accomplished up to 1934, including his suppression of the Opposition, the basic principles of the Stalin Revolution, and the whole system of ideological manipulation, was reaffirmed by Khrushchev and continued to remain above question for the Brezhnev regime.

Notes

1. On the problem of deterministic theory and voluntaristic behavior see Alfred G. Meyer, *Marxism: The Unity of Theory and Practice* (Cambridge, Mass.: Harvard University Press, 1955).

2. V. I. Lenin, "Will the Bolsheviks Retain State Power?" 24 September [7 October] 1917, *Collected Works* (New York: International Publishers, 1929), vol. XXI, book 2, p. 51.

3. See Cyril E. Black, *The Dynamics of Modernization* (New York: Harper & Row, 1966); Adam Ulam, *The Unfinished Revolution: An Essay on the Sources of Influence of Marxism and Communism* (New York: Random House, 1960).

4. Friedrich Engels, *The Peasant War in Germany* (New York: International Publishers, 1926), pp. 135–136.

5. See Robert V. Daniels, *The Conscience of the Revolution* (Cambridge, Mass.: Harvard University Press, 1960), pp. 50–51.

6. Resolution of the Tenth Congress of the Russian Communist Party, "On the Syndicalist and Anarchist Deviation in Our Party," in Lenin, *Selected Works* (Moscow, Foreign Languages Publishing House, 1950–1952), vol. II, book 2, pp. 502–506.

7. Resolution of the Tenth Congress of the Russian Communist Party, "On Party Unity," ibid., pp. 497–501.

8. Alexander Barmine, *One Who Survived* (New York: Putnam, 1945), p. 212.

9. See Daniels, *Conscience of The Revolution,* pp. 183–186, 205–206. In 1990 the Soviet historian Viktor Danilov brought to light a hitherto unknown document, Trotsky's speech to the party leadership in October 1923, in which he explained at some length why he declined to serve as Lenin's chief deputy out of fear that his "Jewish origin" would be seized upon by the anti-Semitic enemies of the Soviet regime. V. P. Danilov, "My nachinaem poznavat' Trotskogo" ("We are Beginning to Get to Know Trotsky"), *Eko* (Novosibirsk), no. 1, 1990, p. 57; Concluding Remarks of Comrades Trotsky and Stalin at the joint session of the plenums of the Central Committee and the Central Control Commission together with representatives of ten proletarian party organizations, 26 October 1923, *Voprosy Istorii KPSS,* no. 5, 1990, p. 36.

10. Trotsky to all members of the Central Committee of the RCP, 16 April 1923, Trotsky Archive (Harvard University), Document No. T794 (in Yu. Fel'shtinsky, ed., *Kommunisticheskaya oppozitsiya v SSSR, 1923–1927,* Benson, Vt.: Chalidze Publications, 1988, vol I, p. 53); Trotsky, *Stalin: An Appraisal of the Man and his Influence* (New York: Harper, 1946), pp. 362–363.

11. Trotsky, *The New Course* (New York: New International Publishing Co., 1943).

12. Ibid., p. 154.

13. Trotsky Archive, T802a, 802b (Fel'shtinsky, *Oppozitsiya,* vol. I, pp. 83–88); English translation in E. H. Carr, *The Interregnum* (New York: Macmillan, 1954), pp. 367–373.

14. Resolution of the Central Committee and the Central Control Commission, 25 October 1923, "O vnutripartiinom polozhenii" (On the Intraparty Situation), *KPSS v rezoliutsiyakh i resheniyakh s"ezdov, konferentsii i plenumov TsK* (7th ed., Moscow: Gospolitizdat, 1954), vol. I, pp. 767–768.

15. According to Anton Antonov-Ovseyenko, son of Vladimir Antonov-Ovseyenko, Trotsky's supporter General N. I. Muralov, commandant of the Moscow Military District at the time, was ready to intervene. A. V. Antonov-

Ovseyenko, "Trotsky as a Military leader," paper presented at the International Trotsky Symposium, Wuppertal, Germany, March 1990.

16. *Pravda*, 7 December 1923.

17. Trotsky, *New Course*, pp. 89–98.

18. Resolution of The Thirteenth Party Conference, "Ob itogakh diskusii" (On the Results of the Controversy), *KPSS v rezoliutsiakh*, vol. I, p. 782.

19. Richard Day, *Leon Trotsky and The Politics of Economic Isolation* (Cambridge, Eng.: Cambridge University Press, 1973), p. 183.

20. Joseph Stalin, "The October Revolution and the Tactics of the Russian Communists," *Problems of Leninism* (Moscow: Foreign Languages Publishing House, 1940), pp. 86–117.

21. Lenin, "The United States of Europe Slogan" (August 1915), *Selected Works*, vol. I, book 2, p. 416.

22. Lev Kamenev, Speech at the Fifteenth Party Conference, *Pravda*, 5 November 1926.

23. See Thomas J. Blakeley, *Soviet Scholasticism* (Dordrecht: Reidel, 1961).

24. Stalin, Report on the Work of the Central Committee, to the Seventeenth Congress of the CPSU(B), *Problems of Leninism*, p. 520; Report on the Work of the Central Committee, to the Eighteenth Congress of the CPSU(B), ibid., p. 662.

25. Alexander Erlich, *The Soviet Industrialization Controversy* (Cambridge, Mass.: Harvard University Press, 1960), p. 59.

26. Ye. A. Preobrazhensky, "Khoziaistvennoe ravnovesie v sisteme SSSR" (Economic Equilibrium in the System of the USSR), *Vestnik Kommunisticheskogo Akademii*, no. 22 (1927), p. 70, quoted, *ibid.*

27. Trotsky, *The Lessons of October* (New York: Pioneer Press, 1937).

28. Daniels, *Conscience of the Revolution*, p. 272.

29. Stalin, Report to the Fifteenth Party Conference, "Ob oppozitsii i o vnutripartiinom polozhenii" (On the Opposition and on the Intra-party Situation), *Pravda*, 5 November 1926. See Daniels, *Conscience of the Revolution*, pp. 273–275.

30. Trotsky Archive, T880a (Fel'shtinsky, *Oppozitsiya*, vol. II, pp. 11–24).

31. Declaration of Zinoviev, Kamenev, Trotsky, Piatakov, Sokolnikov, and Yevdokimov, 16 October 1926, in *Pravda*, 17 October 1926.

32. Stalin, Concluding remarks to the Seventh Plenum of the ECCI, *Pravda*, 19 December 1926.

33. See Trotsky, "The Chinese Revolution and the Theses of Comrade Stalin" (7 May 1927), in Trotsky, *Problems of the Chinese Revolution* (New York: Pioneer, 1932).

34. See Trotsky to Ordzhonikidze, 11 July 1927, as quoted by Stalin, speech to the Central Committee and the Central Control Commission, 1 August 1927, Stalin, *Sochineniya* (Moscow: Gosudarstvennoe Izdatel'stvo Politicheskoi Literatury, 1952), vol. X, p. 52.

35. See the "Declaration of the Fifteen," 27 June 1927 (published as *Avant Thermidor: Révolution et contrerévolution dans la Russie des Soviets—Platforme de l'Opposition de Gauche dans le parti Bolchevique* (Lyons, 1928).

36. Published by Trotsky as *The Real Situation in Russia* (New York: Harcourt, Brace, 1928).

37. *International Press Correspondence*, no. 17, 17 November 1927, pp. 1428–1429.

38. Kamenev, notes on conversation with Bukharin, 11 July 1928, copy in Trotsky Archive, T1897; extracts in Robert V. Daniels, ed., *A Documentary History of Communism* (rev. ed., Hanover, N.H.: University Press of New England, 1984, 1988), vol I, p. 207.

4

Socialist Alternatives
in the Trade-Union Controversy

In the late 1980s the peoples of the Soviet Union and indeed of many other countries began to retrace their historical steps to find the point where they may have tragically taken a wrong turn. They hope to restructure their societies on lines that would have emerged from a different historical choice. This quest calls into question not only the Stalinist and neo-Stalinist system of the recent past, but the basic principle of the socialist organization of society as well. Does this model of social life inherited from the revolutionary experience need to be reshaped, or only cleaned up, or abandoned altogether?

For most of this century socialism has been regarded by both its friends and its enemies as a definite kind of structure of society, something that can be "built." More often than not, in the minds of advocates and critics alike, socialism has been identified with the structure of society that was "built" in the Soviet Union in the 1930s. But when one tries to trace the origins of Stalinist socialism in the years immediately following the Revolution of 1917, it is hard to find a structural model for this or any other conception of the socialist goal.

To be sure, socialism, broadly considered, was the heart of the revolutions of 1917. It was a faith or a goal all across the center and left of the 1917 political spectrum. But this socialism had more the sense of a process than of a structure. Russian revolutionaries of whatever party affiliation seem to have embraced socialism not as a projected set of institutions, but rather as a utopian antithesis to present reality, as an ideal way of life, towards which their society could be led or pushed. To cite the Yugoslav formula, socialism has manifested itself historically not as a fixed system but as "a world-wide process," the climactic point of which, so far, was the Russian Revolution.[1]

The Marxian philosophy, which became axiomatic among most socialists around the world by the early years of this century, did not help to clarify the meaning of socialism. Marxists, subscribing to the doctrine of the natural march of events from capitalism through socialism to communism, gave relatively little thought to the details of the future society. In Russia, before, during, and immediately after the revolution, their attention was absorbed by questions of tactics and even of political survival, while the ultimate details of socialism and communism were expected to be taken care of by the dialectic of history. "No blueprint guided the Bolshevik leaders in devising the new system," writes Thomas Remington. "The ideas they followed consisted either of generalized images of an ideal system or of improvised responses to particular dilemmas."[2] Until nearly the end of the period of War Communism, the character of the socialist institutions and policies established by the Communists was governed more by ad hoc political and economic necessities than by any deliberate, long-run legislative program.

*　　*　　*

It was only after victory in the Civil War, when the Communist leaders began to view their new system in a longer time perspective, that definite conceptions began to be formulated for the road ahead. The occasion that evoked this consideration of future alternatives was the so-called Trade-Union Controversy that agitated the ranks of the Russian Communist Party in 1920–1921. The three principal platforms represented in the discussion, the Leninists, the Trotskyists, and the Workers' Opposition, reflected three fundamentally different conceptions of socialism and of the path to communism.

Each position in the Trade-Union Controversy can readily be placed on the left-right political scale according to the degree of romantic adventurism or of cautious pragmatism that it exhibited. Thus, on the Left stood the Workers' Opposition, espousing the 1917 ideal of workers' control, and confident of a rapid and direct transition to communism. On the Right, contrary to the conventional historiography,[3] I place the Leninists. They were the people who were persuaded by the crisis of War Communism that the Soviet government would have to retreat to a state capitalist system, and only then resume a very long and careful journey to socialism and communism. The Center, as I see it, was occupied by the Trotskyists (and by the slightly more left adherents of the Bukharin platform, who merged with the Trotskyists in the course of the discussion). The Trotskyist position was to pursue socialism rapidly, but in the belief that it was necessary to use the instruments of centralized power and coercion—in other words, a model of barracks socialism.

Each faction in the trade-union debate represented a different source in the revolutionary tradition, and a different psychological orientation toward the prospects of the transition to socialism. The Workers' Op-position expressed the utopian current of thought that went back to the pre-revolutionary Ultra-Left (among both Bolsheviks and Mensheviks) and to the Anarcho-Syndicalist movement.[4] They were close to the Left Communists of 1918, who rebelled not only against the Treaty of Brest-Litovsk, but also against Lenin's efforts to curtail workers' control in industry and restore the managerial hierarchy. Like their forerunners, the Workers' Opposition were confident that socialism could be reached quickly and easily by giving free rein to the masses through the institutions they had created in the course of the revolution, the factory committees (or the trade unions which had absorbed them) and the local soviets. The faith in the masses expressed by the Workers' Opposition paralleled the premises underlying the movement of Proletcult, headed by the same Alexander Bogdanov who had led the Left Bolsheviks between 1905 and 1914. The Ultra-Left rejected the centralist and coercive policies of War Communism as a violation of their democratic-communitarian ideal, which according to their thinking could and should be directly imple-mented and not postponed.

The Leninists of 1920–1921, identified in the Trade-Union Controversy as the adherents of the "Platform of the Ten," included those Bolshevik leaders who were consistently skeptical of the maturity of the masses and cautious about the difficulties to be encountered in the revolutionary transition to socialism. Zinoviev, Kamenev, and Rykov had backed Lenin against the Left Bolsheviks before 1917; they held back on the eve of the October Revolution; and then they supported the pragmatic Brest Treaty and Lenin's polemics against the Left Communists. Socialism under Russian conditions was for them only the end result of a long and difficult evolution while the workers' state endeavored to consolidate its gains. As N. P. Dmitrenko has recently observed, "Lenin . . . emphasized that asserting the possibility of a quick transition to socialism was a manifestation of utopianism or reformism, 'complete theoretical nonsense' and 'the greatest harm.' "[5] Like the Workers' Opposition, the Leninists also turned against the policies of War Communism, but for the opposite reason—simply because they found this system to be ineffective at Russia's current stage of development.

The Trotskyists and Bukharinists taking the middle position in the Trade Union Controversy combined the direct push towards socialism embraced by the Workers' Opposition on the Left, with the more realistic sense of the difficulties lying ahead stressed by the Leninists on the Right. Their position can be traced back both to the impatience of the prerevolutionary Ultra-Left and to the hardening experience that War Communism represented for the entire party. Interestingly enough, their forces included the three men who had served as party secretaries in

1919 and 1920—Krestinsky, Preobrazhensky, and Serebriakov. Following the most uncompromising theories of War Communism as expressed by Trotsky, Bukharin, M. A. Larin, and L. Kritsman, the adherents of the center position rejected what they considered the romantic optimism of the Left as well as the unnecessary caution of the Right. Making a virtue of necessity, they proposed to retain the War Communism methods of centralization, compulsion, and militarization as they pushed ahead toward the quick achievement of socialism.

*   *   *

The first position on the trade unions to take clear shape was that of the centrists, beginning with Trotsky's proposal for the militarization of labor early in 1920. "If we seriously speak of planned economy," he told the Ninth Party Congress, "the working masses cannot be wandering all over Russia. They must be thrown here and there, appointed, commanded, just like soldiers."[6] This objective dictated the function of the trade unions, "not for a struggle for better conditions of labor . . . , but to organize the working class for the ends of production, to educate, to discipline. . . ."[7] Bukharin in his own platform on the unions picked up a phrase first used at the Second Trade-Union Congress in 1919, "governmentalizing" [*ogosudarstvlenie*] of the unions; he called this "the state form of workers' socialism," and expected it to prevail until the state withered away.[8]

The Left and Right positions—Workers' Opposition and Leninist— took shape in reaction to Trotsky's hard-line philosophy. The precipitating event was Trotsky's initiative in the summer of 1920 to merge the Commissariat of Transport with the railroad workers' union and a new, military-style political administration of the railroads, to form the "Central Committee for Transport," *Tsektran*. (Lenin cited this idea in his "Testament" as an example of Trotsky's arbitrariness.) At the Fifth Trade-Union Conference in November 1920, Trotsky proposed to extend the Tsektran system to the entire state sector of the economy, converting the unions from "trade" (*professional'nyi*) to "production" (*proizvodstvennyi*). He dismissed objections to this model as "Kautskian-Menshevik-SR prejudices."[9]

The first concerted criticism of Trotsky's model for the unions and for socialism came from the Ultra-Left, banking on the still surviving 1917 tradition of workers' control and collegial administration in industry. Even the Party Program of 1919 had endorsed this approach: "The trade unions must proceed to the actual concentration in their own hands of all the administration of the whole economy."[10] This was almost word-for-word the position taken by the Workers' Opposition in their theses of January 1921: "The organization of the administration of the economy belongs to the All-Russian Congress of Producers, united in trade-production unions, who elect the central organs which administer the whole economy of the Republic."[11] Both Alexander Shliapnikov for the Workers' Opposition and Osinsky-Obolensky for the Democratic Centralists proposed the concept of a "separation of powers" among the party, the soviets, and the trade unions, or as Osinsky put it, among the "military-soviet culture," the "civil-soviet culture," and the "trade union . . . sphere of culture."[12] Among these, pride of place as the voice of the workers in shaping the new society went to the unions. "Through the creative powers of the rising class in the form of industrial unions," wrote Alexandra Kollontai, "we shall go toward the reconstruction and development of the creative forces of the country; toward purification of the party itself from the elements foreign to it; toward correction of the activity of the party by means of going back to democracy, freedom of opinion, and criticism inside the party."[13]

The position of the Ultra-Left disturbed both Lenin and Trotsky as a threat to the political monopoly of the party apparatus. At the Ninth Party Congress, party secretary Krestinsky literally called the Ultra-Left "counterrevolutionary," and their aspirations to political autonomy were duly repudiated.[14] Nevertheless, under the leadership of Shliapnikov and Kollontai, the Ultras gained strength during the following twelve months, particularly in the metal workers' union and in industrial centers of the south, and organized themselves formally as the Workers' Opposition.

The high point of the Ultra-Left challenge was the Ninth Party Conference, held in September 1920, when all immediate military threats to the Soviet regime had finally been surmounted. The conference seethed with rank and file protests against the bureaucratic trend in the Party, and the leadership of Leninists and Trotskyists temporarily yielded to allow passage of the remarkable resolution, "On the Coming Tasks of Building the Party." Targeting "bureaucratism," this document directed "the attention of the whole party again and again toward putting more equality into practice," and called for "publications which are capable of realizing broader and more systematic criticism of the mistakes of the party and general criticism within the party." Above all it demanded "fully effective practical measures to eliminate inequality (in conditions of life, the wage scale, etc.) between the 'spetsy' and the responsible functionaries on the one hand and the toiling masses on the other. . . . This inequality violates democratism and is the source of disruption in the party and of reduction in the authority of Communists."[15] While Shliapnikov and Kollontai never ceased to reject the charge of syndicalism, the Workers' Opposition clearly had some of that flavor, enough to justify Mikhail Tomsky in calling their ideology "industrialism and syndicalism."[16] That was after Tomsky switched from the union cause to Lenin's group. "Syndicalist deviation," reflecting the alleged "petty-bourgeois element," was the main charge against the Workers' Opposition when the Tenth Party Congress condemned their factional activity.[17]

Lenin's own faction in the Trade-Union Controversy took shape only gradually during the year 1920, as the top party leadership divided over Trotsky's stern approach to the national crisis bequeathed by the Civil War. As early as the Ninth Party Congress, consistently cautious Communists such as Rykov, V. P. Miliutin, and V. P. Nogin objected to economic militarization, even though Lenin at this point stood with Trotsky to use the unions as an instrument of labor discipline.[18] A different emphasis quickly developed, however, around the potential educational and propaganda function of the unions. Still fighting resistance to the restoration of one-man management and bourgeois specialists in industry, Lenin persuaded the Ninth Party Congress to resolve, "The unions must take upon themselves the task of explaining to the broad circles of the working class all the necessities of reconstructing the apparatus of industrial administration . . . , the maximum curtailment of administrative collegia, and the gradual introduction of individual management."[19]

Lenin kept his options open for a time, while anti-Trotsky sentiment grew in the Central Committee. He allowed Trotsky to personify the methods of War Communism, while preparing his own reversal of course and encouraging Zinoviev (a consistent enemy of Trotsky ever since 1917) to develop the anti-Trotsky argument. Trotsky later recalled, "Stalin and Zinoviev were given what one might call their legal opportunity to bring their struggle against me out into the open."[20] The actual break between Lenin and Trotsky came at a meeting of the Central Committee early in November, 1920, when Lenin cast the deciding vote to reject Trotsky's theses on the trade unions, eight to seven.

By the time the debate reached a public forum at the Eighth Congress of Soviets in December 1920, Lenin was moving rapidly away from any administrative role for the unions, in favor of their educational and political function coupled with the presocialist notion of protecting the interests of the workers: "We must use these workers' organizations for the defense of the workers from their state and for the defense by the workers' of our state."[21] Shortly afterwards Lenin's position was endorsed in the Platform of the Ten, emphasizing the unions' functions of "a school of communism," "production propaganda," and "the setting of rates of pay," all of course under the direction of the Party. However, the document still spoke of the unions' "direct participation" in "working out and implementing the comprehensive economic plan," and called on the unions to "undertake the closest participation in the business of organizing and administering industry."[22]

The struggle during the pre-congress debate early in 1921 was the most serious controversy the Communist Party had experienced since Brest-Litovsk. When it began, the extent of Lenin's victory was by no means assured. The Leninists felt compelled to call for the election of delegates to the Tenth Congress on the basis of factional platforms, presumably so that Lenin's personal prestige could decide the outcome; they pushed this rule through the Central Committee by another narrow margin of eight to seven against the Trotskyists.[23] The strategy was successful, even without the aid of the Orgburo and the Party Secretariat, still controlled by the Trotskyists. In one local party meeting after another, regularly reported by *Pravda*, the Leninists overwhelmed both oppositions.

Calling for unity of the party and the suppression of syndicalism, Lenin dominated the Tenth Congress and secured adoption of the famous resolutions embodying these two themes. On these fundamental political questions the Trotskyists went with Lenin, but on War Communism and the unions their line was emphatically rejected. The Tenth Congress essentially adopted the Platform of the Ten, denouncing governmental-izing of the unions and Trotsky's ventures in militarization. In the following months, as the NEP was implemented step by step and the Communists acknowledged their retreat to "state capitalism," the traditional role assigned to the unions became clear. As the Politburo resolved in January 1922, "One of the most pressing tasks of the trade unions is to defend in every aspect and by every means the class interests of the proletariat and its struggle with capitalism."[24]

*   *   *

The two most systematic expositions of the theoretical rationale for War Communism were composed by Trotsky and Bukharin, respectively *Terrorism and Communism* and *The Economics of the Transformation Period*.[25] (How these men managed to find time to write theoretical treatises along with their heavy official responsibilities and the incessant crises of the Civil War is still a mystery.) Trotsky was quite blunt about persevering with War Communism as the road to socialism: "We can have no way to socialism except by the authoritative regulation of the economic forces and resources of the country, and the centralized distribution of labor-power in harmony with the general state plan."[26] He reaffirmed the militarization of labor, compulsory labor service, and the absorption of the unions into the state: "The road to socialism lies through a period of the highest possible intensification of the principle of the state."[27] Bukharin expressed a cloudy optimism, somewhat closer to the Workers' Opposition until the decisive realignment in the party on the eve of the Tenth Congress. He saw "a new network of human systems," while the proletariat "builds its own apparatus." But he came down closer to Trotsky on specifics: "Militarization . . . is a method of self-organization of the working class."[28] With the talent for theoretical rationalization that made him popular as the party's number-one ideologue, Bukharin accepted the use of bourgeois experts, and claimed that the growingly bureaucratic administration of industry was "a contracted, condensed *form* of workers' control of industry."[29] For both men, the system of War Communism would remain the norm for an indefinite period of time, though ultimately they looked to the actual attainment of socialism, when "there will be no need for the harsh military style of management" (Bukharin), and "there will not exist the apparatus of compulsion itself, namely, the State: for it will have melted away entirely into a producing and consuming commune" (Trotsky).[30]

For the Workers' Opposition, by contrast, socialism had to be the direct achievement of the working class if it was to be realized at all. "Who shall build the communist economy?" asked Kollontai. "Who is right—the leaders or the working masses endowed with the healthy class instinct?" This was closer to Rosa Luxemburg's thinking than to Leninism. Kollontai continued,

> Through the creative powers of the rising class in the form of industrial unions we shall go towards reconstruction of creative forces of the country; towards purification of the party itself from the elements foreign to it; towards correction of the activity of the party by means of going back to democracy, freedom of opinion, and criticism within the party.[31]

Alone of the contending factions, the Workers' Opposition understood that the revolutionary victory could be snatched away from the proletariat just as the bourgeoisie had snatched it away from the *sans-culottes* in revolutionary France.

For the Leninists it was enough to assert that the Soviet state was a workers' state, guaranteeing the transition to socialism however long the process might take. Lenin's consistent priorities in economic policy from 1918 on were, first, the supremacy of party control in the economic realm, and second, the restoration of just that conventional managerial authority and engineering expertise that the Workers' Opposition found so repugnant. By 1921, he and his supporters were shedding their illusions both about the county's readiness for socialism (contrary to the Workers' Opposition) and about the socialist character of the methods they had resorted to under War Communism (contrary to the Trotskyists). Beneath the level of the dictatorial state, they were ready to accept a new sort of pluralism, with relatively independent functions for the industrial leadership, the trade unions, and any other social organization or interest, including the intelligentsia. In effect, the Leninists were retreating to Lenin's old image of the "democratic dictatorship of the proletariat and peasantry," in which the vanguard party would hold power while the country continued to mature to the point where real socialism would be feasible.[32] This was the essence of the NEP.

*   *   *

Diversity of revolutionary factions and their competing notions about the future road was by no means unique to the Russian Revolution and the Communists. Every great revolution has generated differences, not only for and against the basic aims of the revolution, but about the definition of those aims and the tempo of their realization. As the revolution gathers momentum and the moderate parties fall by the wayside, power goes to those who are most determined to realize the goals of the revolution by any means, including dictatorship and civil war. But disagreements soon emerge among these committed revolutionaries, representing basic differences in human psychology. The most idealistic and utopian people—the Enragés and the Hébertistes in the French Revolution, the Workers' Opposition and the Democratic Centralists in Russia—persuade themselves that the masses need only to be freed and encouraged and thereby realize the revolutionary ideal. The center position is taken by those of the Robespierrist persuasion who are emboldened by combat and the feel of authority, and believe they can overcome all obstacles by force: "There are no fortresses that Bolsheviks cannot capture," to cite a famous statement made at a later point in Soviet history.[33] Meanwhile, the more cautious elements conclude that the revolution risks destruction unless it falls back and tries to resume the advance more gradually—like the Right-wing Jacobins who overthrew Robespierre. Here, of course, the Russian and French revolutions differ in important detail. In France the leader of the militant center was overthrown and guillotined on the Ninth Thermidor; in Russia the prime leader sided with the Right wing of the revolutionaries, and carried out his own Thermidor, so to speak, while letting the Robespierrist Trotsky take the onus for the excesses of War Communism and the Terror.

In neither the French nor the Russian case, of course, did the Thermidorean Reaction represent a repudiation of the aims of the revolution, but only of its violent excesses. Lenin must be credited with unusual political perspicacity and skill, as a leader of the radical revolution who could see that the time had come for revolutionary retrenchment, and who was able to lead the retreat and maintain the rule of his own party instead of suffering the fate of Robespierre. This strategic maneuver, even more than the victory of October, was arguably the most decisive instance of the impact of Lenin's personality on the otherwise impersonal process of revolution in Russia. He had the flexibility that Trotsky, the purer ideologue, lacked.

Trotsky is perhaps the most difficult figure to explain among the major Communist leaders. In his prerevolutionary career and in his years as an oppositionist after 1923, he resisted the unqualified centralism and discipline usually associated with Leninism, yet from the time of the October Revolution until the Kronstadt Rebellion he was the most ruthless and authoritarian of revolutionaries. To be sure, he anticipated the NEP by proposing to the Central Committee in February, 1920, an end to the uncompensated requisitioning of food products from the peasantry. Failing this, so he says in his autobiography, he insisted that military methods be applied even more systematically.[34] Trotsky's psychological orientation towards power seems to have changed according to whether he held it or not. His tragedy was that he was too big a man to subordinate himself to Lenin or any other individual or party or doctrine, and yet too small a man to do without the moral legitimacy that loyalty to such an individual or party or doctrine provided for him. This contradiction lay at the root of his failure in the fateful political struggle of 1923–1927.

*   *   *

The models of socialism expressed or implied by the three factions in the Trade-Union Controversy were all paralleled at one point or another by subsequent developments in the Soviet Union or the international Communist movement. The semisyndicalist ideal of the Workers' Opposition was reincarnated in the doctrine of "workers' self-management" adopted in Yugoslavia in the 1950s. I am not aware of any direct acknowledgment by Yugoslav theoreticians of their Workers' Opposition ancestry. Milovan Djilas says the idea of self-management came to him when he was re-reading Marx to find arguments against Stalinism after the Soviet-Yugoslav break in 1948, but Edvard Kardelj, one of the most enthusiastic backers of the concept, studied in Moscow in the 1930s and may conceivably have become acquainted with the history of the Russian Ultra-Left at that time.[35]

Lenin's position in the trade-union debate—the nondoctrinaire recognition of the time-consuming difficulties along the path of fundamental social change in an incompletely developed country—has been reiterated everywhere by pragmatic Communist reformers, not least in the Soviet Union today. Interestingly enough, Soviet students of radical Third-World regimes observed in the 1970s and early 1980s that Lenin's NEP model of market socialism and limited state intervention was more appropriate under conditions of "superbackwardness" than Stalin's totally centralized system.[36]

Finally, what of the proposition that Stalin's "command-administrative system" was a direct revival of the War Communism model and of Trotsky's concept of militarized socialism? Or was it a Soviet version of Bonapartism, following the NEP "Directory"? Recent Western scholarship suggests that the phenomenon of Stalinism was more complicated, and that it is necessary to recognize certain distinct phases in the establishment of the Stalin system.[37]

In its first phase, from 1928 to 1931 or 1932, Stalin's "revolution from above" appears in many ways to have been a revival of the "Jacobin" phase of the Russian Revolution. In 1928–1929 the Bukharinists were charging explicitly that Stalin was breaking with the NEP and resorting to the methods of War Communism. The renewed spirit of class struggle and the mood of hysteria directed against bourgeois specialists, beginning with the Shakhty Trial (when a number of mining engineers in the Donets Basin were accused of "sabotage"), recall the views of the Ultra-Left during War Communism. Robert C. Tucker writes of a "culture of War Communism," which he believes lived on among the new Stalinist apparatchiki of the 1920s and then emerged to dominate the political scene of the 1930s.[38] (Perhaps this explains why the former leaders of the Workers' Opposition supported Stalin against the Trotsky–Zinoviev Opposition, though it does not explain the fate that most of them subsequently suffered.) Stalin's measures of centralized mobilization and compulsion obviously recall the Center, Trotskyist position in the trade-union debate. By this time, however, Trotsky had rejected compulsion in favor of economic methods, and consistently criticized the manner in which Stalinist industrialization and collectivization were implemented.[39]

As to the second phase of Stalinism, with its purges and full-blown cult of personality, that is another story. This phase, in my opinion, was marked by a profound shift from ultrarevolutionary to counterrevolutionary policies, together with the physical extermination of the revolutionaries, all "masked by Left phrases," as the expression goes.[40] There is no Russian precedent, even in War Communism, for the kind of regime that Stalin ultimately established.

The experience of Stalinism has made the entire world aware that the socialist organization of economic life is no panacea, that socialism can become a vehicle of horror as well as a vehicle of justice. Socialism in the abstract is not necessarily a guarantor of the interests and well-being of the toiling masses. The assurances of the Communist leaders during the "heroic period" of War Communism that the existence of a "workers' state" justified all the methods of command, coercion, and violence rightly condemned when they were employed under the Old Regime, proved to be a tragic delusion. Under Stalinism and neo-

Stalinism, Marxian socialism became the ideological "false consciousness" legitimating the dominance of the New Class of bureaucrats and specialists, just the outcome that the Communist Ultra-Left of 1918–1921 had feared. To be sure, it is questionable whether the bureaucratic trend can be averted in any modern society; the more practical issue is how it may be controlled to protect the ordinary citizen from arbitrariness and injustice. In contrast to the Trotskyists, the Leninists of 1921 perceived this need, at least dimly and in economic matters, though unfortunately not in the political life of the socialist society.

Notes

1. See Dušan Popović, "Socijalizam kao svetski proces" (Socialism as a Worldwide Process), in *Socijalizam kao svjetski proces* (Belgrade: "Komunist," 1978).

2. Thomas F. Remington, *Building Socialism in Bolshevik Russia: Ideology & Industrial Organization, 1917–1921* (Pittsburgh: University of Pittsburgh Press, 1984), p. 49.

3. See, e.g., Isaac Deutscher, *Stalin: A Political Biography* (New York and London: Oxford University Press, 1949), pp. 222–223.

4. See Robert C. Williams, *The Other Bolsheviks: Lenin and his Critics, 1904–1914* (Bloomington, Ind.: Indiana University Press, 1984), pp. 85–93.

5. V. P. Dmitrenko, "Politika 'voennogo kommunizma': problemy i opyt" (The Policy of "War Communism": Problems and Experience), *Voprosy Istorii KPSS*, no. 2, 1990, p. 80, citing Lenin, *Polnoe sobranie sochinenii*, vol. XL, p. 311.

6. *Deviatyi s"ezd RKP(b): Protokoly* (Moscow: IMEL, 1934), p. 100.

7. Leon Trotsky, *Dictatorship vs. Democracy (Terrorism & Communism): a Reply to Karl Kautsky* (New York: Workers' Party of America, 1922), p. 143.

8. *Vtoroi vserossiiskii s"ezd professional'nykh soyuzov: Stenograficheskii otchet* (2 vols., Moscow: Tsentral'noe Izdatel'stvo Profsoyuzov, 1919), vol. I, p. 97; Nikolai Bukharin, *Oekonomik der Transformationsperiode* (Hamburg: Kommunistische Internationale, 1922), p. 86; "O zadachakh i strukture prof-soyuzov," (On the Tasks and Structure of the Trade Unions), *Desiatyi s"ezd RKP(b): Protokoly* (Moscow: IMEL, 1933), appendix 16, p. 802.

9. Trotsky, "Profsoyuzy i ikh dal'neishaya rol" (The Trade Unions and their Future Role), *Desiatyi s"ezd*, appendix 10, p. 786.

10. "Programma Rossiiskoi Kommunisticheskoi Partii (bol'shevikov)," *KPSS v rezoliutsiyakh i resheniyakh s"ezdov, konferentsii, i plenumov TsK* (7th ed., Moscow: Gospolitizdat, 1954), vol. I, p. 422.

11. *Vsesoyuznaya Kommunisticheskaya Partiya (bol'shevikov) v rezoliutsiyakh s"ezdov, konferentsii, i plenumov TsK* (Moscow: Partiinoe izdatel'stvo, 1931), vol. I, appendix, p. 813.

12. *Deviatyi s"ezd*, pp. 564n32, 123–124.

13. Alexandra Kollontai, *The Workers' Opposition* (Chicago: Kerr, 1921), p. 9.

14. *Deviatyi s"ezd*, p. 44.

15. "Ob ocherednykh zadachakh partiinogo stroitel'stva" (On the Regular Tasks of Party Construction), *KPSS v rezoliutsiyakh*, vol. I, pp. 507–512.

16. *Desiatyi s"ezd*, pp. 371–372.

17. Lenin, *Desiatyi s"ezd*, p. 119; resolution of the Tenth Party Congress, "O sindikalistskom i anarkhistskom uklone v nashei partii" (On the Syndicalist and Anarchist Deviation in Our Party), *KPSS v rezoliutsiyakh*, vol. I, p. 531.

18. See Lenin, "K organizatsiyam RKP(b) po voprosu o poriadke dnia partiinogo s"ezda" (To the Organizations of the RCP(B) on the Question of the Agenda of the Party Congress, 2 March 1920), *Deviatyi s"ezd*, appendix 2, p. 473.

19. "Po voprosu o professional'nykh soyuzakh i ikh organizatsii" (On the Question of the Trade Unions and Their Organization), *KPSS v rezoliutsiyakh*, vol. I, p. 493.

20. Trotsky, *My Life: An Attempt at an Autobiography* (New York: Scribner's, 1930), p. 462.

21. Lenin, "O professional'nykh soyuzakh, o tekushchem momente, i ob oshibakh tov. Trotskogo" (On the Trade Unions, the Current Situation, and the Mistakes of Comrade Trotsky), *Sochineniya* (3rd ed., Moscow: IMEL, 1928–1937), XXVI: 67.

22. "Rol' i zadachi professional'nykh soyuzov (Proyekt postanovleniya X s"ezda RKP, vnesennyi gruppoi 'Desiati')" (The Role and Tasks of the Trade Unions: Draft for a Decision of the Tenth Congress of the RCP, Introduced by the Group of the "Ten"), *Desiatyi s"ezd RKP(b): Stenograficheskii Otchet* (Moscow: Gosudarstvennoe izdatel'stvo politicheskoi literatury, 1963), appendix, pp. 663–674. The ten were Lenin, Zinoviev, Kamenev, Stalin, Tomsky, Kalinin, Rudzatak, Lozovsky, Petrovsky, and Artem-Sergeyev.

23. See *Desiatyi s"ezd*, p. 837n1.

24. Adopted by the Eleventh Party Congress as "Rol' i zadachi profsoyuzov v usloviyakh novoi ekonomicheskoi politiki" (The Role and Tasks of the Trade Unions under the Conditions of the New Economic Policy), *KPSS v rezoliutsiyakh*, vol. I, p. 604.

25. Trotsky, *Terrorizm i kommunizm* (Moscow: Gosizdat, 1920); Bukharin, *Ekonomika perekhodnogo perioda* (Moscow: Communist Academy, 1920).

26. Trotsky, *Terrorism and Communism* (Ann Arbor, Mich.: University of Michigan Press, 1961), p. 142.

27. Ibid., pp. 169–170.

28. Bukharin, "The Economics of the Transition Period," in Nikolai Bukharin, *The Politics and Economics of the Transition Period*, Kenneth V. Tarbusk, ed. (London: Routledge and Kegan Paul, 1979), pp. 104–105, 142.

29. Ibid., p. 143.

30. Ibid., p. 144; Trotsky, *Terrorism and Communism*, p. 169.

31. Kollontai, *The Workers' Opposition*, pp. 4, 15, 17.

32. See Lenin, "Two Tactics of Social Democracy in The Democratic Revolution" (July 1905), *Selected Works* (Moscow: Foreign Languages Publishing House, 1950–1952), vol. I, book 2, pp. 86–90.

33. Joseph Stalin, "The Tasks of Business Executives" (Speech delivered at the first All-Union Conference of Managers of Socialist Industry, 4 February

1931), in J. Stalin, *Problems of Leninism* (Moscow: Foreign Languages Publishing House, 1953), p. 458.

34. Trotsky, *My Life*, pp. 463–464.

35. Milovan Djilas, *The Unperfect Society: Beyond the New Class* (New York: Harcourt, Brace & World, 1969), pp. 220–223. Cf. Bogdan Denitch, *The Legitimation of a Revolution* (New Haven: Yale University Press, 1976), pp. 152–153; Dennison Rusinow, *The Yugoslav Experiment, 1948–1974* (Berkeley and Los Angeles: University of California Press, 1977), pp. 50–51.

36. See, e.g., G. I. Mirsky, *Tretii mir—Obshchestvo, vlast', armiya* (Moscow: Nauka, 1976).

37. See Robert V. Daniels, "Stalin: Revolutionary or Counterrevolutionary?" *Problems of Communism*, September–October 1989; Sheila Fitzpatrick, ed., *Cultural Revolution in Russia* (Bloomington: Indiana University Press, 1978).

38. Robert C. Tucker, "Stalinism as Revolution from Above," in Robert C. Tucker, ed., *Stalinism: Essays in Historical Interpretation* (New York: Norton, 1977).

39. See, e.g., Richard B. Day, *Leon Trotsky and the Politics of Economic Isolation* (Cambridge, Eng.: Cambridge University Press, 1973), pp. 182–185.

40. See below, chs. 9 and 10. On the two phases of Stalinism, see Claudio Ingerflom, "Soviet Totalitarianism, Myth & Reality," *Liber*, February 1990, citing Francesco Benvenuti and Silvio Pons, *Il sistema di potere dello stalinismo* (1988) and Gabor Rittersporn, *Simplifications staliniennes et complications sovietiques* (1988).

5

Forging the Apparatus: The Secretariat and the Local Organizations in the Russian Communist Party, 1921–1923

An acutely significant episode in the history of Soviet Russia was the development of the organizational machinery of the Communist Party in the years immediately following the Civil War. It was this period which witnessed the true realization of Lenin's prerevolutionary ideal of the monolithic party, despite the paradox that the model of conspiratorial discipline was designed for the accomplishment of the revolution, not the organization of the postrevolutionary society.

The Communist Party in 1921 was confronted with the dilemma of pursuing socialist goals in a country admittedly unprepared for such a program. Forces of dissatisfaction were growing on both the left and the right, and sometimes in combination, as manifested by the Kronstadt revolt. With the New Economic Policy, the Party undertook a long-term strategic retreat, but only at the cost of alienating substantial elements in its own following. To preserve the illusion that there could be no correct "proletarian" policy other than that espoused by the party leadership, the determined suppression of such left-wing discontent as that manifested by the Workers' Opposition was called for.

The decisive steps were taken at the Tenth Party Congress in March 1921: the left-wing opposition groups were denounced as a "petty-bourgeois" deviation; organized factions were banned in the name of party unity; and the Party's machinery of organizational control and discipline was shaken up and invigorated. The Trotskyist party secretaries

Reprinted with permission from *American Slavic and East European Review*, vol. 16, no. 1 (February 1957), pp. 32–49.

(Krestinsky, Preobrazhensky, and Serebriakov) were ousted in favor of a new crew (Molotov, Yemelian Yaroslavsky, and V. M. Mikhailov), among whom one influence was especially strong—Stalin's. The appointment of Stalin to the new post of general secretary in 1922 was largely the formal recognition of power which he already wielded.

There ensued a complex process whereby the party Secretariat, pursuing its function of rooting out dissension and building the Party into an efficient instrument of political control and supervision, became more and more a power unto itself. The trend toward a military mode of organization and operation did not cease until the entire political life of the country came under the domination of a hierarchy of individual party secretaries, all under the supreme command of one man, General Secretary Stalin. Decisive in this process was the establishment of control by the central Secretariat over the local party organizations, which gave Stalin the foundation for controlling the party congresses and through them, in time, dominating the entire policy-making summit of the Party and the state. This paper is intended to elucidate some of the processes whereby the paramount influence of the Secretariat was established.

*   *   *

Though the party Secretariat had been formally established in 1919, along with the Politburo and the Orgburo, under the headship of Krestinsky, its effectiveness was severely limited during the first two years of its existence; the party press of that period is replete with complaints about the organizational inadequacies of the party machinery. Local spontaneity was as much the rule as central direction in the affairs of the Party, and such over-all supervision of party organizations and personnel as could be managed appears to have been applied largely for military purposes—the mobilization of party members for the war effort, and the maintenance of political discipline in the armed forces. Speaking at the Ninth Party Congress in 1920, Krestinsky admitted widespread defects of a "business, practical, organizational character," while his critics stressed the failure of the Party's central machinery to make itself felt at the local level.[1] A graphic example of the state of fluidity in the Party is provided by a Central Committee circular letter at the time when the Ukraine was reconquered late in 1919; this was a special pronouncement made in an effort to ban movement of party members to the Ukraine unless they made application through the proper channels and received official assignments.[2]

The principle was well established in the course of the Civil War that a party member, especially one engaged in full time party work or in work assigned to him by the Party, was bound by decisions of the Party's top organizational bodies to transfer or relieve him. As the

Eighth Party Congress resolved, "The whole matter of assignment of party workers [*rabotniki*] is in the hands of the Central Committee of the Party. Its decision is binding for everyone. . . . The Central Committee is entrusted with the carrying out of the most determined struggle against any *mestnichestvo* or separatism in these questions."[3] Once the system of assignment was established, it was easy to extend the considerations involved from military need or administrative efficiency to the liquidation of political disputes and dissension through transferring the offenders. By Krestinsky's admission, this had already become a customary practice in 1920.[4] The first large-scale use of this authority of reassignment came in April 1920 when the entire Central Committee of the Communist Party of the Ukraine was disbanded. Declared the order from Moscow,

> The Central Committee of the Russian Communist Party considers it necessary to transfer from the Ukraine for work in Great-Russia those of the responsible party workers whose active participation in the still fresh struggle has unavoidably made it difficult to carry on agreed-on and friendly work . . . on the basis of the decisions reached by the Ninth Congress of the Party.[5]

With the continued resort to such action, particularly after the shakeup of 1921, the nominally democratic election of local party secretaries became a complete sham.

By 1923 local party secretaries were generally appointed, de facto, by the higher instance in the secretarial hierarchy, although the legal fiction of "recommendation" and election by local committees was still retained. At the same time the development of the Party's secretarial institutions confirmed the cleavage between responsible officials and party workers on the one hand and the rank-and-file on the other. The military pattern was becoming complete: to the chain-of-command, discipline, and assignment of personnel by higher authority, was added the distinction of officers and enlisted men. Trotsky, going into open opposition in the fall of 1923, complained bitterly of this trend:

> In the fiercest moment of War Communism, the system of appointment within the Party did not have one-tenth of the extent that it has now. Appointment of the secretaries of provincial committees is now the rule. That creates for the secretary a position essentially independent of the local organization. . . . There has been created a very broad stratum of party workers, entering into the apparatus of the government of the Party, who completely renounce their own party opinion, at least the open expression of it, as though assuming that the secretarial hierarchy is the apparatus which creates party opinion and party decisions. Beneath this

stratum, there lies the broad mass of the Party, before whom every decision stands in the form of a summons or a command.[6]

There were two agencies under the Secretariat through which this situation was brought into being. The "Organization and Instruction Department" (*organizatsionno-instruktorskii otdel*) had cognizance over the affairs of local party organizations and the liaison between them and the central institutions of the Party. The "Record and Assignment Department" (*uchetno-raspredelitel'nyi otdel* or "*uchraspred*") was responsible for matters pertaining to individual party members, particularly the collection of information and making of recommendations bearing on the transfer and promotion of the Party's "officer corps" of full-time workers. Both of these agencies commenced operations in 1920, but began to exercise a significant influence only in 1921 and 1922, with the new secretarial regime under Stalin.

The basic rationale for the Secretariat's assignment operations was laid down by the Tenth Party Conference in May, 1921:

> The fundamental tasks of party and soviet work at the present moment demand the concentration of main attention to the appropriateness of the assignment of party forces, which is directly and primarily connected with the promotion of new party workers and the transfer of these from less responsible to more responsible work. . . . The system of transfer of party workers must be constructed on the basic principle of the primacy of general party and soviet work. . . .[7]

The effect of the latter point was the complete subordination of local considerations, preferences, and autonomy to the power of the Party's central institutions, which were given the right to dispose over the full-time staff of party officials, even those who were nominally elected to their posts by the membership or representative gatherings of local organizations.

A report of the Record and Assignment Department to the Twelfth Party Congress described the duties of the organization as

> detailed and attentive accounting of the commanding cadre of the Party; reassignment of party forces to strengthen the most important provincial organizations; selection of organizers for party work; review of the directors of *oblast'*, *guberniya*, and *uyezd* party organizations and the upper grade of secretaries of cells; replacement of workers who do not measure up to the standards set forth by the party congress. . . .[8]

By this time the operations of the department had become quite extensive; during the year between the Eleventh and Twelfth Party Congresses it handled some 10,000 assignments of party workers, of whom roughly half were of the grade known as "responsible." Higher-ranking officials were assigned by the Secretariat after the department had processed their records. A program of "planned exchange" of party workers was undertaken, under which regular rotation of party officials between the central institutions and the local organizations was to be carried out. Special attention was devoted to the 600 men occupying the key provincial posts of *guberniya* party secretary, president of the executive committee of a *guberniya* soviet, *guberniya* trade-union secretary, and head of the organizational or agitation-propaganda department of a *guberniya* party committee.[9] By 1923, even these latter posts in the *guberniya* organizations were being filled through appointments by the Secretariat.[10]

Reports in *Izvestiya TsK* (the Party's journal for organizational affairs, revived in 1989) spoke with pride of the work of the Central Committee in assigning, removing and transferring local party secretaries during 1922. "Selection of secretaries of *guberniya* committees and *oblast'* committees" was the frank title of one of these articles. It reported that in this period thirty-seven *guberniya* secretaries were removed or transferred by the central party authority, and forty-two new men were sent out "with recommendations for the post of secretary."[11] Some organizations had their secretaries changed several times a year, and some secretaries found themselves transferred from post to post at a corresponding frequency.

The system of controls by the Secretariat over the whole staff of full-time party workers and officials was gradually extended and intensified from the top downward. According to the system prevailing in 1922, party workers were classified for purposes of assignment into four levels— *uyezd*, *guberniya*, regional and republic, and nation-wide. Each class was subject to the jurisdiction of the appropriate party authority on the next higher level, with the highest class coming directly under the jurisdiction of the Orgburo (in such cases the Secretariat officially made recommendations, not assignments). At first the Secretariat, acting through the Record and Assignment Department, concentrated on establishing detailed records and firm controls down to the *guberniya* level; towards the end of 1922 and the beginning of 1923 this work was completed to the satisfaction of the heads of the apparatus, and intensive work was begun in extending the full system of central accounting and controls over personnel down to the *uyezd* level.[12]

All of these developments contributed to the authority of the general secretary, for whom the Record and Assignment Department was simply an executive agency. In rationalizing this system of tight controls over the party officialdom it was explained that

The transition to broad organizational work in soviet and party construction demanded from the Party serious attention to the choice of directors for the various branches of work. The period of broad mobilizations, upon which main attention was focused two to four years ago, has now been succeeded by the epoch of all-round accounting of party forces, the training and promotion of new cadres of party workers, and complete direction by the Party in all matters of assigning party workers.[13]

With this system in effective operation, whereby every responsible party official was to be assigned to his post by the Secretariat in Moscow, it is difficult to see how the party leadership found room for retaining the fiction of free election of local party secretaries and other officials by the rank-and-file.

*   *   *

Direct control over individual personnel in the party apparatus was one of the long arms by which the Secretariat exerted its influence. The other was its power exercised over local party organizations through supervision and control activities. The agency responsible for this aspect of the Secretariat's operations was the Organization and Instruction Department, whose functions were, as described at length in its report to the Twelfth Congress,

> to establish relations of the Central Committee with local organizations, in order to make possible daily study of the condition of each organization and the activities going on in it; to strengthen the apparatus, bring about a vital link with the localities, to improve the conditions of information so they embrace and reflect the work of the localities; to draw nearer to the life and work of local organizations down to the lowest cells; to single out the most important industrial centers and establish a direct link with them and, on this basis, to carry on planned work directed toward the strengthening and improvement of party organization, liquidation of disputes, improvement of methods of general party work, accounting and treatment of those new undertakings in the area of party work in the localities which have significance for the Party.[14]

The department was thus designed to serve as the eyes and ears of the Secretariat in matters concerning the local party units. Its head in 1922 and 1923 was, significantly, one of Stalin's most steadfast lieutenants, Lazar Kaganovich.[15]

A special concern of the Organization Department was conflicts among the responsible personnel in local organizations—i.e., manifestations of opposition strength and activity. On the basis of the picture assembled by the Organization Department, the assignments of party workers were planned in conjunction with the Record and Assignment Department, to implement the organizational policy of the Secretariat and root out opposition:[16] "The Central Committee considered as its duty the constant observation of the internal affairs of local party organizations, trying in every way to eliminate from the localities those frictions and dissensions known under the name of '*skloki*.'"[17]

By critics of the apparatus these "*skloki*" were partially explained as themselves a result of the control operations undertaken by the Secretariat. Preobrazhensky complained at the Twelfth Congress,

> Approximately 30% of all secretaries of our *guberniya* committees . . . were, as the expression goes, 'recommended' by the Central Committee. I am very much afraid, comrades, that if this matter continues further, and the practice of 'recommendation' becomes a system, then we may find that we have this in many organizations: comrades who have come to the locality and who don't meet with sufficient support—often for no reason at all they do not meet with support—and as a result they group around themselves several comrades who disagree with the local people, and as a result we get a state within the state.[18]

This formation of interest groups within the party apparatus on the local level paralleled the emergence on the top level of the group of party officials centered around Stalin.[19]

In spite of the additional resistance stirred up by the efforts of the party apparatus to further its own power, the resources of the Secretariat proved adequate to its task. "Experience has shown," it was euphemistically reported in 1922, "that lively direction and instruction are among the basic means for the solidification of the organization, the real invigoration of work, and the liquidation of disputes."[20] The effectiveness of these operations was highly satisfying to the Secretariat and to the party leadership. Reported Molotov at the Eleventh Congress, "Now, after a year of party work, it is possible to say in all firmness that the basic groupings and tendencies which existed within our Party have disappeared; now in both political and organizational respects, as a militant Communist organization, our Party is a stronger, more solid organization."[21]

A particularly important transmission belt in the organizational machinery was the institution of "responsible instructors." These individuals, reminiscent of the Carolingian *missi dominici*, were high-ranking party workers who travelled around the country as representatives of the Central Committee, to visit, inspect, and advise the local organizations: "The basic link, joining the Central Committee with the localities, is the instructors, through whom the Central Committee executes its direction of the work of the party organizations."[22] The instructors regularly attended meetings of provincial party committees and conferences, to which they conveyed the wishes of the Central Committee: "The responsible instructors . . . attend the sessions of the respective *guberniya* committees and propose a series of concrete measures for the elimination of specified defects and abnormalities."[23] The claimed efficacy of these missions was striking: "In the course of the year's work there has not been even one case at all significant in which the practical proposals of the instructors have not been adopted by the *guberniya* committees."[24]

Supplementing the system of instructors was the practice, begun in 1921, of reports to Moscow in person by provincial secretaries. Occasionally conferences of local secretaries were held, especially when nationwide party conferences or congresses brought most of the ranking party officialdom to Moscow. Sometimes, in addition, the chiefs of the local organization departments were called upon to report directly to Moscow.[25]

In some instances, notably in the case of certain nationality frictions, the party center resorted to an extreme form of intervention in the affairs of local organizations. "Plenipotentiaries" were dispatched by order of the Central Committee "with the right of veto regarding those decisions of the local organizations which interfered with the proper conditions of party and soviet work."[26]

Liaison between the center and the local organizations was far from perfect, as contemporary records indicate only too well. The pages of *Izvestiya TsK* are replete with complaints about inadequacies in the links between the various levels in the party pyramid. Nevertheless, though the secretarial apparatus was imperfect, its importance was decisive. The superiority of the apparatus against the Opposition in 1923 and thereafter demonstrates clearly the power of even a mediocre organization against an opponent virtually without any at all. Moreover, the apparatus was able to concentrate its strength where it counted most. Personnel controls were imposed as vigorously as possible at the top level, and as a result, even if the organization had its weak spots, it was in fact the decisive nationwide force.

There was a prevailing sense that lower party organizations ought to be under the tutelage of the next higher organizations. It was in this spirit that the Central Committee took upon itself the task of "inspecting," "instruction," and "checking the structure of the apparatuses of the *guberniya* committees."[27] Extremely significant was the remark that local party organizations, if left in isolation from the central apparatus, tended to come under the influence of "anti-party forces."[28] This illustrates the need faced by the Secretariat of shifting the centers of decision-making upward as rapidly as possible, under the guise of "directing nationwide party work," in order to forestall the development of centers of local autonomy which might become bases for opposition activity. Local party organizations were, in the ideal scheme toward which the Secretariat was striving in its organizational policy, organs for the execution of central decisions rather than for the formulation of local opinion and the exercise of local autonomy. In this direction the Eleventh Party Conference of December 1921 provided in its resolution "On Strengthening the Party" that *guberniya* committees should curtail their discussions and policy-making sessions, and concentrate on "the direct execution of party tasks,"[29] leaving decision-making to Moscow.

* * *

Some idea of the impact of the new party machinery on a local party organization can be gained by examining the course of events in particular organizations as illustrative examples. The Samara organization is especially interesting in this respect because it was the only case in which the Workers' Opposition got control of a *guberniya* committee.[30]

From the spring of 1920, i.e., from the beginning of the existence of the Workers' Opposition as a clearly defined group in the Party, the Samara organization was dominated by that faction.[31] The reason for this is obscure; the Samara region was not particularly industrialized. However, from the proletarians who were in the *guberniya*, the Workers' Opposition apparently enjoyed almost solid allegiance.[32] Beyond this there is apparently the factor of a local strong-man, who in this unusual case happened to line up with an opposition faction rather than with the party organization. He was Yu. K. Milonov, the president of the Samara *guberniya* economic council from 1918 on. From this position he apparently gained ascendancy over the *guberniya* party committee, of which he was made secretary before 1921.[33]

Milonov was a delegate of the Samara organization to both the Ninth and Tenth Party Congresses, and at the latter he made a vigorous speech defending the record of the Workers' Opposition in Samara and attacking the bureaucratic tendencies of the party leadership.[34] Under his leadership, the Samara Workers' Oppositionists elected ten or eleven of the fifteen delegates which the organization sent to the Tenth Congress.[35]

This triumph was short-lived. The party apparatus, rapidly being built up organization-wise, and armed by the Tenth Congress with drastic powers to operate against manifestations of factionalism, soon found an opportunity to come to grips with the situation in Samara. As Molotov reported frankly,

The Central Committee has in the recent period exerted quite decisive interference in the work of several party organizations. The most decisive and radical measures were taken by the Central Committee in regard to the Samara party organization. Here the Central Committee was compelled to resort to definite and strong measures.[36]

The pressure was applied gradually. In response to evidence of friction and malfunctioning of the Samara organization, the Central Control Commission dispatched a commission of three to investigate. They allegedly found a disastrous drop in the membership of the *guberniya* organization from 13,000 to 4,500, and complete inability of the op-positionist *guberniya* committee to cope with the chaotic situation resulting from famine conditions in the area.[37] In the words of Molotov, in the Samara organization there was "a complete absence of party discipline and party ties between the responsible comrades on the one hand and the party masses on the other."[38]

The action which Moscow finally took was drastic indeed. The entire *guberniya* committee was ousted, by the use of the Secretariat's power to transfer party workers at its discretion. In their place a new committee was installed by virtue of the same authority, leaving the rank and file in Samara no voice at all in the changeover.[39] Molotov strove to justify the affair:

Leaving the organization any longer in such a situation was intolerable. This was the only *guberniya* organization where the Central Committee removed the whole upper group of party and soviet workers. . . . This was the only case of appointment which was necessitated, and the Central Committee does not regret it.[40]

The newly appointed secretary of the Samara organization was I. I. Minkov, a stalwart of the party apparatus who had been transferred from Moscow. His loyalty to the apparatus is attested by his reward with appointment as a candidate member of the Central Control Commission in 1923, followed by promotion to full member in 1927.[41] His installation in Samara was a striking example of the manner in which the new, close-knit secretarial hierarchy under Stalin's leadership was using the campaign that Lenin had called for against the Opposition as an opportunity for installing itself in the seats of power.

Different circumstances in which the party apparatus similarly used and developed its power can be seen in the case of the Tula *guberniya* organization, where the force of the apparatus was brought to bear to sustain a local secretary against local unrest and criticism. Zh. I. Meyerzon had served as the secretary of the Tula *guberniya* party committee since the fall of 1920.[42] He became a supporter of the Stalin group, as is attested by the appearance of his name in 1932 as a secretary of the Transcaucasian regional party organization, and his appointment in 1934 to the Commission of Party Control.[43] (He disappeared in the purge of 1937–1938.)

The Tula party organization was the scene of considerable strife among the membership. It was severely hit by the purge of 1921, 34 percent of its members being expelled.[44] An organizational report for the year preceding the Eleventh Party Congress mentioned certain local troubles, without elaborating: "We point to Tula and Nizhegorod, which experienced for a certain time a period of internal local struggle in the organizations. At present these organizations are among the best in vitality and solidarity."[45] The struggles which broke out in the Tula organization were sufficiently disturbing to the party leadership to warrant the dispatch of a special commission to investigate; it was headed by V. V. Kuibyshev, then a candidate member of the Central Committee.[46]

If the sanguine conclusion regarding the efficacy of the action taken with respect to the Tula organization is anything more than pure verbiage, the party Secretariat was seriously in error in its evaluation. Internal dissension in the organization quickly resumed, with a faction forming in opposition to the secretary, Meyerzon. Again a special commission was sent to the scene, this one with much more rank represented— Feliks Dzerzhinsky of the Central Committee, M. F. Shkiriatov of the Central Control Commission, and N. A. Kubiak, a responsible instructor of the Central Committee who was shortly to become a Central Committee candidate member himself. Meyerzon was upheld against the opposition. In the fall of 1922 A. A. Sol'ts of the Central Control Commission was dispatched to Tula to watch over the interests of the Moscow party leadership at the *guberniya* party conference.[47]

In spite of all this obvious pressure by the central apparatus, the factional friction in Tula not only continued, but grew worse. When the delegates to the Tenth Congress of Soviets assembled in December, 1922, L. S. Sosnovsky (destined to become a member of the Trotskyist Opposition in the fall of 1923) spoke up in a meeting of the Communist fraction to protest the candidacy of Meyerzon for the Central Executive Committee: "This was like a spark, from which blazed out a sharp conflict in the Tula organization. The basis for the conflicts in the Tula organization had existed previously over the course of several years."[48] A special point in Sosnovsky's objection to Meyerzon was the fact that the latter had become a Bolshevik only in 1919, after a period as a Bundist (i.e., a member of the Jewish Social-Democrats), during which he was actually arrested by the Soviet government for agitation on behalf of the Bund. Previously the party leadership had instituted the requirement that all *guberniya* secretaries have pre-1917 status in the Party. In cases like that of Meyerzon, however, where this rule would have worked against the power of the secretarial machine, its application was suspended.[49] Following the report of a third commission sent to Tula, the Orgburo handed down a decision definitively upholding Meyerzon and censuring his critics for disrupting the unity and effective work of the Tula organization.[50] Even this action did not put an end to the opposition. Only with the *guberniya* conference of March 1923, at which Rykov and M. K. Muranov laid down the line for the Central Committee and demanded the restoration of unity in Tula, does the factionalism appear to have died away.[51]

It is impossible to say whether the opposition in Tula was ideologically related to the broader Left Opposition movements or whether it was simply an affair of local issues and personalities, as claimed in the official party reports describing it. Nevertheless, it serves as a good illustration of the efforts which the party apparatus was prepared to make to keep local organizations properly functioning in the secretarial hierarchy. It shows, moreover, the prevailing manner of thinking about relations between the party center and local organizations. The center was the guiding body, continually supervising and educating local organizations to keep them up to its standards. It was the source of doctrinal correctness and political wisdom. In this atmosphere it was impossible for the majority of lesser party functionaries to avoid a sense of dependence on the omniscient center. This condition was one further factor militating against the effective operation of the democratic processes of rank-and-file decision-making which were officially incorporated in the party statutes.

*   *   *

An additional step in strengthening the secretarial hierarchy was taken in 1920 and 1921 with the introduction of a new organizational echelon between the center and some of the 112 *guberniya* organizations. This consisted of "regional bureaus" of the Central Committee, which together with the central committees of the Communist parties of the lesser Soviet republics served as intermediaries to maintain closer links with the *gubernii*. They were headed by high-ranking party workers, who were in some cases actually members of the Central Committee. The most important of the regional bureaus were the Siberian (headed by Yaroslavsky to 1922 and then by Stanislav Kosior, a purge victim in 1938), the Far Eastern (headed by Kubiak, who also disappeared in 1937–1938), the North Caucasus (headed by Anastas Mikoyan from 1922 to 1926), and the Turkestan (subsequently Central Asian, headed by

Kuibyshev to 1922 and then by Yan Rudzutak, another Stalinist *apparatchik* ultimately purged).[52]

The regional bureaus served as special representatives of the authority of the Central Committee, to supplement in distant areas the system of instructors and secretarial reports to Moscow. The names which figure in the bureaus are of special significance: particular care must have been taken by Stalin as dominant figure in the Orgburo and as general secretary after 1922, to place reliable people in these strategic posts. From these vantage points the party apparatus was able to secure firm control of the local organizations within the regional jurisdictions by purges and administrative pressure. It was thus able to build up additional bases of strength against the actual and potential forces of opposition whose support was concentrated in the more heavily populated areas of European Russia.

The case of the Siberian regional bureau can serve as an illustration of the importance of these organizations for the effective operation of the Party's secretarial machinery. In Siberia the local organizations of the Party were notoriously weak during the period after the end of the Civil War. One factor contributing to this was the sparsity of workers to leaven out the preponderance of people with peasant backgrounds in these organizations.[53] Another reason was the extreme difficulty of finding qualified party workers willing to go to Siberia; some people even quit the professional party service altogether rather than face such an assignment, which was to them tantamount to exile.[54] These particularly onerous conditions made it especially hard in this case to build up a local apparatus under the direct control of the party center in Moscow. This deficiency in the local implementation of central authority was reflected in the spirit of independence of the local organizations, particularly in the Omsk *guberniya* committee and in the organization of the Yenisei territory. The latter was apparently a stronghold of the Democratic Centralists, and, in accordance with the concern of this group for local autonomy, it strongly opposed the establishment of a regional bureau.[55]

The Siberian bureau was set up in 1920 after the conquest of Siberia from the Whites, in order to supply a temporarily dictatorial authority to build up the party organization in that region.[56] Its initial chief, Yaroslavsky, was one of Stalin's leading supporters and later head of the Union of Atheists. Since 1919 he had been a candidate member of the Central Committee, and in 1921 he received a double promotion to full member and to the Secretariat. He continued to represent the Central Committee in Siberia, with understandably great authority accruing from his rank.[57] In 1922, when he moved up to the Central Control Commission, he was succeeded in Siberia by Kosior.

Drastic action was taken by the Siberian bureau under the leadership of Yaroslavsky and Kosior to bring the local organizations under the firm control of the Secretariat. The Yenisei organization, where the Democratic Centralists were strong, was not inclined to heed the directions of the regional bureau, and in consequence of this was purged; the bureau employed its assignment authority to remove excessively independent local officials and replace them with more reliable party workers. Much the same thing happened in the case of the Omsk organization, although in this case the bureau had a more difficult time. As a result of friction with the Omsk *guberniya* committee, the bureau ordered the Omsk organization to depose the chairman of its committee. The members of the local committee refused and threatened to quit the Party if their wishes were not respected. Finally, the Central Control Commission was called in to discipline the recalcitrants, and reassignments, in the customary pattern, restored order in the Omsk party organization.[58]

To implement the operations of the Siberian regional bureau, the Secretariat in Moscow dispatched to Siberia in the course of 1922 a specially mobilized group of eighty party workers. In contrast to previous practice, when local organizations were simply ordered to furnish a certain number of men and left free to choose whomever they saw fit, this group was selected individually by the Secretariat.[59] This reflects the growing efficiency of the Record and Assignment Department of the Secretariat and illustrates its important role in the building of a tight party machine—making sure that the proper individuals went where they were most needed.

One of the Siberian delegates at the Eleventh Party Congress voiced a strong protest over the operation of the regional bureau, and criticized it for an excessive concentration of power at the expense of the local organizations.[60] He objected, moreover, to the fact that the regional bureau, instead of being elected by the regional party conference representing the membership, was still appointed by and responsible to the Central Committee in Moscow. The bureau had originally been constituted in this fashion as an emergency measure during the Civil War, but in this as in so many other instances the Party failed to make the reconversion from wartime to peacetime methods. The Siberian party organization continued to be ruled in a military fashion, and the democratic rights of the membership remained a very tenuous fiction indeed.

*   *   *

The translation of secretarial influence into domination of the top councils of the Party was for Stalin the decisive step. He accomplished it by bringing to bear all the resources of organizational supervision and personnel selection in order to control the election of provincial delegates to the national party congresses. At all important provincial party conferences, where the delegates were elected, the Secretariat was careful to have the views of the party apparatus represented either by one of the responsible instructors, or by a member of the Central Committee itself.[61] In this manner, the party leadership in Moscow was able to exert great influence over the local party organizations. The prestige of a man of Central Committee rank or just below was sufficient to sway many hesitant comrades into supporting the policy or candidates recommended by Moscow.

At the party congresses themselves (the Eleventh and Twelfth being the decisive ones) Stalin was careful not to challenge the position of any established leaders. Instead, he used his organizational influence to install his supporters from the apparatus in the new Central Committee seats which were created at each congress. His packing operation was eminently successful.

Special emphasis was constantly placed in the Party's organizational pronouncements on the policy of "systematic promotion of new party workers and the transfer of party workers to more responsible work."[62] The Tenth Congress resolved,

> The Congress regards it as the duty of the Central Committee and its Orgburo to follow attentively the outstanding workers and draw them directly into responsible work at the center and locally. The Congress considers that one of the greatest deficiencies in party work is the circumstance that up to now the Party has still not been able to give sufficient room for their development.[63]

Detailed instructions were issued for examining, recommending and promoting functionaries at all levels of the party organization. On the face of it, this seemed to be a commendable effort to bring new blood into the upper councils of the Party and give an opportunity to deserving younger people to show their ability. In practice it meant that the officials so promoted became more dependent than ever on the party apparatus for their status; owing their political existence to the Secretariat, they could hardly be anything but its willing creatures.

This quickly became the situation even on the highest level to which the policy of promotion was applied, i.e., in the Central Committee. In 1922 and especially in 1923, a host of new candidate members were elected to the Central Committee. Most of them were provincial functionaries with no national reputation at all. At the Eleventh Congress, of the eight new candidates, three—A. Y. Badaev, P. I. Lebedev, and D. Z. Manuilsky—had become known before the revolution, but the others were strangers to most of the Party (though one later achieved note—Mikoyan).[64] Fourteen new candidates were selected at the Twelfth Congress, of whom only three had achieved any prominence—Kaganovich, N. A. Skrypnik, and Kosior. These functionaries were simply being rewarded for loyal service in the party machinery. Essentially the same process was taking place in the Central Control Commission, which, by the reform authorized at the Twelfth Congress, was vastly enlarged to a total of fifty members and ten candidates. In return for their elevation to political prominence by the good graces of the Secretariat, these new members of the Party's leading circles performed loyally in accordance with the wishes of the leadership of the secretarial group, headed by Stalin.

The combined result of the Secretariat's effectiveness in selecting new "leading cadres" and of the loyalty which it was able to command from them is attested by examining the subsequent careers of these new candidates selected at the Eleventh and Twelfth Congresses. Of the twenty-two men, all but five definitely continued to pursue flourishing careers as late as 1930; virtually all of these seventeen rose to full member of the Central Control Committee or to high posts on the Central Control Commission.[65] The other five were dropped from the Central Committee by 1925 and no record is available of their subsequent careers. None of the twenty-two ever appeared in the Opposition during the whole stressful period of factional controversy up to 1930. Such were the loyal *"apparatchiki"* drawn forth by the plan to "give room for the development" of "the outstanding party workers." Through this process, by the spring of 1923, with Lenin out of the picture and the other party leaders largely ineffective in matters of organization, Stalin was well started on the road to total power.

Stalin's success, in retrospect, was not the unique product of cunning, force, or the magic of personal politics. Stalin gained against his rivals in the measure that his politics were depersonalized; he rose as the unimposing representative, unfeared until too late, of the Party's secretarial hierarchy. Organization and its manipulation, on the lines here described, were the key to political victory in Soviet Russia. During his climb to power Stalin was the incarnation of Lenin's model of the Party, and little else; more than any other man, the General Secretary *was* bolshevism.

Notes

1. *Protokoly s"ezdov i konferentsii Vsesoyuznoi Kommunisticheskoi Partii (b): Deviatyi s"ezd RKP(b)* (Moscow, Partiinoe Izdatel'stvo, 1933), p. 41.

2. Circular of the Central Committee, dated 12 December 1919, published in *Izvestiya Tsentral'nogo Komiteta*, 14 January 1920.

3. Resolution of the Eighth Party Congress, "Po organizatsionnomu voprosu (On the Organizational Question), *Kommunisticheskaya Partiya Sovetskogo Soyuza v rezoliutsiyakh i resheniyakh s"ezdov, konferentsii, i plenumov TsK* (Moscow, Gosudarstvennoe Izdatel'stvo Politicheskoi Literatury, 1954), vol. I, p. 444.

4. *Protokoly: Deviatyi s"ezd*, pp. 47–48.

5. Central Committee order of 7 April 1920, text in M. Ravich-Cherkassky, *Istoriya Kommunisticheskoi Partii (bol'shevikov) Ukrainy* (Khar'kov: Gosudarstvennoe Izdatel'stvo Ukrainy, 1923), appendix 12.

6. Trotsky to the Central Committee, Oct. 8, 1923, extracts quoted in Max Shachtman, "The Struggle for the New Course," in Leon Trotsky, *The New Course* (New York: New International, 1943), p. 154.

7. Tenth Party Conference, "Plan raboty TsK RKP (b)" (Work Plan of the CC, RCP(B)), *KPSS v rezoliutsiyakh*, vol. I, p. 576.

8. *Izvestiya TsK*, March 1923, p. 28.

9. Ibid., pp. 34–41.

10. Ibid., pp. 53–56.

11. Ibid., p. 51.

12. Ibid., pp. 33–34. This was the origin of the "nomenklatura," i.e., the classification of officials by rank, and by extension the whole body of officials so classified.

13. Report of the Central Committee for the period March 1922–April 1923, *Izvestiya TsK*, April 1923, p. 45.

14. *Izvestiya TsK*, March 1923, p. 3.

15. *Protokoly: Odinnadtsatyi s"ezd RKP(b)* (Moscow: Partiinoe Izdatel'stvo, 1936), Index of Names, p. 791.

16. *Izvestiya TsK*, March 1922, pp. 18–19.

17. Ibid., p. 13.

18. Ye. A. Preobrazhensky, in *Dvenadtsatyi s"ezd rossiiskoi kommunisticheskoi partii (bol'shevikov): Stenograficheskii otchet* (Moscow: Gosizdat, 1923), p. 133.

19. The process conforms closely to the phenomenon of "protective nuclei" forming within Soviet bureaucratic hierarchies, described by Barrington Moore in *Soviet Politics: The Dilemma of Power* (Cambridge, Mass.: Harvard University Press, 1950), p. 290.

20. *Izvestiya TsK*, March 1922, p. 15.

21. *Protokoly: Odinnadtsatyi s"ezd*, pp. 48–49.

22. *Izvestiya TsK*, March 1923, p. 7.

23. Ibid., p. 8.

24. Ibid.

25. Ibid., pp. 9–10.

26. Ibid., March 1922, pp. 15–16.

27. Ibid., p. 5.

28. Ibid., p. 13.

29. Resolution of the Eleventh Party Conference, "Po voprosu ob ukreplenii partii, v sviazi s uchetom opyta proverki lichnogo sostava ee" (On the Question

of Strengthening the Party, in Connection with Taking Account of the Experience of Verifying its Personal Composition), _KPSS v rezoliutsiyakh,_ vol. I, p. 595.

30. V. M. Molotov, Organizational Report to the Eleventh Party Congress, _Protokoly: Odinnadtsatyi s"ezd,_ p. 57.

31. _Protokoly: Desiatyi s"ezd RKP(b)_ (Moscow: IMEL, 1933), note 48, pp. 848–849.

32. Yu. K. Milonov, _ibid.,_ p. 86.

33. Ibid., Index of Names, p. 925.

34. Ibid., pp. 84–87.

35. Ibid., Note 48, pp. 848–9.

36. _Protokoly: Odinnadtsatyi s"ezd,_ p. 57.

37. Z. Ya. Litvin-Sedoi, ibid., p. 193.

38. Ibid., p. 57.

39. _Izvestiya TsK,_ March 1922, p. 35.

40. _Protokoly: Odinnadtsatyi s"ezd,_ pp. 57–58.

41. Ibid., Index of Names, p. 799.

42. _Izvestiya TsK,_ January 1923, p. 75.

43. _Protokoly: Odinnadtsatyi s"ezd,_ Index of Names, p. 798.

44. _Izvestiya TsK,_ March 1922, p. 20.

45. Ibid., p. 15.

46. Ibid., January 1923, p. 75.

47. Ibid.

48. Ibid., April 1923, p. 42.

49. Ibid., p. 46.

50. Ibid., January 1923, p. 75.

51. Ibid., April 1923, pp. 42–43.

52. Ibid., March 1922, p. 14. For persons appointed to the bureaus see _Protokoly: Odinnadtsatyi s"ezd,_ Index of Names.

53. Resolution of the Eleventh Party Congress, "Ob ukreplenii i novykh zadachakh partii," (On the Strengthening and New Tasks of the Party) _KPSS v rezoliutsiyakh,_ vol. I, p. 621.

54. _Izvestiya TsK,_ March 1922, p. 33.

55. Ibid., April 1923, p. 38.

56. Yakov Shumiatsky, _Protokoly: Odinnadtsatyi s"ezd,_ p. 450.

57. Ibid., p. 187.

58. _Izvestiya TsK,_ April 1923, pp. 38–39.

59. Ibid., p. 47.

60. Shumiatsky, _Protokoly: Odinnadtsatyi s"ezd,_ pp. 449–450.

61. _Izvestiya TsK,_ March 1923, p. 10.

62. Tenth Party Conference, Work Plan of the CC, _KPSS v rezoliutsiyakh,_ vol. I, p. 576.

63. Resolution of the Tenth Party Congress, "Po voprosam partiinogo stroitel'stva" (On Questions of Building the Party), ibid., vol. I, p. 521.

64. For composition of the Central Committee, see "TsK-VKP(b)," _Bol'shaya sovetskaya entsiklopediya,_ (first edition, Moscow: "Sovetskaya Entsiklopedia" Institute), vol. LX (1934), p. 555.

65. See _Protokoly: Odinnadtsatyi s"ezd,_ Index of Names.

6

Evolution of Leadership Selection in the Central Committee, 1917–1927

Under Stalin and his successors the Central Committee of the Communist Party of the Soviet Union was an institutionally defined bureaucratic elite, bringing together in the nominally leading body of the Party all the leading figures in the central and local echelons of the major functional hierarchies in Soviet society.[1] With few exceptions, membership in the Central Committee reflected the official job assignment of the particular member, and the individual's rank—Politburo member, Politburo candidate, Central Committee member, Central Committee candidate, Central Auditing Commission—corresponded to the status imputed to the job he held. The selection of jobs to be represented was governed by a set of unwritten laws that nevertheless operated with very strict regularity, to specify the proportions of seats from the party apparatus, the civil government, the military, the trade unions, and the miscellaneous "public organizations" that made up the rest of the institutional fabric of Soviet society. Similar rules of status determined representation geographically among the Party and government people, as between the center, the union republics, and the major regional entities.

Two major areas of inquiry arise in considering the distinctive status characteristics of the Central Committee elite in a historical context. One is the intriguing parallel, superficial at least, between the Soviet status system and the rank and status practices of the imperial government before the revolution. The other area especially inviting inquiry is the historical emergence of the elite membership rules during the early years

This chapter originally appeared in *Russian Officialdom*, edited by Walter Pintner and Don Rowney (Chapel Hill: University of North Carolina Press, 1980). Reprinted with permission.

of the Soviet regime. Pursuit of this developmental phenomenon may shed some light on the actual process whereby prerevolutionary political patterns reemerged, as many authorities hold, under the revolutionary banner.[2]

*   *   *

From the inception of the Russian Social Democratic Workers' Party, ancestor of the Communists, through the Brezhev era, the Central Committee was, according to the statues, the responsible decision-making organ of the Party. To this extent, the institution was originally unexceptional among Western as well as Russian political party organizations. Elected—at least pro forma—by the party congress, the Central Committee was supposed to exercise leadership in the interim between congresses, during which time, according to Lenin's dictates of "democratic centralism," its decisions were binding on all the party membership.

Until well after the revolution the makeup of the Communist Central Committee was governed by genuine elections at the party congresses, however much they may have been influenced by factional controversies and leadership pressure. Congress delegates voted for as many individuals as there were seats on the Central Committee, and the appropriate number with the highest votes were declared elected. Candidate members were originally the runners-up, but by 1920 they were being voted on separately after the roster of full members was announced.[3] Under these conditions the membership of the Central Committee was naturally drawn from well-known revolutionary activists and key figures in the central party leadership.

From the revolution until Lenin fell ill after the Eleventh Party Congress in 1922, the size of the Central Committee was relatively stable—twenty-one members and ten candidates elected at the Sixth Congress in August 1917, trimmed to fifteen and eight at the Seventh Congress in March 1918, held to nineteen and twelve as late as 1920, then raised incrementally to twenty-seven and nineteen by 1922. Through 1920, at least, the numbers were small enough so that most aspirants were being voted on by the congress delegates on the basis of personal or direct knowledge. However, or perhaps for this reason, election to the Central Committee was sensitive to personal popularity and the interplay of the factional controversies that freely animated the life of the party during the War Communism period. Some individuals (A. S. Bubnov, for instance) reached, fell, and returned to the Central Committee as many as three times.

In 1921, at the Tenth Party Congress, the first signs appeared of a basic change in the actual manner of selecting Central Committee members. This was the practice of making up a semiofficial slate of aspirants, to be voted on de facto as a group by the congress delegates. The occasion happened to be the most acute crisis ever experienced by the Soviet leadership, when it came under attack both externally from peasant rebels and the naval mutineers at Kronstadt, and internally from the Left and Ultra-Left factions represented by Trotsky and the Workers' Opposition. Having decisively defeated his critics within the Communist Party in the pre-congress delegate selection, Lenin evidently decided to use his influence not only to oust several key oppositionists from the Central Committee but to expand the body from nineteen to twenty-five, thereby creating in all nearly a dozen openings for new people.

The fact that a slate of recommended official candidates was prepared for the congress delegates to vote on is made clear by the totals of individual votes announced after the ballot. Lenin was everyone's choice, with 479 votes. But nearly unanimous votes were received by numerous other people, tapering down to 351 for the twenty-fourth member, the newcomer I. Ya. Tuntul. Only F. A. Artem-Sergeyev, an incumbent, fell appreciably below the rest of the slate with 283, for the last slot, and he was far ahead of the next contender, the deposed Trotskyist party secretary Krestinsky with 161.[4]

Fourteen of the new Central Committee were holdovers, all with outstanding reputations, representing from Lenin on down the top posts at the center in government, in the Party, and in the trade unions.[5] Among the eleven members newly elected or promoted from candidate rank, the territorial principle stood out instead: party leaders from Siberia (Yaroslavsky), the Caucasus (Sergo Ordzhonikidze), and the Ukraine (Molotov, moving into the national secretariat), plus the government chiefs from the Ukraine (G. I. Petrovsky) and Petrograd (N. P. Komarov). Though transitory and overlapping assignments at this early stage make it hard to define some individuals' functions, one of the new members at the center (V. M. Mikhailov) is identifiable as a former Cheka official moving into the party secretariat; two (M. V. Frunze and K. Y. Voroshilov) represented the army; and two (Shliapnikov and I. D. Kutuzov) were added to the trade-union representation in a move to co-opt the Workers' Opposition.[6] (The function of the remaining individual, Tuntul, is unknown.)

Among the candidate members of the Central Committee, only four of the twelve incumbents of 1920 were held over in 1921, probably on grounds of reputation as much as function. Two, the commissar of labor and the Siberian government chief, were former full members; one, the outgoing mine-union chief newly installed as senior deputy people's commissar, was a former candidate. Eight entirely new candidates reflected strongly the territorial principle—two from the Ukraine, one from the Caucasus, one from Turkestan, one from Petrograd, and one from the

Urals—plus one more trade unionist and one man (Osinsky) to conciliate the "Democratic Centralist" opposition group. Lenin thus made up the slate of Central Committee members and candidates to punish the Trotskyists, tame the Ultra-Left, and award Central Committee status to loyal but not widely known provincial functionaries who would have stood little chance in the earlier style of elections to a smaller body of stellar personalities.

At the Eleventh Party Congress in 1922 (Lenin's last), balloting for Central Committee members presumably took place in the usual fashion, though no individual vote totals were announced. The membership was increased by two more (from twenty-five to twenty-seven, with a rise in candidates from fifteen to nineteen). There happened to be much less turnover than the year before (mainly reflecting the elimination of the Workers' Opposition and Democratic Centralist members). Individual political distinction seems to have governed most of the new choices. However, among eight men newly installed as candidate members, territorial representation (Petrograd, Turkestan, the Ukraine) prevailed where direct filling of vacancies (mostly trade unionists) did not.

The year 1923 saw Joseph Stalin's signal breakthrough in setting up a personal political organization in the Party, following his designation as general secretary the year before. Turning Lenin's proposal for an expanded Central Committee to his own advantage, Stalin persuaded the Twelfth Party Congress to increase the body from twenty-seven to forty.[7] This substantial expansion, together with three vacancies, gave him sixteen slots to fill.

Slate making was in evidence once again when the Twelfth Congress came to the election of the Central Committee, though the mathematics of it were covered up, as they were the year before, by a motion at the congress to withhold announcement of individual vote totals.[8] Three of the new candidates of 1921 were now promoted, together with two of the 1922 group (Manuilsky and Mikoyan), and two ex-candidates, while four former members were restored. Among them these eleven represented the party in the Northwest region (P. A. Zalutsky), Nizhnii Novgorod (N. A. Uglanov), Azerbaidzhan (Sergei Kirov), the Ukraine (Manuilsky), the North Caucasus (Mikoyan), and the Urals (D. Y. Sulimov), plus a second Moscow secretary (Mikhailov), together with the government and trade unions in Petrograd (Komarov and G. Y. Yevdokimov, Moscow already being represented) and the deputy commissar of War (M. M. Lashevich). Some of these selections—the Petrograders and Lashevich— represented politicking by Zinoviev to promote his friends and aides in the same way that Stalin was operating in most other parts of the country. Only Grigory Piatakov was an individual recognized in his own right as a stellar industrial administrator. Of the five noncandidates directly installed as members, two were industrial administrators (A. D. Tsiurupa, head of Gosplan, and K. V. Ukhanov, head of the electrical industry), while three represented still more regional party organizations—the Far East (Kubiak), Yekaterinburg in the Urals (M. M. Kharitonov), and the Ukraine (Ye. I. Kviring).

At the candidate level, promotions and demotions together created fourteen vacancies in 1923, again filled mainly by leaders of territorial party organizations—Tver, Perm, the Don, Samara, and Siberia, with additional men from Moscow, the Northwest Bureau, and the Ukraine. Four new candidates represented government in Transcaucasia and Turkestan, plus one more from the Ukraine. One, Kaganovich, was the new head of the Organization and Instruction Department in the central Secretariat. Stalin—and Zinoviev in his own northwestern area—were clearly bent on making the Central Committee a council of their regional party secretaries. In the course of this effort, patterns of precedence were beginning to appear that held true into the 1980s: priority of party representation over government (more in toto, and more at the full-member level), and higher rank and/or more representation for the key provinces—Moscow, Petrograd, and the Ukraine.

The Thirteenth Party Congress of May 1924 was the first to come after Lenin's demise and the open break between Trotsky and the party leadership. It was the occasion for another substantial expansion in the ranks of the Central Committee, this time from forty to fifty-two. While practically all incumbents were confirmed in office,[9] six candidates were promoted, representing the Don, Ural, and Far Eastern party organizations, the central Secretariat (Kaganovich), the chief military commissar (Bubnov), and the metal workers union. Nine newcomers directly installed as members included two from the Donets province, two more from the recently renamed city of Leningrad (Zinoviev's people, one, Klavdiya Nikolaeva, becoming the sole woman on the Central Committee as head of the Women's Division of the Secretariat), and one more from the Moscow party organization, plus two trade unionists (Tomsky's aide A. I. Dogadov, and the miners' chief I. I. Shvarts) and two economic administrators (G. M. Krzhizhanovsky of Gosplan and L. B. Krasin of Trade). These selections reinforce the picture of a body composed heavily of territorial party chiefs (mostly the people recently installed by Stalin) together with top functional administrators—party, governmental, industrial, military, and trade union—at the center.

The twenty-one new Central Committee candidate members introduced in 1924 to fill the vacancies created by promotion and expansion continued to fit the same pattern. Among them were a host of additional provincial party leaders, including Tula, Samara, Ivanovo,[10] Kharkov and Podolia in the Ukraine, Belorussia, two more from the Urals, three from Turkestan, and one more each from Moscow and Petrograd. Three central party functionaries on the slate were the heads of Agitprop and the Komsomol, and the deputy chief of the Women's Division. Three more trade unionists were included, two representing the Moscow Province unions specifically and one the national teachers' union. One industrial administrator, heading the machinery industry, was added, and one candidate (K. A. Rumiantsev) cannot be identified in terms of his employment but may have come from the central party apparatus.

At the Fourteenth Party Congress in December 1925, when Zinoviev broke with Stalin and went down to defeat, the Central Committee was once again substantially enlarged—this time by eleven men, from fifty-two to sixty-three. In this manner Stalin continued to build his power base while minimizing the head-on confrontations that would be implied in removing his leading opponents. These new slots, combined with one death (War Commissar Frunze), three drops (of lesser Zinovievists), and two demotions to candidate status (the Zinovievists Lashevich and Nikolaeva), opened up seventeen membership positions. Nine were filled from the candidate ranks and eight from outside. Administrators (the commissar of labor, V. V. Shmidt, the deputy Gosplan chairman, I. T. Smilga, the machinery industry chief, A. F. Tolokontsev, the Northwest Industrial Bureau head, S. S. Lobov, along with Foreign Commissar G. V. Chicherin) figured prominently in this expansion, while party leaders were included from Tula and the Donetsk regions, together with second-line secretaries from Moscow and the Ukraine, and the new head of the Women's Division (A. B. Artiukhina). Others brought in were the deputy Leningrad government chief, the new head of the Ukrainian trade unions, and the chief army commissar for the Russian Republic (N. M. Shvernik), plus a leading party journalist (I. I. Stepanov-Skvortsov). Three cannot be identified as to job.

At the candidate level, expansion (from thirty-five to forth-three), promotions, and drops opened up an even larger number of new slots than the year before, a total of twenty-five (after allowing for the three demotions from member to candidate status). These openings were filled by a very mixed crew—eight regional party officials (including Andrei Zhdanov of Nizhnii Novgorod), a functionary from the Institute of Party History, and another from the Comintern (V. V. Lominadze), four regional government officials (the prime minister of Azerbaidzhan and the number-two people for Moscow, Leningrad, and the Transcaucasian federation), two oil-industry officials, two more trade unionists (textiles and another Ukrainian leader), the chief of the nascent Kolkhoz movement, and the deputy commissar of war (I. S. Unshlikht, recently shifted from the GPU). Three new candidates are not identifiable as to position. The breadth of selections at both levels suggests that Stalin was now broadening his political base, or that he was temporarily heeding the wishes of Rykov and Tomsky to stress industrial and trade-union appointments.

The Fifteenth Party Congress, held in December 1927, a year later than the date that the rules called for, saw the dramatic expulsion of the Left Opposition headed by Trotsky and Zinoviev. The unprecedented number of eight Central Committee members was dropped for oppositionist activity. This move, together with two deaths (Dzerzhinsky and Krasin), a transfer to the Central Control Commission (Ordzhonikidze), and an expansion of eight seats, created nineteen vacancies in all. Most were filled by promoting candidates (twelve) or by transfers from the Central Control Commission (Kuibyshev and I. A. Piatnitsky, and Lenin's widow, Nadezhda Krupskaya, enjoying honor without influence). Direct appointments included such specialties as the party leader of Belorussia, the head of the GPU (V. P. Menzhinsky), the new head of the Ukrainian trade unions, and a leading party intellectual (A. I. Stetsky). Twenty-four candidate vacancies were created by expansion, promotion, and drops, and these were filled by a wide variety of party, governmental, and trade-union functionaries: new party secretaries from the Don, Donetsk province, Lugansk province in the Donbas, Azerbaidzhan, and the Tatar Autonomous Republic, two additional men from Moscow, and the secretary of the Red Trade-Union International (S. A. Lozovsky); also the government chiefs of Georgia and the Far East region, together with the commissar of finance, the head of the metal industry, and the chairman of the Ukrainian economic council; the chief of the air force; and the leader of the agricultural workers union. Eight new candidates remain unidentified as to function.

*   *   *

With the seventy-one members of 1927, the Central Committee had reached a level that was to hold constant through the postpurge Eighteenth Congress of 1939, although the candidate roster continued to creep up marginally. Therefore, 1927 is a logical stopping place to review systematically the personnel structure of the Central Committee as it had evolved up to that time.

The 121 members and candidate members of 1927 break down into functional groups as follows: party apparatus, fifty-five; civil government, thirty-six; trade unions, ten; military, three; police, one; miscellaneous, two (the head of the Kolkhoz Union and, more or less in her own right or as a cultural figure, Krupskaya); position undetermined, one member and twelve candidate members. In comparison with the ratios of functional representation in the post-Stalin regime, the party and government proportions remained nearly constant. However, the trade unions were much higher in 1927, and the military distinctly lower, suggesting an interesting shift of imputed prestige from the proletariat to the armed forces since the 1920s. Other evidence of sensitivity about the working-class base of the regime at that time was the heavy representation from the Donets Basin industrial area (both party and industrial administrators) and the status accorded Commissar of Labor Shmidt as a full Central Committee member and candidate member of the Orgburo.

Within the party sector, the 1927 allocation of CC member and candidate seats was: central apparatus (including Comintern representatives), fifteen; Russian Republic, twenty-five; Union Republics, fourteen (including future Central Asian republics). Again the proportions are not radically different from the later distribution. The varying status of particular areas was already clearly reflected, as it has been systematically in more recent times. Within the Russian Republic, the Moscow organization had six members and candidates, headed by a candidate member of the Politburo with seats on the Orgburo and Secretariat (Uglanov). Leningrad had three, headed by a candidate member of the Politburo (Kirov). At this time in certain parts of the Russian Republic groups of provinces (*gubernii*) were combined into *oblasti* (not to be confused with the present use of the term as a province), and these large entities were all represented by their party chiefs—the North Caucasus (Politburo candidate A. A. Andreyev and two Central Committee candidates), the Urals (Orgburo member Sulimov and two Central Committee candidates), Siberia (one member), and the Far East (one member). In addition, a cluster of *gubernii* surrounding Moscow (Tula, Orel, Ivanovo, and Vladimir, roughly corresponding to the present *oblasti*,) had full CC membership status for their first secretaries, while another group trailing down the Volga (Nizhnii-Novgorod, the Tatar Autonomous Republic, Samara, and Saratov) had candidate status. Among the Union Republics the pecking order was fairly clear: seven member or candidate slots for the Ukraine (headed by Politburo candidate Kaganovich); two for Uzbekistan; one for Belorussia; one for the Transcaucasian Regional Bureau as a whole, and one for Azerbaidzhan in particular. The Central Asian territories yet to become Union Republics had two members as well (who both happened to be Russians).

On the government side the distribution of member and candidate positions was: central (USSR), nineteen; RSFSR (central and local), ten; Union Republics, seven (five from the Ukraine, one from Azerbaidzhan, and one from Georgia). Allowing for the difference in organizational structure, involving in 1927 no great proliferation of industrial ministries, the distribution of central seats among the key commissars and industrial chiefs was essentially similar to the post-Stalin allocation where every cabinet-level post was included. Local government chiefs included Moscow

(Orgburo candidate Ukhanov) and Leningrad (Komarov), each with one deputy; and the regional (*oblast'*) administrations for the Northwest, Siberia, and the Far East (all at the candidate level).

Within its more limited numbers the 1927 trade-union representation followed a similar pattern: central, seven seats (Chairman Tomsky, a Politburo member; Secretary A. I. Dogadov; and the union chiefs of four different industries); Russian Republic, two (Moscow, with Orgburo candidate status, and Leningrad); Union Republics, two (both from the Ukraine). Rank distinctions also figure among the industrial unions: metalworkers, Orgburo candidate; miners, Central Committee member; textiles and agricultural workers, Central Committee candidates.[11]

Further systematic status relations emerge from a comparison of geographical representation between the various functional sectors. For any entity, the party apparatus had more representation, at an equal or higher rank, followed by the government and then the trade unions. Geographical units received representation both in numbers and in rank in close proportion to their demographic and economic importance. This rule held true in the apportionment among Union Republics and among regions within the Russian Republic. All of these hierarchical relationships continued in the post-Stalin party; in fact, massive expansion of the Central Committee allowed the implicit principles of apportionment to operate in a much more refined way.

The expansion of the Party's Central Auditing Commission to nine members in 1927 brings it into the scope of this representational analysis along with the Central Committee. Apart from their new chairman (former head of the Central Control Commission in the Ukraine) and the rector of the Sverdlov party university, the members of the Central Auditing Commission were all leaders of regional party or government bodies in the Russian Republic. This list clearly anticipated the regular practice in the later Stalin and post-Stalin years, of making the Central Auditing Commission an honorable-mention category for functionaries in a variety of capacities whose jobs carried a status just below those distinguished by Central Committee membership or candidate rank.

The picture of functional apportionment and rank allocation as of 1927 demonstrates very clearly how the leadership institutionalized in the Central Committee had acquired by that time the basic characteristics of status and representation that still prevailed under the post-Stalin regime. Within the short span of five years under Stalin's domination of the party organization, the central leadership elite (Central Committee members and candidates) was expanded more than two and a half times and almost totally realigned from an elected group of the articulate and politically popular to a body de facto appointed on the basis of bureaucratic constituencies.

*   *   *

There is ample precedent in prerevolutionary history for such a status-based bureaucratic leadership body as the Central Committee rapidly became under Stalin's leadership. Russia had a long tradition of consultative policy sounding-boards, de facto appointed by the man in charge and apportioned among representatives of the key political institutions and social groups. Kerensky used the device in 1917 in the absence of any nationally elected body, when he convened the Moscow State Conference in August 1917 and the Petrograd Democratic Conference in September. In the nineteenth-century empire the State Council was such a body, appointed by the emperor from among the top figures in the nobility and the bureaucracy, including cabinet ministers and provincial governors-general. As a legislative advisory body whose recommendations the tsar might or might not respond to, it conferred more status than power on its members—like Stalin's Central Committee. Status within the State Council was further refined by the distinction between the upper group of sixteen, who participated in one of the council's subcommittees (legislative, police and church, general policy, and economic affairs) and the remainder, who attended only the general sessions.[12] The distinction anticipates the Communist differentiation of the Politburo, Orgburo, and Secretariat out of the membership of the Central Committee.

Long before the creation of the State Council by Alexander I and Mikhail Speransky, similar procedures provided for some form of top-status consultative body putting the heads of the various component institutions and interests of the realm in touch with the tsar (but more to underscore their subservience than to limit his arbitrary will). Such were the Boyar *Duma* (Council of Nobles) and the *Zemskii Sobor* (Assembly of the Land) before the time of Peter the Great, and the Senate as it functioned during the eighteenth century. Peter's Table of Ranks crystallized the old Russian tradition of prescribed status and precedence relationships (especially *mestnichestvo*) in a new, superficially rational and seemingly Western mold. Throughout the subsequent operation of this system there was a compulsion to equate the status of a function and some badge of personal rank of the individual, in a manner that Western societies observe only in military service. At the uppermost level the most common way of underscoring this consideration of rank was membership at the appropriate grade in those bodies in contact with the tsar. Exactly the same holds true of the Central Committee.

None of the foregoing is meant to suggest that Stalin was consciously or specifically guided by a knowledge of imperial bureaucratic practices when he set about expanding and packing the Central Committee of the CPSU. Such knowledge was and is rather esoteric when it comes to the details. But what Stalin does appear to have been guided by was a feel for what would be most acceptable in the Russian milieu for his choice of members to serve in the nominal governing body of the Party. The canons of such acceptability, in turn, seem to be a deeply established traditional expectation that the top body should represent the key institutional functions and geographical areas in some proportion to the importance of the respective functions and areas, and that the representatives of each functional or geographical unit should be the top appointed functionaries in that unit. These were criteria for inclusion in the slate of nominees for the Central Committee that no one seemed able to quarrel with. Conveniently these criteria dovetailed with the circumstance that the top provincial functionaries were Stalin's own appointees to party secretaryships. Stalin built his own power by paralleling the model of the imperial bureaucratic elite.

Stalin's political tactics exemplify a widespread, though not commonly recognized, mechanism, not only in Russia but in other situations following abrupt social and political change, that serves to explain the "return of the repressed," patterns of behavior resembling the Old Régime. Pragmatic and opportunistic leaders rising to the surface in the wake of a revolution sense the political steps that will be acceptable and effective because they are familiar and expected within the context of the particular culture, even if they are not particularly liked. (The change of ideological labels can allay in part this last reservation.) In Russia this mechanism, broadly conceived, helps account for the Bolsheviks' ability to establish a new autocracy with old, scarcely disguised bureaucratic and police methods, and to have this regime accepted by the Russian nation.

Notes

1. For an analysis of the eventual principles of Central Committee composition, see Robert V. Daniels, "Office Holding and Elite Status: The Central Committee of the CPSU," in Paul Cocks, Robert V. Daniels, and Nancy Whittier Heer, eds., *The Dynamics of Soviet Politics* (Cambridge, Mass.: Harvard University Press, 1976).

2. See, e.g., Zbigniew Brzezinski, "Soviet Politics: From the Future to the Past?" ibid.

3. *Deviatyi s"ezd RKP(b): Protokoly* (Ninth Congress of the Russian Communist Party, Bolsheviks: Minutes, Moscow: State Press for Political Literature, 1960), p. 398.

4. *Desiatyi s"ezd RKP(b): Protokoly* (Tenth Congress of the Russian Communist Party, Bolsheviks: Minutes, Moscow: State Press for Political Literature, 1963), p. 402.

5. Government: Lenin, prime minister; Kalinin, chief of state; Trotsky, commissar of war; Dzerzhinsky, head of the Cheka; Rykov, chairman of the Supreme Economic Council; Kamenev, chairman of the Moscow Soviet; Rakovsky, prime minister of the Ukraine. Party: Stalin, Politburo and Orgburo member; Bukharin, editor of *Pravda* and leading theoretician; Zinoviev and Radek, Comintern leaders. Trade unions: Tomsky, chairman; Rudzutak, secretary; Artem-Sergeev, new head of the miners.

6. Biographical data for this study has been drawn from a variety of sources, but most particularly from the index of names in the Minutes of the Eleventh Party Congress (*Odinnadtsatyi s''ezd RKP(b): Protokoly*, Moscow: IMEL, 1936) and from *Who Was Who in the USSR* (prepared by the Institute for the Study of the USSR; Metuchen, N.J.: Scarecrow Press, 1972).

7. See Robert V. Daniels, *The Conscience of the Revolution* (Cambridge, Mass.: Harvard University Press, 1960), pp. 190–197. Stalin wanted to double the membership of the Central Committee, in order to "bring new, fresh, party workers into the work of the Central Committee," individuals whom he qualified in anticipation as "independent people . . . but not independent of Leninism, . . . independent people free from personal influences, from those habits and traditions of struggle within the Central Committee which have been formed among us and which often cause alarm within the Central Committee" (Stalin, *Dvenadtsatyi s''ezd RKP(b): Stenograficheskii otchet* (Twelfth Congress of the Russian Communist Party, Bolsheviks: Stenographic Report, Moscow: Press for Political Literature, 1968), p. 61). Trotsky led the opposition to the proposed expansion, holding out for a small body that could continue to exercise quick day-to-day decision-making authority.

8. *Dvenadtsatyi s''ezd*, p. 661.

9. One—Lenin—had died; one—Kuibyshev—was transferred to the Central Control Commission, which ruled out Central Committee membership, and one—Karl Radek—was dropped for his activities on behalf of Trotsky.

10. Presumed from incomplete data.

11. This count is one short; an additional trade-unionist (G. P. Melnichansky) had been head of the textile union but was probably an assistant to Tomsky at this time.

12. *Entsiklopedicheskii slovar'* (Encyclopedic Dictionary, St. Petersburg: Granat, 1893), vol. XVII, pp. 415–416.

7

Trotsky on Proletarian Democracy and Party Bureaucracy, 1923–1937

Trotsky was a man of baffling paradoxes. From staunch enemy of Leninism in the prerevolutionary emigration, he became its most ardent champion in the revolution and in the Civil War. From revolutionary hero, his fate was to become the devil-figure in the political theology of the postrevolutionary regime.

To many minds, Trotsky has appeared only as the revolutionary master of ceremonies, the Civil War commander, the firebrand of international revolution, the Stalinist before Stalin, perhaps deserving of his fate. These images have their basis in historical fact, but they still miss a major part of the real Trotsky, as much as, say, impressions of Lenin or Bukharin based only on their records during the War Communism era would neglect how they changed later on. The same holds for Trotsky, whose political outlook changed profoundly during the succession struggle that broke out in 1923. But his outlook did not change enough to enable him to break out of the doctrinal loyalties that bound him to Stalin's sacrificial altar. Trapped between the rigidity of his theoretical commitments to Marxism and Leninism, and the embittering political adversity that afflicted him in mid-career, Trotsky was truly the protagonist of a Greek tragedy played on the Soviet stage.

*　　*　　*

The Trotsky of the 1920s and 1930s cannot be properly understood without reference to the prerevolutionary context. Trotsky's disputes with Lenin are well known. It was Trotsky who wrote as early as 1904 of Lenin's model for the party, "These methods lead, as we shall yet see, to this: the party organization is substituted for the party, the Central Committee is substituted for the party organization, and finally a 'dictator' is substituted for the Central Committee."[1]

This warning about Lenin's centralism did not mean that the author of the theory of permanent revolution was any less committed in his revolutionary fervor. Between the revolutions of 1905 and 1917 Trotsky was part of the radical democratic tendency that included both Left Mensheviks and Left Bolsheviks. When he joined the Bolshevik ranks in the summer of 1917 with such other left-wing Mensheviks as Radek and Rakovsky, Lenin's growing party was at its nadir of Leninist organizational rigor, and the radical democrats could well find it a logical and comfortable vehicle for their revolutionary enthusiasm.

Six years later the Communist Party had gone through the steeling experience of civil war, and had converted itself from a mass revolutionary movement to a disciplined organ exercising a monopoly of power in the new revolutionary state. Trotsky changed along with most of the party, as circumstances brought him to the command of a revolutionary army and put a premium on the most desperate methods in a life-or-death struggle with the counterrevolution. After 1921, circumstances took another turn, and Trotsky found himself all but excluded from the collective leadership formed by the old Leninists when their revolutionary chief was stricken with terminal illness. In the fall of 1923 it was not the Trotsky of the Civil War but the Trotsky of the old radical democracy who decided to speak out against that leadership and their violation of the workers' democracy that was supposed to be the Communist norm.

*   *   *

Trotsky set forth a qualified democratic agenda in the fall of 1923 that guided his political activity for the rest of his life. Some of his statements were secret at the time (a tactical error); some were never published in full until perestroika opened some of the party archives.[2] His first and most extensive public statement in this critical vein came in the form of his so-called "New Course Letter" and accompanying articles, published in December 1923, first in *Pravda* and then in pamphlet form. These materials were made accessible to the outside world twenty years later by Trotsky's American follower Max Shachtman, in the volume, *The New Course*.[3]

By the time Trotsky commenced his behind-the-scenes feud with his Politburo colleagues, he had fully formulated a denunciation of the bureaucratization of the party and the violation of workers' democracy being perpetrated since Stalin became General Secretary. He never really improved upon the charges he made in his letter of 8 October 1923 to the Central Committee:

> The pressure of the period of War Communism ought to give place to a more lively and broader party responsibility. However, this present regime

. . . is much farther from workers' democracy than the regime of the fiercest period of War Communism. The bureaucratization of the party apparatus has developed to unheard-of proportions by means of the method of secretarial selection.[4]

Trotsky's critique was echoed a week later in the "Declaration of the Forty-Six," the eminent party figures who were the backbone of Trotsky's following:

The Party is to a significant degree ceasing to be that living self-acting collective. . . . We observe more and more a progressive division of the Party, no longer concealed by hardly anyone, into the secretarial hierarchy and the 'laymen,' into the professional party functionaries, selected from above, and the simple party masses, who do not participate in its group life.[5]

While Trotsky's enemies maneuvered for time and position in the face of these unsettling charges, they allowed him to compose the reformist manifesto that was adopted as a resolution by the Politburo on 5 December 1923, and published in *Pravda* December 7.[6] The statement targeted

a whole series of negative tendencies . . . : sharp divergences in the material position of members of the Party in connection with differences in their functions . . . ; the growth of connections with bourgeois elements and ideological influences from the latter; departmental narrowing of horizon . . . ; a danger of losing the perspective of socialist construction as a whole and of the world revolution . . . ; bureaucratization of the party apparatuses and the rise everywhere of a threat of cleavage between the Party and the masses.

But the resolution offered only a restricted definition of the alternative: "Workers' democracy signifies freedom of open discussion by all members of the party of the most important questions of party life, freedom of controversy about them, and also electiveness of the leading official individuals and collegia from below upwards. However, it does not suggest freedom of factional groupings." The resolution went on at length to promise all manner of reforms to restore party democracy and to fight "the bureaucratic perversion of the party apparatus and party practice."

Having won these concessions, Trotsky then overplayed his hand by publishing under his own name his "New Course" letter,[7] warning against unnamed "conservative-minded comrades" motivated by "a profound bureaucratic distrust of the Party," who might try to evade the December 5 resolution. Claiming victory, he asserted, "The Party must subordinate to itself its own apparatus without for a moment ceasing to be a centralized organization." This was the proverbial attempt to square the circle. "Democracy and centralism are two faces of party organization," Trotsky tried to explain. "The question is to harmonize them in the most correct manner." He unabashedly attacked his colleagues who had passed the resolution for tactical reasons: "During the last period there was no such equilibrium. The center of gravity wrongly centered in the apparatus." And to turn the knife in the wound, "History offers us more than one example of degeneration of the 'old guard.' " Then Trotsky directly charged bad faith:

> Before the publication of the decision of the Central Committee on the "new course," the mere pointing out of the need of modifying the internal party regime was regarded by bureaucratized apparatus functionaries as heresy, as factionalism, as an infraction of discipline. And now the bureaucrats are ready formally to "take note" of the "new course," that is, *to nullify it bureaucratically.*

Indeed, this was bound to be the response when Trotsky called for a purge:

> The renovation of the party apparatus . . . must aim at replacing the mummified bureaucrats with fresh elements. . . . The leading posts must be cleared out of those who at the first word of criticism, of objection, or of protest, brandish the thunderbolts of penalties before the critic. The "new course" must begin by making everyone feel that from now on nobody will dare terrorize the party.

Trotsky's challenge, seconded by his followers in the Moscow party organization (notably Preobrazhensky, Radek, and the former Democratic Centralist Sapronov), prompted a sudden *volte-face* on the part of his rivals in the leadership, led by Zinoviev. A torrent of invective commenced in the press and in party meetings on the theme of Trotsky's factional disloyalty; it culminated in the resolution of the Thirteenth Party Conference in January 1924 denouncing the leadership's critics as a "petty-bourgeois deviation."[8] Thus ended the most serious opposition challenge to the bureaucratic trend in the Soviet system. With it ended any further deepening of the Opposition's case for democracy. To the end of the Left Opposition's struggle in 1927, Trotsky and his friends did no more than echo the lines they had spoken and written in 1923, while they went down to a pitiful political defeat.

*   *   *

The Thirteenth Party Congress in May 1924, the first after Lenin's death, was the occasion of Trotsky's celebrated confession, "Comrades, none of us wants to be or can be right against the Party. In the last analysis the Party is always right, because the Party is the sole historical instrument that the working class possesses for the solution of its fundamental tasks." But these words, spoken in the peroration of a long address to the congress stressing again the danger of bureaucracy and the need to boost the working class as a social force, were clearly intended to be sarcastic. And Trotsky qualified his recantation immediately: "I for my part believe that I am only fulfilling my duty as a party member who warns his party about what he considers to be a danger. . . . Not only an individual party member but even the Party itself can make occasional mistakes."[9]

Earlier in his speech Trotsky went back to cite the resolution of December 5 as an authoritative warning about the party's course, and even quoted a speech by Bukharin of that period:

> Our cell secretaries . . . are usually appointed by the district committee. . . . As a rule, the voting takes place according to a definite pattern. They come into the meeting and ask: "Is anyone opposed?" And since everyone is more or less afraid to voice dissent, the individual who was appointed becomes secretary of the cell bureau. . . . Since it is considered bad form for anyone to speak against the "leadership," the matter is automatically settled. . . . This entire system eliminates the internal life of the party.[10]

As Trotsky's critique of the bureaucratic trend sharpened, his view of the trouble broadened and his understanding of it deepened. Before he went into open opposition, bureaucracy seemed largely a problem of the governmental machinery, stemming mainly from the holdover of tsarist personnel and their habits. Trotsky spoke out in the spring of 1923 to underscore Lenin's last articles about bureaucratic malfunctions and cultural backwardness, and complained of "a state machine of which it has been said that it is . . . little different from the old tsarist machine." This was "bureaucratism," the red tape, petty squabbles, avoidance of responsibility, and public-be-damned attitude popularly attributed to the old *chinovniki*. But Trotsky was still confident that the Party, as a healthy new organization of alert workers, would eventually overcome these survivals of prerevolutionary days.[11]

What drove Trotsky into opposition in 1923, or at least coincided with that move, was his perception that bureaucracy had seriously invaded the Party as well. In an addendum to his "New Course" articles, he warned of the deleterious influence of bureaucratic habits upon party members serving in the government, and attributed "bureaucratism" to "the heterogeneity of society, the difference between the daily and the fundamental interests of various groups of the population . . . , the lack of culture of the broad masses." These conditions "could place the revolution in peril." But salvation still lay with the Party, despite its own increasingly bureaucratic habits of appointment from the top down: "As the voluntary [sic] organization of the vanguard, of the best, the most active, and the most conscious elements of the working class, it is able to preserve itself much better than can the state apparatus from the tendencies of bureaucratism."[12] It would seem that if the dictatorship of the proletariat suppressed bourgeois elements more systematically it would be more democratic for the workers—a paradox that Trotsky did not attempt to resolve. Nor did it ever occur to him that a society with a high level of culture might incline as much or even more to bureaucratic forms of organization, as all of modern sociology, following Max Weber, is well aware. Trotsky's only theoretical source was Marx, mainly the notion that the bureaucracy could achieve temporary autonomy as the mediator between contending classes.[13] Of Engels' warning about the bureaucratic state organs becoming "the masters of society,"[14] Trotsky seems to make no mention.

When the turn of Zinoviev and Kamenev came in 1925 to fall under the relentless wheels of Stalin's apparatus, Trotsky called a plague on both of the bureaucratic houses in Moscow and in Leningrad. The Leningrad Opposition was to him at best a "bureaucratically distorted expression of the political anxiety felt by the most advanced section of the proletariat."[15] After he formed the United Opposition bloc with Zinoviev and Kamenev in 1926, Trotsky returned to the theme that the root of the bureaucratic trouble was the Communists' failure to develop industry and expand the working class fast enough:

> The bureaucratization of the party . . . is an expression of the disrupted social equilibrium, which has been and is being tipped to the disadvantage of the proletariat. . . . It is absolutely clear that a change of regime in the direction of workers' democracy is inseparable from a change in economic policy in the direction of genuine industrialization and a rectification of the line of the party leadership toward genuine internationalism."[16]

But to the end of his Soviet career, Trotsky refused to say that the regime had lost its essential Marxian virtue. "Our state is a proletarian state, though with bureaucratic deformations," he still maintained in November 1926, after he, Zinoviev, and Kamenev had been ousted from the Politburo.[17]

A somewhat more contextual and sociological conception of the bureaucratic trend emerged in the final months of the Left Opposition's existence. "The question of Soviet bureaucratism is . . . at bottom . . . a question of the class role played by the bureaucracy," stated the September 1927 Opposition platform, linking the growth of bureaucracy with the pro-kulak, anti-worker line that the Left attributed to the party leadership. The country was becoming dominated by "an innumerable caste [*sloi*] of genuine bureaucrats," contributing to the tendency toward a Soviet Thermidor.[18] Workers newly recruited into the bureaucracy, Trotsky observed, were fusing with the class enemy:

> The proletarian part of the state apparatus, which was earlier sharply divided from the cadres of the old bourgeois intellectuals and did not trust them, in the last few years has separated itself more and more from the working class and, in its style of life, has drawn closer to the bourgeois and petty-bourgeois intellectuals, and has become more susceptible to hostile class influences."[19]

*   *   *

Stalin's break with Bukharin's right wing of the Party in 1928 had little immediate effect on Trotsky's thinking, though many of his supporters "capitulated" to Stalin on the ground that the latter had substantially adopted the program of the Left. Trotsky was now more direct about the danger of a "Bonapartist" coup in the interest of the petty-bourgeoisie: "The further the Stalin regime goes, the more it appears as a dress rehearsal for Bonapartism. . . . On its back the power is sliding over from the proletariat to the bourgeoisie. . . . Stalinism is Kerenskyism moving from left to right."[20] But he still dreamed that his group could "mobilize the proletarian core of the Party" to save the workers' state from the "monarchist-Bonapartist principle" of the bureaucratic and petty-bourgeois Thermidoreans.[21]

During the weeks just before his expulsion from the USSR, Trotsky contemplated a more systematic treatise on the problem of bureaucracy, but he actually left only fragments.[22] "The bureaucracy," he insisted still, "was never an independent class. In the last analysis it always served one or the other," even if it "towers over and above society, including the class which it serves."[23] Trotsky was hanging on to the traditional Marxian class formulation by a very thin thread, one that his friend Rakovsky was just then breaking altogether.

Rakovsky, the Bulgarian from Rumania who had joined the Bolsheviks and served as prime minister of the Soviet Ukraine, was sent to Astrakhan at the same time that Trotsky was exiled to Alma Ata. Together with a handful of co-exiles Rakovsky endeavored to work out his own explanation of the social nature of Stalinism:

> When a class seizes power, a certain part of this class is transformed into agents of the power itself. In this way the bureaucracy arises. In the proletarian state, where capitalist accumulation is not permitted for members of the ruling party, this differentiation is at first functional, but then it becomes social. I do not say class, but social. I mean that the social position of the Communist who has an automobile at his disposal, a good apartment, regular leaves, and earns the party maximum, is distinct from the position of that same Communist if he works in the coal mines where he gets fifty to sixty rubles a month."[24]

Up to this point Rakovsky did not go in principle beyond Trotsky, but with the passage of time he and his group made the leap to a distinctly new position: "Before our eyes a great *class of rulers* has been *taking shape* and is continuing to develop."[25] Here, in embryo, was the "New Class" theory later embraced and amplified by other Marxists or ex-Marxists—Bruno Rizzi, James Burnham, Milovan Djilas, Rudolf Bahro, Michael Voslensky.[26] Rakovsky still tried to make his insight fit the terms of Marxian sociology by means of some forced redefinitions: "The unifying factor of this unique class is that unique form of private property, governmental power."[27] The Left Opposition was finally vindicated by this theoretical breakthrough, if not by political victory: "The Opposition of 1923–1924 foresaw the vast harm to the proletarian dictatorship which stems from the perversion of the party regime. Events have fully justified its prognosis: the enemy crept in through the bureaucratic window."[28]

*   *   *

Exile abroad did not immediately alter Trotsky's own perception of the Stalin regime, still in some mysterious sense a "workers' state," however much it was perverted by "bureaucratic deformation" and threatened by outright bourgeois counterrevolution. He recognized now that postrevolutionary fatigue had led to "an unquestionable reduction in the level of direct mass intervention," while "the party has been artificially diluted with a mass of half-raw recruits." These weaknesses allowed the bureaucracy to assume more and more power and independence: "The government official is increasingly filled with the conviction that the October Revolution was made precisely in order to concentrate power in his hands and assure him a privileged position." In turn, the bureaucrats "seek a peaceful Thermidorean switching back on to the track leading to bourgeois society."[29] Trotsky still could not conceive of any socio-political alternative besides the proletariat and the bourgeoisie: "Soviet power . . . is falling increasingly under the influence of bourgeois interests. . . . Not just the state apparatus, but the party apparatus as well, is becoming, if not the conscious agent, then at least the effective agent of bourgeois conceptions and expectations."[30]

As year followed year in exile, Trotsky became progressively more absorbed in the factional infighting and doctrinal hair-splitting among Communists outside the Soviet Union. Despite the tragic unfolding of Stalin's experiment with revolution from above, Trotsky would not bend the rigid Marxian framework of his own views. To be sure, he wrote in the spring of 1930, "The bureaucracy has restored many characteristics of a ruling class and that is very much how the working masses consider it," but he hastened to add, "From the Marxist point of view, it is clear that the Soviet bureaucracy cannot change itself into a new ruling class."[31] This conclusion permitted him to hope that his supporters could still somehow rouse "the proletarian nucleus of the Party to reform the regime in a struggle against the plebiscitary Bonapartist bureaucracy."[32] Meanwhile this same bureaucracy, hoping to wind down the revolution, "feels it has been double-crossed by its leader since 1928," leaving Stalin to depend on "the open and cynical establishment of the ple-biscitary-personal regime," against the "tens of thousands of old Bolsheviks and hundreds of thousands of young potential Bolsheviks [who] will rise up at the moment of danger."[33]

By 1933, despite all his past protestations against splitting the Communist Party, Trotsky decided that the time had come to repudiate the whole Communist International and to organize his followers everywhere into a new International. Nevertheless, the new International would make "the defense of the workers' state from imperialism and counterrevolution" one of its cardinal principles.[34] Trotsky would not yield on the proposition that Moscow still represented the dictatorship of the proletariat, albeit "a sick dictatorship."[35] He took particular umbrage when the French Socialist Lucien Laurat and the emigré Russian ultra-leftist Gabriel Miasnikov picked up the idea, like Rakovsky's in 1930, that the Soviet state represented a new form of class rule exploiting the proletariat; Trotsky thought he quashed the notion by linking it with the anarchist misgivings published well before the Russian Revolution by Jan Machajski. "The bureaucracy," he asserted, could not be a class, because it "has no independent position in the process of production and distribution. It has no independent property roots"—the point of Marxian dogma that still blinded Trotsky about the emerging Stalinist reality. "The biggest apartments, the juiciest steaks and even Rolls Royces are not enough to transform the bureaucracy into an independent ruling class." In short, "We have to deal not with *class exploitation* in the scientific sense of the word, but with *social parasitism*,"[36] a fine distinction which did not alter the outcome: "In the last analysis, the stifling of workers' democracy is the result of the pressure of class enemies through the medium of the workers' bureaucracy."[37] In consequence, "The bureaucracy can be compelled to yield power into the hands of the proletarian vanguard only by *force*." Even so, the greater danger of civil war was posed by the lurking forces of bourgeois counterrevolution.[38]

*   *   *

Trotsky's famous summation of his analysis of Soviet society came in his book, *The Revolution Betrayed: What is the Soviet Union and Where is it Going?*, written in Norway in 1936 and published in 1937 in English, French, and Spanish.[39] Much of his argument was a reiteration of what he had been saying in his many polemical statements of prior years— the Soviet regime was not yet socialist but only "a preparatory regime transitional from capitalism to socialism"; it was still a workers' state in its metaphysical essence.[40] Though the bureaucracy, which "has neither stocks nor bonds," still fell short of the definition of a ruling class, Trotsky finally went so far as to term it "an uncontrolled caste alien to socialism." He now conceded that the bureaucracy had already consummated the Soviet Thermidor.[41] Stalin's regime was "a variety of Bonapartism—a Bonapartism of a new type not before seen in history," ruling in a manner that Trotsky himself called "totalitarian."[42] Only a new proletarian revolution could restore the Soviet Union to the socialist path: "There is no peaceful outcome for this crisis."[43]

Perhaps most significantly, in this reassessment, Trotsky finally gave up the Leninist proposition that the working class could legitimately have only one political party to represent it. He now claimed that the Bolshevik suppression of other parties soon after the October Revolution had only been intended as "a temporary evil," which unfortunately gave rise to "the monopoly of an uncontrolled bureaucracy." Then his crucial new realization: "Classes are heterogeneous. . . . One and the same class may create several parties."[44] As to the CPSU, "The ruling party which enjoys a monopoly in the Soviet Union is the political machine of the bureaucracy."[45] A few months later Trotsky reaffirmed these conclusions, ending his Odyssey of theory in terms prophetic of the East European revolutions of 1989: "It is necessary to prepare the arena for two parties . . . , maybe three or four. It is necessary to smash away the dictatorship of Stalin. . . . If this new political upheaval is successful, the masses, with these experiences, will never permit the dictatorship of one party, of one bureaucracy."[46]

In the last year of his life, shaken by Stalin's purges on the one hand and the "New Class" heresies of some of his followers on the other, Trotsky toyed with the possibility that democratic proletarian socialism might *not* be the natural outcome of the revolution as per Marx. If it turned out that the proletariat suffered a "congenital incapacity to become a ruling class," one would have to acknowledge that "in its fundamental traits the present USSR was the precursor of a new exploiting regime on an international scale."[47] But Trotsky could not accept this alternative prospect, certainly not as one excluding his lifetime ideals. Baruch Knei-Paz comments, "He, at least, would remain a socialist, out of moral conviction if not out of 'scientific' certainty."[48]

*   *   *

Trotsky was an eloquent observer of the evolution of Soviet Russia after Lenin left the scene, and of the degeneration of the revolution into postrevolutionary despotism. Yet he was a total failure politically in trying to arrest or redirect that evolution. Not surprisingly, from the early 1920s to the time of his death, Trotsky's thought was constantly colored by his own fall from power. A profound resentment of having been upstaged, defeated, and condemned by lesser mortals than he, comes through in almost everything he wrote from the very beginning of the struggle to succeed Lenin.

Trotsky was particularly galled by reminders of his belated adherence to Bolshevism and charges that he was less than a totally devoted follower of the Marxist-Leninist party line. In response, he wrote reams of exegetical self-justification, to prove in one instance after another that he was correct in all matters of Communist theory, and that his critics were the ones who had fallen into error. As Trotsky said himself in replying to the Politburo during the opening phase of the controversy, "I will examine the disputed questions point by point, giving exact quotations and references to documents that are readily accessible for verification."[49] To fend off his critics he clung to Lenin as a veritable oracle: "We proceed from the fact that, as experience has irrefutably shown, on all more or less fundamental questions over which any of us differed with Lenin, *Vladimir Ilyich was entirely right.*"[50]

Yet most of what Trotsky was able to publish or otherwise disseminate during the succession struggle fell on deaf ears, or was turned back against him as material for still more charges of heretical thinking. Could Trotsky not have known that his tiresome diatribes, however well documented by references to the collected works of Lenin, would have little or no impact on the enemies who were politically determined to destroy him? Indeed, many spokesmen for the party leadership relished in baiting Trotsky, as the extant records of debate between them vividly show.[51] An alternative explanation is that Trotsky was really speaking and writing, not in the vain hope of persuading his enemies, but to establish a record vindicating himself, for his own self-satisfaction and for posterity.

In furthering this purpose, the task Trotsky obsessively set for himself was to prove that despite his prerevolutionary differences with Lenin, he had become a loyal Bolshevik in 1917 and had unswervingly followed Lenin ever since. His fatal mistake was to accept the 1921 ban on factions within the Party as a non-debatable premise. Trotsky thereby put himself in a position where he had to prove that he was not what he really was. When confronted with the charge of factionalism, which obviously was the kind of activity he was pursuing from 1923 on, he could only try to deny that his oppositional efforts constituted factional activity within the terms of the ban, while suggesting at the same time that any actual factionalism appearing in the Party was a symptom of the growing oppressiveness of the party bureaucracy. He wrote in July 1926, for example, "That a ruling party, under conditions of revolutionary dictatorship, cannot accept a regime of contending factions is absolutely unquestionable. One need only add that it is absolutely inevitable for an apparatus regime to breed factions from its own midst."[52] In 1927 the Left Opposition went to great lengths to deny that it advocated a split in the Communist ranks. "We will struggle with all our force against the formation of two parties," they declared in their platform for the Fifteenth Party Congress, "for the dictatorship of the proletariat demands as its very core a united proletarian party."[53] Thus Trotsky and his followers rejected precisely what the country needed. They would not accept and defend the real logic of their own position, which was to say that bureaucratism in the Party showed the faults of Lenin's centralist conception of organization, and that factional freedom—or better yet, multi-party freedom—had to be allowed in order to fight effectively against the bureaucratic trend. At no time did Trotsky or his followers propose any concrete democratic procedures to record the voice of the rank-and-file of the Party, let alone of the non-party masses, in formulating policy alternatives and in the choice of leaders.

Trotsky's formulation of the democracy–bureaucracy problem was inhibited not only by his political commitment to the precepts of Leninism, but also by his theoretical anchorage in the utopian propositions of Marxism. He never lost faith in the revolutionary and democratic qualities of the proletariat, despite civil war ravages among the experienced, prerevolutionary industrial workers (death in battle, return to the village, promotion into the bureaucracy). He never gave up belief in the "workers' state," even when it became encrusted with "bureaucratic deformations." Throughout the 1920s Trotsky and his supporters held unshakably to their belief that the workers would spontaneously show democratic responsibility—and support the Left Opposition—if only the party bureaucracy got off their backs and pushed a pro-worker program of faster industrialization and higher wages. In reality, party cells in the factories were among the least responsive to the Opposition, and the "Lenin Enrollment" of 1924 made the proletarian rank and file in the party even more manipulable by the apparatus.

Trotsky failed to see that the proletariat was not the new revolutionary vanguard being generated by industrial society. Nor could he see that the bourgeoisie as commonly understood was not the real alternative for postrevolutionary social dominance. This role was being steadily assumed, as some of Trotsky's followers ultimately realized, by the bureaucracy itself, state and party in the Soviet Union, governmental and corporate in capitalist countries. Thus the tide of social evolution was on the side of those who accommodated themselves to the bureaucratic reality, whatever slogans they might toss off to appease other elements who thought the revolution belonged to them. The only true options, as the world has seen in so many recent instances, are whether to let that bureaucratic reality rule by fiat, in the name of some disproven revolutionary dogma, or to subject it to the democratic mechanisms of restraint and control that theorists too sure of themselves used to dismiss as "bourgeois."

Notes

1. Lev Trotsky, *Nashi politicheskie zadachi* (Geneva: Russian Social Democratic Workers' Party, 1904), p. 54.

2. The principle documents were Trotsky's letters to the Central Committee and the Central Control Commission, 8 and 23 October 1923, known until recently only from the summaries and extensive quotations published by the *Sotsialisticheskii Vestnik* (Berlin), 28 May 1924. The full texts were published in *Izvestiya TsK*, no. 5, 1990, pp. 165–173, and no. 10, 1990, pp. 167–181.

3. Leon Trotsky, *The New Course*, edited and with introduction by Max Shachtman, together with Shachtman, "The Struggle for the New Course" (New York: New International Publishing Co., 1943). Republished in Russian, Lev Trotskii, "Novyi kurs," *Molodoi Kommunist*, no. 8, 1989.

4. Trotsky, *The New Course*, p. 154.

5. Declaration of the Forty-Six, 15 October 1923, Trotsky Archive, Houghton Library, Harvard University, document T802a; Yu. Fel'shtinsky, ed., *Kommunisticheskaya oppozitsiya v SSSR, 1923–1927: Iz arkhiva L'va Trotskogo* (4 vols., Benson, Vt.: Chalidze Publications, 1988), vol. I, pp. 83–85; *Izvestiya TsK*, no. 6, 1990, pp. 189–191. English translation in E. H. Carr, *The Interregnum: A History of Soviet Russia*, vol. IV (New York: Macmillan, 1954), pp. 367–373.

6. On the circumstances of the adoption of the resolution, see Robert V. Daniels, *The Conscience of the Revolution* (Cambridge, Mass.: Harvard University

Press, 1960), pp. 222–223. The resolution is sometimes attributed to the Central Committee.

7. *Pravda*, 11 December 1923; Trotsky, *The New Course*, pp. 89–98.

8. *Kommunisticheskaya Partiya Sovetskogo Soyuza v rezoliutsiyakh i resheniyakh s"ezdov, konferentsii, i plenumov TsK* (7th ed., Moscow: Gospolitizdat, 1954), vol. I, p. 782.

9. *Trinadtsatyi s"ezd RKP(b): Stenograficheskii otchet* (Moscow: Gosudarstvennoe Izdatel'stvo Politicheskoi Literatury, 1963), pp. 158–159; Naomi Allen, ed., *Leon Trotsky: The Challenge of the Left Opposition* (3 vols., New York: Pathfinder Press, 1975–1981), vol. I, pp. 161–162.

10. Nikolai Bukharin, speech at a meeting of the Krasnaya Presnia district organization, December 1923, quoted by Trotsky, *Trinadtsatyi s"ezd*, p. 148; Allen, *Leon Trotsky*, vol. I, pp. 149–150.

11. Trotsky, *Zadachi XII s"ezda RKP* (Speech at a conference of the Communist Party of the Ukraine, 5 April 1923; Moscow: Izdatelstvo Deviatogo Yanvaria, 1923), p. 24; "Tasks of the Twelfth Congress of the Russian Communist Party," in *Leon Trotsky Speaks* (New York: Pathfinder Press, 1972), p. 155.

12. Trotsky, "Bureaucratism and Revolution (Outline of a Report that the Author Could not Deliver)," first published in his pamphlet, *Novyi Kurs*; Trotsky, *The New Course*, pp. 45–46.

13. Cf. Karl Marx, *The Eighteenth Brumaire of Louis Bonaparte* (New York: International Publishers, 1926), pp. 130–131; *The Civil War in France* (Chicago: Kerr, n.d.), p. 42.

14. Friedrich Engels, 1891 introduction to Marx, *The Civil War in France* (New York: International Publishers, 1940), p. 20.

15. Trotsky, "Blok s Zinov'evym (k dnevniku)" 9 December 1925, Trotsky Archive T2972, Fel'shtinsky, *Oppozitsiya*, vol. I, p. 154; "A 'Bloc' with Zinoviev (For a Diary)," Allen, *Leon Trotsky*, vol. I, p. 386.

16. Trotsky, "V Politburo" (To the Politburo), 6 June 1926, Trotsky Archive T2986; Fel'shtinsky, *Oppozitsiya*, vol. I, pp. 235, 238; translated as "Party Bureaucratism and Party Democracy," Allen, *Leon Trotsky*, vol. II, pp. 68, 72.

17. Trotsky, Speech to the Fifteenth Party Conference, 1 November 1926, *Pravda*, 6 November 1926; Allen, *Leon Trotsky*, vol. II, p. 162.

18. "Proekt platformy bol'shevikov-lenintsev (oppozitsii) k XV S"ezdu VKP(b) (Krizis partii i puti ego preodoleniya)," September 1927, Trotsky Archive T1007, Felshtinsky, *Oppozitsiya*, vol. IV, pp. 139, 151; English translation, "The Real Situation in Russia and the Tasks of the Communist Party," in Leon Trotsky, *The Real Situation in Russia* (New York: Harcourt, Brace and Co., 1928), pp. 95, 124.

19. Trotsky, "At a New Stage," *Die Fahne des Kommunismus*, 21 and 28 December 1927, Allen, *Leon Trotsky*, vol. II, pp. 490–491.

20. Trotsky, "Who is Leading the Comintern Today," *The Militant*, 15 August and 30 November 1928, Allen, *Leon Trotsky*, vol. III, p. 205; "The Danger of Bonapartism and the Opposition's Role" (21 October 1928), *The Militant*, 1 February 1929, Allen, *Leon Trotsky*, vol. III, p. 274.

21. Trotsky, "Our Differences with the Democratic Centralists," 11 November 1928, *Contre le courant*, 6 May 1929, Allen, *Leon Trotsky*, vol. III, p. 294; "The

Crisis in the Right-Center Bloc" (November 1928), *Contre le Courant*, 22 March 1929, Allen, *Leon Trotsky*, vol. III, p. 328.

22. Trotsky, "Marxism and the Relation between Proletarian and Peasant Revolution" (December 1928), Trotsky Archive, Allen, *Leon Trotsky*, vol. III, pp. 347–351; "Philosophical Tendencies of Bureaucratism" (December 1928), Trotsky Archive, Allen, *Leon Trotsky*, vol. III, pp. 389–409.

23. Ibid., vol. III, p. 391.

24. Khristian Rakovsky, "Pis'mo o prichinakh pererozhdeniya partii i gosudarstvennogo apparata" (Letter on the Causes of the Degeneration of the Party and of the State Apparatus, 6 August 1928), *Biulleten' Oppozitsii*, no. 6, October 1929, p. 15.

25. Kh. Rakovsky, V. Kossior, N. Muralov, and V. Kasparova, "Obrashchenie oppozitsii Bolshevikov-Lenintsev v TsK, TsKK VKP(b); ko vsem chlenam VKP(b)" (Appeal of the Bolshevik-Leninist Opposition to the CC and the CCC of the AUCP(B), and to all members of the AUCP(B), April 1930), *Biulleten' Oppozitsii*, no. 17–18, November–December 1930, p. 16.

26. Cf. Bruno Rizzi, *La Bureaucratisation du monde* (Paris: Hachette, 1939); James Burnham, *The Managerial Revolution* (New York: John Day, 1941); Milovan Djilas, *The New Class: An Analysis of the Communist System* (New York: Praeger, 1957); Rudolf Bahro, *Die Alternative: Zur Kritik des real existierenden Sozialismus* (Koln: Europäische Verlagsanstalt, 1977); Michael Voslensky, *Nomenklatura: The Soviet Ruling Class* (Garden City, N.Y.: Doubleday, 1984).

27. Rakovsky et al., "Obraschchenie," p. 16.

28. Kh. Rakovsky, V. Kossior, and M. Okudzhava, Theses of August 1929, *Biulleten' Oppozitsii*, no. 7, November–December 1929, p. 9.

29. Trotsky, *Chto i kak proizoshlo?* (Paris: De Nevarre, 1929), translated in *The New York Times*, 1 March 1929, as "Trotsky Reveals Origins of His Fall"; *Writings of Leon Trotsky* (New York: Pathfinder Press, 1975), vol. I, pp. 47, 50.

30. Trotsky, preface to *La Révolution défiguré* (Paris: Reider, 1929), *Writings of Leon Trotsky*, vol. I, p. 118.

31. Trotsky, "K kapitalizmu ili k sotsializmu," *Biulleten' Oppozitsii*, no. 11, May 1930, p. 9; "Toward Capitalism or Socialism?" *Writings of Leon Trotsky*, vol. II, p. 207.

32. Trotsky, "K XVI-mu s"ezdu VKP(b)" *Biulleten' Oppozitsii*, no. 12–13, June–July 1930, p. 5; "Toward the Sixteenth Congress of the CPSU," *Writings of Leon Trotsky*, vol. II, p. 261. Oddly enough, in commenting on the 1930 statement of Rakovsky and his associates which among other things explained the bureaucracy as a new class, Trotsky overlooked the point altogether. Trotsky, "Introduction to the Rakovsky Declaration," 22 October 1930, *The Militant*, 15 January 1931, *Writings of Leon Trotsky*, vol. III, pp. 49–50.

33. Trotsky, "Chto dal'she? (K kampanii protiv pravykh)," *Biulleten Oppozitsii*, no. 17, November 1930, p. 23; "What Next in the Campaign Against the Russian Right Wing?" *The Militant*, 1 January 1931, *Writings of Leon Trotsky*, vol. III, pp. 63–65.

34. Trotsky, Declaration of the Bolshevik-Leninist Delegation at the Conference of Left Socialist and Communist Organizations (Paris, 17 August 1933), *The Militant*, 23 September 1933, *Writings of Leon Trotsky*, vol. VI, p. 42.

35. Trotsky, *The Soviet Union and the Fourth International* (New York: Pioneer Publishers, 1934), *Writings of Leon Trotsky*, vol. VI, p. 104.

36. Ibid., pp. 112–113.

37. Trotsky, Declaration at the Conference of Left Socialist and Communist Organizations, *Writings of Leon Trotsky*, vol. VI, p. 43.

38. Trotsky, "The Soviet Union and the Fourth International," *Writings of Leon Trotsky*, vol. VI, p. 104.

39. Garden City, N.Y.: Doubleday, Doran & Co., 1937. Cf. Richard B. Day, "Democratic Control and The Dignity of Politics—an Analysis of *The Revolution Betrayed*," *Comparative Economic Studies*, XXIX:3 (fall 1987).

40. *The Revolution Betrayed*, p. 47.

41. Ibid., pp. 149, 255.

42. Ibid., pp. 278, 279.

43. Ibid., p. 287.

44. Ibid., pp. 266, 267.

45. Ibid., 270.

46. Trotsky, Statement to the Preliminary Commission of Inquiry, John Dewey, Chairman, in *The Case of Leon Trotsky: Report of Hearings on the Charges Made Against Him in the Moscow Trials* (New York: Harper, 1937), pp. 440–441.

47. Trotsky, "The USSR and War," in *In Defense of Marxism* (New York: Pioneer Publishers, 1942), p. 9.

48. Baruch Knei-Paz, *The Social and Political Thought of Leon Trotsky* (Oxford: Oxford University Press, 1978), p. 426.

49. Trotsky to the Politburo, 24 October 1923, as quoted in *Sotsialisticheskii Vestnik*, 28 May 1924, p. 11; Allen, *Leon Trotsky*, vol. I, p. 60.

50. Trotsky, "In Defense of the Opposition Bloc" (September 1926), *Mitteilungsblatt* (Berlin), no. 2, January 1927; Allen, *Leon Trotsky*, vol. II, p. 110.

51. See, e.g., "Rech' Trotskogo na zasedanii ob"edinennogo plenuma 6 avgusta 1927 g.," Trotsky Archive T2992; Fel'shtinsky, *Oppozitsiya*, vol. IV, pp. 52–67; translated as Trotsky, Speech to the Joint Plenum of the CC and the CCC, 6 August 1927, Allen, *Leon Trotsky*, vol. II, pp. 270–290.

52. Trotsky, "V Politburo," Fel'shtinsky, *Oppozitsiya*, vol. I, p. 235; "Party Bureaucratism and Party Democracy," Allen, *Leon Trotsky*, vol. II, p. 69.

53. "Proekt platformy," Fel'shtinsky, *Oppozitsiya*, vol. IV, p. 174; *The Real Situation in Russia*, p. 194.

8

Soviet Socialism:
From Redistribution to Production

Despite a century and a half of the most diverse developments in the history of socialist thought, it is still the habit of most followers of any school of socialism to regard their own beliefs as the sole, exclusively valid form, all others being perversions. Any discussion of the subject would be considerably clearer if we detach the definition of socialism from particular preferences for particular socialist forms. We can then treat socialism as a broad category of socioeconomic forms which must be judged on their individual merits.[1]

What distinguishes Marxian socialism from all other forms is a theory of how socialism is to come about, as the natural consequence of the historical laws of class struggle and revolution that Marx thought he had discerned. As to the specific characteristics of the future socialism, Marx was always advisedly vague; he added little to the hopes and plans of the Utopian socialists of the generation preceding him. Marx's socialism was utopianism with a difference: the earlier ideal of a stateless collectivism with complete distributive justice was now reinforced with a sophisticated theory of social and economic development. Marx was the first philosopher in history to incorporate in his thought the full importance of economic development through technical progress and industrialization, which by multiplying society's capacity to produce would finally give some realistic substance to the old dream of abolishing human misery. The stark facts—largely overlooked by Marx's Utopian predecessors—were that given the limits on productivity in pre-industrial society, no redistribution of the wealth of the small privileged class would make much of a dent on the average in the poverty of the vast majority. Redistribution would only undermine the culture-bearing class,

This chapter is a revised version of "Toward a Definition of Soviet Socialism," *New Politics*, vol. 1, no. 4 (1962), pp. 111–118. Reprinted with permission.

and it could be evaded by any group with the drive and the power to spare itself from reduction to the average level of misery.

The crucial function of economic development is, according to Marxism, to furnish the material prerequisites for the effective socialist redistribution of wealth in the name of justice. This developmental function is not the responsibility of socialism, but is the distinctive work of capitalism. The Marxian law here is rigorous: socialism must follow capitalism, but by the same token capitalism must precede socialism. Where capitalism has not entered the picture to play its "progressive" role, the productive capacity and the propertyless proletarian class will not exist to provide the indispensable foundation for socialism.[2]

The great paradox of Marxism is that the proletarian socialist revolution envisioned by Marx never came to pass in the more advanced industrial countries where he expected it, but instead proclaimed itself in Russia where the economic transformation under capitalism was still in an early stage. Russia in 1917—by the admission of all schools of Russian Marxism—still dismally lacked the industrial maturity and proletarian majority required for socialism. It was for this reason that the Mensheviks and even right-wing Bolsheviks opposed the attempt at a "socialist" revolution going beyond the "bourgeois democracy" of the Provisional Government. The rationale for the Bolshevik seizure of power was drawn from Trotsky's theory of permanent revolution—the contention that a working-class uprising in Russia would inspire general socialist revolution in the riper countries of the West. When the great world-revolutionary hopes of 1917–1919 faded away in the early 1920s, the supposedly proletarian socialist regime of the Russian Communists was left hanging in mid-air, as it were, without much of the industrial and proletarian base which was presumably the prerequisite for it.

Lenin conceded as much in reply to Menshevik criticisms. His solution was to claim that the Soviet government could deliberately create its own cultural and economic prerequisites for the goal of socialism.[3] Meanwhile the "workers state" would protect the interests of the proletariat while the country operated under the nationalized economy of "state capitalism." No heed was given to the divergence of this doctrine from the Marxian conception of the conditioning of political forms by economic relationships. In reality the Soviet system had already departed from the Marxian framework.

Lenin's position was the starting point for two sharply contrasting approaches toward socialism—exemplified by Trotsky and Bukharin respectively—which set the theoretical stage for the great factional controversies in the Communist Party in the mid-1920s. Trotsky wanted to take the offensive, with a state-planned industrialization drive which, by expanding industry, would build up the proletarian class "base" for the "dictatorship of the proletariat" and keep it from collapsing for lack of a foundation. Bukharin took the cautious approach of long-term "peaceful co-existence" with the peasantry—not only the Soviet peasants, he pointed out with considerable insight, but also the great peasant majorities of Asia and the colonial territories.[4] Stalin's theoretical contribution of "socialism in one country" was less a policy directive than a political maneuver to try to use Lenin against Trotsky. All factions were concerned to build up the Soviet economy and avoid international risk, and the issue was only whether the existing Soviet system was theoretically secure socialism. Trotsky, in opposition, said no; Stalin and Bukharin, seeking doctrinal security, insisted on a positive answer. Stalin began doing deliberate violence to the scriptures by quoting Lenin out of context to make it appear that Russian socialism did not depend on the success of international revolution. He insisted on an act of faith in a socialist Russia, and was soon enforcing this faith with all the force of the totalitarian state.[5]

* * *

The history of the theoretical gyrations performed by the Soviet leaders to square their power and their practices with the Marxian perspective leads naturally to a fundamental question: can Soviet Communism in any real sense be regarded as the proletarian socialism predicted by Marx? Or should we not approach it as quite a different phenomenon, entirely outside the Marxian framework, which only makes claim to the Marxian label—which in effect is using Marxism as "ideology" or "false consciousness" in the service of a distinctly new movement?

The Russian Revolution and most instances of significant Communist strength are products not of a great proletariat and industrial maturity, but of the stresses of early industrialization and the alienation of the intelligentsia. This is particularly the case in countries outside Western Europe and North America; the Communist movement was typically a response to the challenge of Westernization. Its ambitions were those of anti-Western Westernizing nationalists, for whom the anti-capitalist and anti-imperialist phraseology of Marxian socialism provided an irresistible theoretical vehicle. It makes no difference that the country concerned was not ripe for the Marxist revolution and might not yet have entered its bourgeois phase; the Marxist revolutionary appeal is psychological rather than logical. As Adam Ulam demonstrated in *The Unfinished Revolution*,[6] Marxism has typically reached its greatest strength— in late nineteenth-century Germany, in early twentieth-century Russia, in Asia in the second quarter of this century—when a country is just beginning its most rapid transformation.

The Marxist revolution—or rather, the revolution of the Westernizing intelligentsia with a Marxist "ideology"—really rests on the possibility of the *diversion* of a society's development away from capitalism and into revolutionary socialism. This socialism is not the successor to capitalism but an alternative, which is likely to be ruled out if capitalism is allowed to develop too far. Such diversion is made more likely by various circumstances—by the lack of a liberal democratic development prior to the onset of industrialization; by overly rapid industrialization (such as foreign capital permits); and above all by difficult anti-colonial struggles or the military defeat of the traditional government, as in the cases of Russia and of China.

Once such a revolutionary regime is in power, it has to contend with the problems of economic development that would have been handled by capitalism had it not been overthrown. Since the new regime is socialist in principle, it begins to apply its socialist forms of economic organization and control to the task of economic development. An utterly new kind of socialist ideal then emerges—not the socialism of redistributive justice, but what I term "production socialism." Production socialism tries to do capitalism's job of accumulating capital and developing the productive forces of society. This fundamentally altered economic content of socialism in the USSR underlay the sad history of the Communist betrayal of democratic and equalitarian ideals and the creation of the permanent bureaucratic apparatus of what can well be termed "state capitalism."

*   *   *

The foregoing represents schematically what happened in Soviet Russia in the 1920s and then became the model for the whole international Communist movement. Lenin fought with the left-wing Communists as early as 1918 over the restoration of hierarchical authority in industry and the army. In 1920 Trotsky proposed the militarization of labor and the trade-unions, in order to create a machine that could mobilize the effort which Russia's dire economic straits required. In the early 1920s Trotsky and Preobrazhensky borrowed the industrial planning model of the German "Kriegssozialismus" of World War I, and for the first time anywhere laid down the basic principle of planned industrial development by the socialist state. The novelty of the idea is attested by the resistance it encountered on the part of Trotsky's political opponents, who for years, under the inspiration of Bukharin, insisted that development could only proceed in the capitalistic fashion of stimulus (even of state-owned industry) by market demand. Preobrazhensky frankly added the principle of "primary socialist accumulation"—deliberate exploitation of the people (especially the peasants) by the socialist state, in order to squeeze out the surplus required for industrial capital formation.[7]

The theory of the new production socialism worked out by the Trotskyists awaited only its adoption by the dominant political force in the country. This was precisely what happened in 1928 when Stalin, having crushed the Trotsky Opposition, plagiarized their ideas and turned against the cautious Bukharinists. The resulting Five-Year Plans of intensive industrialization provided the foundation for the Communist economy, both dynamically and structurally, through the Brezhnev era. Soviet economic development has been based on the use of the dictatorial state to accumulate capital—by taxes, obligatory farm deliveries, wage control, and monopoly state trading profits—and to channel this capital through the central planning system into the construction and equipment of heavy industry. Ownership, and basic production decisions as represented in the plan, were of course in the hands of the state, individual enterprise being tabooed altogether regardless of considerations of efficiency and incentive. Below the level of ownership and the plan, however, the requirements of industrial effectiveness led the Soviet regime at an early date to revert to almost all the familiar capitalist forms—or rather, to the bureaucratic forms which corporate capitalism and state-owned industry can have in common: the managerial hierarchy and individual responsibility, in preference to the workers' control and committee administration which was the Communists' initial ideal; salary differentials, bonuses, and piece wages; strict industrial discipline; and a fully monetary, profit-and-loss accounting system. The Soviet enterprise differed but little from the capitalistic corporation except that the profit motive was replaced by plan-fulfillment, and there was of course no significant labor-management bargaining.

The Stalinist system was undeniably a form of socialism—emphatically so, in the broad sense of the term as social control over economic activity. The particular kind of socialist control which distinguished this system was the all-embracing bureaucratic hierarchy embodied in the totalitarian state. As its purpose this socialism set for itself not distributive justice but the development of industrial production and national power. We can well visualize it as the capitalist corporation on the scale of the national state, where the whole country is a company town (with insurance and pension plans, to be sure) and the citizen-stockholders are manipulated by the managers in rigged meetings. Add to this, of course, the oriental political habits of Russian despotism and the quasi-religious requirements of theoretical indoctrination which the system inherited from its Marxist background, and we have all the essentials of Stalinist society.[8]

*   *   *

This description of Soviet socialism would not be complete without reference to a particular school of early socialist thought which, by coincidence, Soviet developments remarkably paralleled. This is the doctrine of the French Utopian, Henri de Saint-Simon, whose writings in the first quarter of the nineteenth century sketched out a model of the new industrial society as organic, hierarchical, enlightened by science and technology, and infused with moral concern for the welfare of the workers.[9] Saint-Simon's socialism was frankly elitist, with careers open to the technically talented—a form of "meritocracy," if you will—and its emphasis on natural obedience and the propagandizing of virtue had strongly totalitarian implications. The irony is that the socialism of Marx's Russian followers conformed in practice much more closely to that of the precursor whom the Marxists meant to reject. Saint-Simon's insights about the coming forms of industrial society were so accurate that his ideas would have made a much less unrealistic "ideology" for the industrializing totalitarianism established by the Russians in the name of Marx.

Some neo-Trotskyist analysts have tried to combine the Marxian conception of the class struggle with a sort of Saint-Simonian view about the bureaucratic industrial society. People like James Burnham and Milovan Djilas have represented Soviet socialism as a new type of class society—the "managerial revolution" or the "new class"—succeeding the bourgeoisie.[10] This is a dubious effort as far as salvaging the Marxian class analysis is concerned, but it does appropriately emphasize the non-proletarian nature of the Stalinist system. It was a form of society that paralleled the function of early capitalism, and to this end borrowed and exaggerated the bureaucratic institutions of mature capitalism.

As such, Soviet socialism was an outstanding success in the task it set itself, of rapid industrialization and the achievement of a self-sufficient military potential. This is not to say that the same results could not have been accomplished in a capitalist-mercantilist manner, as in Japan and Imperial Germany. The Soviet system was not the only developmental alternative, even though it worked. What Soviet socialism could not offer was any substantial progress toward the freedom and the egalitarian justice of the nineteenth-century socialist ideal.

It might seem that when the industrial transformation of the USSR had been largely accomplished, a liberalization could follow with more scope for democratic procedures and egalitarian ideals. This was the fond hope of neo-Marxists who felt that industrialism meant democracy and that the economic success of Soviet totalitarianism was, so to speak, sowing the seeds of its own destruction. In point of fact, stable democracy is a product of the pre-industrial commercial societies of Western Europe of the seventeenth and eighteenth centuries, and wherever industrialization has commenced without a prior liberal political base—i.e., outside of the North Atlantic community—democracy has not been able to achieve a stable existence. Far from laying the groundwork for democracy, Soviet economic development entailed a profound bureaucratization of political and economic life.

Even when the original justification for "primary socialist accumulation" by dictatorial means had passed, the bureaucratic structure of the Communist Party and the Soviet state had an ongoing life of its own, and for decades after Stalin's death no force appeared which could effectively challenge it. Systems of organized power can—Marx to the contrary notwithstanding—perpetuate themselves for long periods of time after the conditions which brought them into being have disappeared. European feudalism endured almost a thousand years after it performed its function of restoring order out of Dark Age anarchy. The bureaucratic hierarchy of Soviet socialism may prove equally hard to undo.

Notes

1. On definitions of socialism, see above, ch. 1.

2. Marx did concede that Russia might be able to skip capitalism and develop directly into socialism on the basis of the country's traditional communal agriculture, if the simultaneous international success of socialism provided a favorable setting. His Russian followers—both Menshevik and Bolshevik—were more orthodox than the prophet and insisted on the preparatory function of capitalism. See Marx to the Editor of *Otechestvennye Zapiski,* 1879, Karl Marx and Friedrich Engels, *Selected Correspondence, 1846–1895* (New York: International Publishers, 1942), pp. 352–355; Marx and Engels, preface to the Russian edition of *The Communist Manifesto,* 1882, quoted, ibid., p. 355; Engels to N. F. Danielson, 24 February 1893, ibid., pp. 508–510.

3. V. I. Lenin, "Our Revolution: Apropos of the Notes of N. Sukhanov" (January 1923), *Selected Works* (Moscow, Foreign Languages Publishing House, 1950–1952), vol. II, book 2, pp. 726–727.

4. Nikolai Bukharin, "Teoriya permanentnoi revoliutsii" (The Theory of Permanent Revolution), *Za leninizm: sbornik statei* (Moscow and Leningrad: Gosizdat, 1925), pp. 355–356.

5. On socialism in one country, see above, ch. 3.

6. Adam Ulam, *The Unfinished Revolution* (New York: Random House, 1960), pp. 6–10.

7. See Alexander Erlich, *The Soviet Industrialization Debate,* (Cambridge, Mass.: Harvard University Press, 1960).

8. See Alfred G. Meyer, "USSR Incorporated," *Slavic Review,* XX:3 (fall 1961).

9. See, e.g., *The Doctrine of Saint-Simon: An Exposition, First Year, 1828–1829* (Boston: Beacon Press, 1958), esp. introduction by Georg G. Igers.

10. On the theory of the "New Class," see above, ch. 7.

9

Stalinism as Postrevolutionary Dictatorship

It is currently fashionable on both sides of the Atlantic to say that Marxism is dying and that socialism has failed. Actually, as far as the Soviet Union is concerned, socialism in the original Marxian sense has long been dead. Joseph Stalin killed it. He killed it more than half a century ago, in the course of the revolution from above and the purges that he carried out between 1929 and 1938.

To suggest this antagonism between Stalin and his ideological heritage is immediately to become involved in the long-standing debate among scholars and polemicists alike as to whether Stalin betrayed Lenin's revolution or merely carried it to its logical conclusion. Actually there are both truth and error in each position; there were both continuities and contrasts as the Lenin phase of the Russian revolutionary experience led into the Stalin phase.

The simplistic argument that Stalin was merely the continuator of Lenin's vision of totalitarian socialism is still common in Anglo-American academic circles, and it is now shared by some Soviet reformers. To my mind, this view rests on a fundamental misunderstanding of the nature of revolution as a long process of related but contradictory stages. In turn, failure to grasp the process makes it difficult to understand the Gorbachevian phase of the revolutionary experience. Mikhail Gorbachev suggested shortly after coming to power that he was leading a new "revolution."[1] If so, what was it a revolution against, and how did that negativity define the new era? Obviously, against Stalinism and its neo-Stalinist legacy. But what did that system really represent in the context

This chapter was originally presented as a paper for the international conference "The Age of Stalinism," sponsored by the Gramsci Institute and the University of Urbino, Italy. The conference proceedings in Italian have been published in Aldo Natoli and Silvio Pons, eds., *L'età dello stalinismo* (Rome: Riuniti, 1991), pp. 17–34.

of revolutionary history? Was Gorbachev rebelling against 1917 or against a different political and social order that was a consequence of 1917? Would his "revolution" therefore assure real change? These questions underscore the necessity today of understanding the historical place of Stalinism.

Revolution, as we all know, is one of the most complex as well as dramatic and controversial phenomena in history. Revolution is not an event but a process, not just a subjective act of revolutionaries, but an objective response of a society to conditions of profound historical transformation. As François Furet has recently observed about the French Revolution, the revolutionary experience is replete with ironies and surprises—"a very great event that took a bad turn."[2] Engels understood this hazard: nothing really happens according to the intentions of the people who thought they were leading the process at each stage, and even less according to their announced self-justifications.[3] For Hegel, this was the great irony of history: "The owl of Minerva only begins its flight as darkness falls."[4] We make history blindly, and understand the meaning of our actions only when it is too late to alter the consequences.

To speak of revolution as a process means simply that a series of events is causally interconnected: one thing leads to another, one phase leads to another, even if the successive stages and events are qualitatively different and unintended by the actors responsible for prompting them. I take the Brinton model of the revolutionary "fever"—proceeding from moderate beginnings to an extremist crisis and then through a "Thermidorean" phase of recovery back to normalcy—as a point of departure.[5] However, the Brinton scheme is too simple in and of itself to describe adequately most of the great revolutions of history and their place in the evolution of their respective societies.

The most serious weakness of the Brinton model is that it stops too soon. The revolutionary process does not end with the Thermidorean Reaction. Instead, this phase is characteristically accompanied or followed by the development of a new, aggressive authority, under a variety of ideological labels, that synthesizes elements of the revolution and the Old Regime. This new phase has been recognized by a host of writers, from Trotsky on, as "Bonapartism." I prefer a term less bound to a particular figure or country, and hence I call this phase "postrevolutionary dictatorship." Its obvious manifestation in the history of the USSR is the era of Stalinism.

*   *   *

The essence of the postrevolutionary dictatorship is the restoration of authority and routine, usually more systematic, despotic, and "modern" than the Old Regime, after the chaos and fanaticism of the earlier revolutionary phases. In Weberian terms it is the "routinization of charisma," responding to modern economic needs and inevitably leading to "bureaucratization."[6] In the twentieth century, postrevolutionary dictatorship has taken the institutional form of totalitarianism. Indeed, totalitarianism is nothing more nor less than postrevolutionary dictatorship with modern means of surveillance and coercion. The "totalitarian model" does not have to be rejected completely; instead, it needs to be understood as a historical conception limited to the postrevolutionary context. In this restricted sense the totalitarian model is not only useful but illuminating.

Like any other generalized phenomenon in history, the postrevolutionary dictatorship manifests wide variations of detail in different times and different places. It may announce itself under the banner of the revolution and the Left, or under the banner of counterrevolution and the Right. In either case ideology masks the actual integrating function of the postrevolutionary regime as it combines both revolutionary and prerevolutionary symbols, forms of authority, and dominant social elements in the totalitarian socio-political structure. Those who prefer the Hegelian language will see here the "synthesis" of the Old Regime "thesis" and the revolutionary "antithesis," but it is a synthesis coming much quicker and much more to the disadvantage of revolutionary values than the theorists of Marxism anticipated.

The postrevolutionary dictatorship is most often created by a successor or enemy of the original revolutionary leader, though it may be installed by the original leader himself, as it was by Oliver Cromwell in the English Puritan Revolution. Its actual social basis, like that of the earlier stages of a revolution, depends on a country's overall stage of development. It may vary in the particular balance of revolutionary and counterrevolutionary elements combined in its institutional and policy synthesis, but it is always aggressive, towards external or internal foes or both, and it is always nationalistic and chauvinistic (within whatever limits may be imposed by the international correlation of forces).

Postrevolutionary dictatorship takes hold at a characteristic point in the revolutionary process, when utopian enthusiasm has spent its force in terror or civil strife or war, leaving society exhausted and cynical, and when the popular longing for a return to order and authority outweighs attachment to the announced values of the revolution. These characteristic circumstances of the Thermidorean phase create the opportunity for an individual strong man, controlling whatever is the most effective organization of power bequeathed by the revolution, to make himself a personal dictator. For Cromwell and Bonaparte, it was the revolutionary army. For Stalin, it was the apparatus of the revolutionary party. In any case, the power base of the dictatorship, set against the disruption of old loyalties and values, traditional and revolutionary alike, gives the postrevolutionary dictatorship extraordinary scope for personal leadership and influence. Thus the exact character of any postrevolutionary dictatorship becomes unique and indeterminate.

*   *   *

If each instance of the postrevolutionary dictatorship is unique, what was distinctive to the Russian case and to Stalin's personal role? The most unusual feature in its time, though it has been replicated in subsequent Communist revolutions, was the organizational and ideological continuity that Stalin maintained between the revolutionary era and his own regime. He himself came out of the apparatus of the party of revolutionary extremism, and made this apparatus the foundation of his postrevolutionary rule. At the same time Stalin insisted on the formal observance of the revolutionary ideology, now designated "Marxism-Leninism," which played a key role for him in legitimizing his rule internally and propagandizing it externally. It was possible for him to use the doctrine for these purposes because he commanded the power to reinterpret its meaning as he chose, to make it serve the radically changed social structure over which he presided. In other words, Stalin turned Marxism into a system of ideological "false consciousness" in the original Marxian sense of the term.[7]

Distinctive in Stalin's postrevolutionary dictatorship, though not altogether unique, were its bureaucratic social base and its cultural conservatism. In any revolution, the social class or segment that emerges from the revolutionary process as the dominant or hegemonic element is not the same as the elements who contributed the most fire to the extremist stage. In the Russian Revolution, workers and peasants were instrumental in bringing the extremist party to power, and saw many of their sons rise to high rank under the new regime, but they never exercised class power as such. Instead, the successor to the dispossessed landlords and bourgeoisie as the nation's dominant social force was the new party bureaucracy—in other words, what is now commonly known as the "New Class." It was the New Class, expanded and elaborated, that became the basis, the instrument, and the beneficiary of the postrevolutionary dictatorship. Its position was reflected in Stalin's repudiation of the goal of egalitarianism and in his enumeration of the three "strata"—workers, collective farmers, and the "toiling intelligentsia" within the nominally "classless" society of socialism.[8]

Along with the social dominance of the New Class, Stalin's postrevolutionary dictatorship was distinguished by a cumulative trend toward conservatism in its cultural and social policies.[9] Revolutionary experiment in everything from education and labor relations to criminology and family law was rejected, and replaced (in the name of Marxism) by highly traditionalist policy norms attempting to put the burden on individual discipline and responsibility in addressing every kind of social and economic problem. The much-touted "New Soviet Man" was but the image of an artificially imposed Protestant Ethic restated in Marxist language. In cultural life the advent of absolute party authority was accompanied or followed by corresponding reversions from revolutionary to traditionalist norms—though still in Marxist language—with the suppression of modernism in all the arts as "degenerate bourgeois formalism," and even the rejection of modern discoveries in such scientific fields as physics and biology. Most distinctive of all in Stalin's return to conservative models was his embrace of nationalism, above all Russian nationalism. (This was ironic for Stalin the Georgian; it underscored "the Great-Russian chauvinism of the Russified non-Russian," as Lenin once termed it.) This shift entailed the repudiation of the anti-nationalist Marxist history written prior to the 1930s; the compromise with the Russian Orthodox Church effected during the Second World War; and the freeing of foreign policy from ideological constraints that became so evident in the mid and late 1930s.

Like any postrevolutionary dictator, Stalin placed the imprint of his own style and personality on the policies of the state. As best one can judge in retrospect, he was guided by no higher vision than his own personal glory and his vindictiveness toward past rivals and suspected enemies. I leave it to the psychohistorians to fathom the roots of his conduct in the recesses of his psyche. What does strike the conventional historian was Stalin's pursuit of immediate, short-term political success, in both internal and international matters, and his skill and shrewdness in maneuvering to achieve one limited goal after another. Contrary to the image Trotsky has composed, Stalin was not ignorant in matters of ideology; he was quite adroit in the manipulation of ideological arguments and precedents to embarrass his opponents and justify his own positions, as he first demonstrated during the socialism in one country controversy of the mid-1920s. In the pattern of his policy choices, his personal predilections of cultural conservatism and Russophilia come through distinctly, along with his unusual passion for doctrinal legitimacy, a deep resentment or contempt for genuine intellectual commitment, and an elemental anti-Semitism.

Was Stalin insane? If so, as Soviet critics from Khrushchev to the present have hinted, his was far from the only instance in history of a megalomanic despot. This is a type of personality that the postrevolutionary situation invites to take power. Mad or not, Stalin was clearly unrestrained by normal ethical standards, though the Bolshevik tradition had already reasoned such considerations out of the way as an impediment to the class struggle. As one expedient and amoral action led to another, he wove a web of criminality and mendacity of an extent without precedent in modern times. By all accounts, he developed a paranoid suspiciousness about potential plots and enemies on every hand, although it is in the nature of any despotism to generate opposition that can only take the form of conspiracy. If Stalin's fear was unfounded, it is the lack of effective opposition to his capricious rule that is the surprising thing, not the fear. The autocrat's suspicion of enemies in his realm becomes a self-fulfilling prophecy.

Stalin's historic role was a great one, even greater than the glories that his sycophants attributed to him. As a devotee of short-run maneuver and problem-solving, dressed up at each point in ideological legitimacy, he managed a regime that was maximally responsive to the deeper forces in Soviet society. In this manner he reflected Russia's postrevolutionary need for stability and authority; the challenge of modernization and military self-sufficiency; the universal trend toward the bureaucratic organization of modern political and economic life; and the resources of the Russian tradition of "orthodoxy, autocracy, nationality" as a form of reconciling all these needs. These challenges and Stalin's responses to them were all essential constituents of the postrevolutionary synthesis in Russia.

But this synthesis was accomplished in a form uniquely governed by Stalin's personal actions and decisions. One especially oppressive feature was his attachment to the letter of Marxist-Leninist orthodoxy and his imposition of pervasive and stultifying controls in intellectual life in order to sustain his own ideological authority. This was but one facet of his mania for total control, building on but far exceeding the tsarist tradition of autocratic centralism, and contributing to the most extreme form of totalitarianism to emerge anywhere in the contemporary world. Finally, Stalin personally inspired an atmosphere of terror and violence that caused his country untold damage and suffering.

It is a distraction from some of the worst aspects of Stalinism to suggest that any other Communist leader—Trotsky, for example, as Soviet historians sometimes suggest nowadays—would necessarily have behaved the same way. While it is impossible to draw any firm conclusions from a "what if" exercise in history, the difference between Trotsky and Stalin as personalities and as policy makers was clear enough to assure that a Trotsky dictatorship would have been very different from Stalin's. To argue that someone else would necessarily have taken the same path Stalin did, is to say that Stalin's personality, his lust for power and legitimacy, his pathological criminality, did not make any difference. This is the opposite extreme from the Khrushchev fallacy of blaming the evils associated with the Stalin era solely on the leader's personality. In the case of postrevolutionary Russia we cannot underestimate the role of the individual in history, any more than we can hold a utopian doctrine, an impersonal system, or an abstract law of history exclusively responsible.

*   *   *

Stalin's postrevolutionary dictatorship did not take final form all at once. Like its counterparts in other revolutions it unfolded by stages, as the leader responded to the challenges confronting him and then to the new problems created by his own responses. Under cover of doctrinal continuity, Stalin adjusted to the social and economic realities of a country coming out of revolution that in other instances were addressed by more avowedly counterrevolutionary regimes or monarchical restorations.

The personal impact of Stalin is often described as a "revolution from above," when the all-powerful leader imposed violent and disruptive change upon the country he commanded.[10] The Russian precedents usually cited are Peter the Great, ordering the nation into the Western cultural orbit in order to restore its military competitiveness, or Ivan the Terrible, crushing the independence of the nobility in order to give the nation the strength of an absolute autocracy. Recognizing the parallels with himself, Stalin had his official historians restore both of these tsar-revolutionaries to the pantheon of national heroes.

Strictly speaking, a "revolution from above" is a misnomer, if "revolution" means the violent overthrow of a political system. However, we can accept "revolution from above" in the metaphorical sense as a radical and coercive change of policy imposed by the governmental leadership. Stalin's early years in full authority, the era of the First Five-Year Plan from 1929 to 1932, were clearly a time of revolution from above in this sense.[11] This was the form of his postrevolutionary dictatorship in its first phase.

The features of Stalin's revolution from above—the "Stalin Revolution," as I have termed it—are familiar.[12] It instituted total socialization and even militarization of the economy through collectivization of the peasants, the elimination of the private commercial enterprise of the Nepmen, the institution of comprehensive central planning in lieu of the market socialism of the NEP, and the subordination of the rights of industrial labor and the trade unions to the needs of the state for greater production and surplus value. In turn, the new economic institutions required more bureaucratic control and a hierarchical distribution of power from the leader down through the party apparatus. At the same time, control from above was extended to all other organized social institutions and activities, including cultural and intellectual life. This is why we can accurately say that the Soviet system became totalitarian in the early 1930s.

A number of writers consider these years a period of "cultural revolution," sometimes with the upheaval of the 1960s in China in mind.[13] It is true that Stalin was able to tap a certain residue of ideological fervor and class struggle feeling among younger intellectuals and workers, and perhaps poor peasants, and to mobilize this sentiment in campaigns against kulaks, saboteurs, and bourgeois culture in general.[14] But in Stalin's case cultural revolution was not the work of a new social force from below that the leader merely unleashed as Mao Tse-tung did. Rather, it was a matter of manipulating the social antagonisms of the Thermidorean stage to reinforce the totalitarian aims of the dictatorship. Culture became in the eyes of the leadership an instrument of propaganda and control.

The underlying national need addressed by all these steps was, of course, modernization. To be sure, Stalin's effort did not begin with an entirely undeveloped society, but rather from the mid-point at which industrial progress under tsarism had been stopped short by World War I and the revolution. This is not to say that Stalin's methods of modernization were the most effective or that they were rationally arrived at. There is much evidence that he made his key decisions of 1928 initiating the Stalin Revolution without any broad conception of a new era of policy, but only as a series of short-run political maneuvers to secure victory over the Bukharin faction of party moderates. Ironically, the foreign threats of fascistic imperialism commonly cited even today in justification of Stalin's totalitarian path of accelerated modernization did not materialize until the program had already been underway for two or three years. Furthermore, there is serious question whether Stalin's methods put the country in the best position to resist outside aggression when it finally came in 1941.[15]

Struggle, it seems, is in the nature of the postrevolutionary dictatorship. If it is not strong enough to engage in revolutionary imperialism against the outside world, as Bonaparte and Hitler did, then it turns against its own people or vulnerable minorities among them, as Cromwell did. Stalin declared war on the peasantry, forcing them, under cover of socialist slogans and the class struggle against all those defined as "kulaks," back into a form of serfdom. Bukharin, vainly resisting this course, called it "military-feudal exploitation of the peasantry."[16] Nevertheless, collectivization had a rational, if inhumane, goal, namely to exploit agriculture in order to finance rapid industrial construction. It was Stalin's methods, making struggle an end in itself, and annihilating suspected enemies by the millions, that were irrational and ultimately counterproductive. Recent reconstructions of the economic record show that the violent way in which collectivization was actually carried out weakened Soviet agriculture so severely that the rural sector became a net consumer of resources, not a source for profitable exploitation.[17]

The second phase of Stalin's postrevolutionary dictatorship is not widely recognized as a period distinct from the first. Beginning in 1931, and moving more clearly by the end of the First Five-Year Plan the following year, Stalin took advantage of his now unlimited power in matters of policy and doctrine to order the sweeping changes in social, cultural, and intellectual policies that I have already noted. As these shifts accumulated between 1932 and 1936, they evidenced a consistent pattern: the rejection of ultra-radical experiments in social thought and cultural life, and the substitution of traditionalist values and norms in one area after another. The entire operation was camouflaged, however, by preserving the vocabulary of Marxist-Leninist orthodoxy and designating the new, conservative line "Marxist" while old ideas advanced in the name of Marxism were denounced as bourgeois and counterrevolutionary. In sum, following the Revolution from Above of 1929–1931, the period 1932 to 1936 was a time of Counterrevolution from Above.

There were pragmatic reasons for much of Stalin's shift in the conservative direction, and these again reflected the underlying needs and possibilities of a postrevolutionary society still facing the challenge of modernization. With the slogan, "Cadres decide everything," he recognized the necessity of bureaucratic organization and elite authority in modern industrial life, as well as the convergence of this need with the Russian tradition of bureaucratic centralism. Accepting these realities, Stalin proceeded accordingly on both the practical and theoretical planes. He boldly confronted the ideological heritage of egalitarianism when he asserted in 1934, "Equalization . . . , levelling the requirements and the individual lives of the members of society . . . has nothing in common with Marxism, with Leninism."[18] It was sufficient for his sense of doctrinal rectitude that he could proclaim the abolition of classes while extending as permanent policy the wide differentiation in wage and salary levels that had first been reluctantly accepted during the NEP to reward responsibility and encourage productivity. Educational policy abruptly felt the new winds in 1931–1932, when radical libertarian experimentation was condemned and replaced by a combination of revived academic traditionalism for the elite and practical literacy and vocational training for the masses. The party "maximum" on money incomes was abandoned, and proletarian preference in education and party life gave way to de facto preference to the children of the elite. All of these steps reflected Stalin's postrevolutionary accommodation to the social reality of the New Class, to the emergent *egemonia* of the bureaucratic stratum, if one may use that expression.

Along with his adjustment to the requirements of a stratified industrial society, Stalin swept away practically everything that had been attempted in the name of the revolution for the past fifteen years in the realm of social experiment and cultural innovation. The guiding spirit in the social thought of the pre-Stalin era was "withering-away"—the withering-away of any and all coercive social institutions in a spirit of Rousseauian utopianism. Not only was the state supposed to wither away, but along with it law, and the school, and in the minds of some, the family. Now all of these institutions were rehabilitated as pillars of socialist society. The traditional leftist approach to individual deviance and failure as the consequences of adverse social conditions and class deprivation was rejected in favor of the philosophy and practice of individual responsibility and coercive discipline. The nation was restored both as a historical category and as a focus of loyalty. All these steps embodied the essence of conservative social control as it would have been advocated by Edmund Burke, for example, horrified though he would have been at the despotic Russian manner of restoring such control.

At the same time, artistic experimentation in the modernist vein, in which Russia had been an international leader both before and after the revolution, was swept aside and replaced by the most conventional norms—a sort of Soviet Victorianism, one might say. Exactly what connection this reversal in cultural standards had with the emergence of the New Class, to what extent it reflected the personal tastes of Stalin, his entourage, or the sons of workers and peasants newly arrived in the bureaucracy, is difficult to say. Some writers have employed literary sources to argue the point,[19] and Roy Medvedev has suggested a petty-bourgeois theme in the tastes of the new elite and their allegiance to Stalin.[20]

The international environment was not a decisive factor in the first phase of Stalin's postrevolutionary dictatorship. In the so-called "Third Period" of the Comintern, Stalin had to go out of his way to generate a sense of political polarization between Communists and everyone else, for the short-run purpose of undermining the influence of his rivals in the Bukharin camp. In practical matters, Soviet trade with the capitalist world actually increased during the First Five-Year Plan, at the same time that Stalin was pounding the nationalist drum about catching up or being beaten as had so often happened to Russia in the past. In the second phase of Stalinism the international threat was clearly more serious, as the menace of Japanese and then German expansionism became a reality. This new circumstance obviously contributed to Stalin's ideological *volte-face* in regard to Russian nationalism as a source of popular loyalty, and to his shift from revolutionary rhetoric to conventional alliance diplomacy between 1933 and 1935 (diplomatic relations with the United States, membership in the League of Nations, the doctrine of Collective Security, and the Popular Front line for the Comintern).

* * *

In the comparative perspective of revolution, Stalin's conservative shift in his Counterrevolution from Above is not in the least surprising. The essence of postrevolutionary dictatorship is to synthesize the new and the old, the revolutionary and the traditional, selecting from each source in the immediate interest of political expediency but in a manner cumulatively reflecting the requirements of a society that has been overstretched and torn by the revolutionary experience. Again, it needs to be reiterated that the most unusual thing about Stalin's fulfillment of this role was his success in covering the vast transformation in the nature and policies of his regime with the language of revolutionary orthodoxy.

In some historic instances of revolution the process of postrevolutionary consolidation went so far as to take the form of monarchical restoration, when military defeat (Bonaparte) or the death of the leader (Cromwell) opened up the opportunity for avowed counterrevolutionaries to take control of the state. They could not undo the revolution's most basic changes in institutions, social values, and the mix of class elements enjoying *egemonia* in society. They did effect great changes in leading personnel and in the literal symbols of authority and belief, carrying the trends of the postrevolutionary synthesis even further and more openly in the conservative direction.

Of course, Russia experienced no overt monarchical restoration, though one can imagine something akin to it had Hitler waged political warfare more intelligently in 1941 and accomplished the outright overthrow of Stalin's regime. Yet in terms of changes in personnel and symbols, Stalin went almost as far as any monarchists might have. I would suggest that the third period of his postrevolutionary dictatorship, the years of the Great Purge and immediately thereafter, saw what may be regarded as the functional equivalent of a monarchical restoration. In personnel, the purges decimated the cadres of Old Bolsheviks. Literally anyone of stature over the age of 35, in the party, the government, or the military—in other words, anyone old enough to remember the revolution, save the members of the Politburo and a few ideological acolytes—was liquidated or sent to a longer drawn-out death in the camps. Significantly, similar fates befell most refugee foreign Communists who had sought asylum in the USSR from fascist dictators at home. One might suppose that the purges, so deadly for the leading members of the New Class, had put an end to that form of social structure, but the reality is the contrary. The New Class was simply restaffed—to be sure, with sons of peasants who gave it a less intellectual and more nativist cast than before—but its bureaucratic mentality and its pursuit of rank and privilege became even more pronounced. A compulsive sense of status reminiscent of unreformed tsarism set in within the party's own leadership, evidenced in the unwritten but consistent rules by which membership in the Politburo and the Central Committee was awarded on the basis of bureaucratic rank and function from Stalin's time to Gorbachev's.[21]

Simultaneously with the purges, Stalin became the object of official adulation and glorification as the omniscient and omnicompetent ruler, beyond anything seen in the history of Russian monarchy or that of most other countries. Rank and hierarchy were restored in the most visible ways, from military titles and diplomatic uniforms to official limousines and Kremlin Hospital privileges. The State Labor Reserves and the forced labor of the Gulag amounted to a restoration of serfdom in the industrial sector as well as the agricultural. Thus Russia returned to the methods used by Peter the Great to lay the foundation for what he intended to be a modern state. The national minorities, prime victims of the collectivization era and the purges, had to yield, as they did for centuries before the revolution, to the primacy of the Great Russians and the russification of their own histories and cultures. Implicit and later overt anti-Semitism became a hallmark of the new regime as it had been of the Old.

Other symbolic steps toward national tradition came during or immediately after World War II, the "Great Patriotic War of the Soviet Union." The Comintern was abolished and with it the serious underwriting of foreign revolution for its own sake; the "Internationale" was supplanted as the national anthem by the "Hymn of the Soviet Union"; and compromise was reached with the Orthodox Church, though not a full embrace, since Stalin had his own orthodoxy in the form of Marxism-Leninism as a state religion. Tellingly, the revolutionary title of "People's Commissar" yielded to the reactionary "Minister."

Soviet international behavior followed Stalin's restorationist course *pari passu*. His diplomacy became even more opportunistic and cynical, climaxing in the pact with Hitler in 1939 (in justification of which Molotov first enunciated the doctrine of the "coexistence of states with different social systems").[22] In the war years Stalin became nakedly imperialist and Pan-Slavist in his foreign ambitions, as manifested both by his territorial annexations during the period of the Non-Aggression Pact and by his determination to dominate Eastern Europe (and Iran and Manchuria) at the end of the war. Celebrating the surrender of Japan, Stalin hailed the rectification of Russia's territorial losses of

1905[23]—in a war in which he himself, as a good Bolshevik at the time, had advocated the defeat of the Tsarist government. All that was unusual, if Stalin were compared with his imperial forebears, was the use of an international revolutionary doctrine and an international movement loyal to Moscow because of that doctrine as instruments to protect or advance the interests of the Russian Empire.

* * *

The process of revolution, as history shows, does not end with the postrevolutionary dictatorship or counterrevolution or even with a restored monarchy. There remains one more distinctive step, when the nation throws off the burden of postrevolutionary conservatism and finally comes to terms in a non-fanatic way with its original revolutionary inspiration. Thus, in England, the Puritan Revolution, Cromwell's dictatorship, and the Stuart Restoration were followed by the Glorious Revolution of 1688, when the parliamentary supremacy of the early revolutionary years was restored. In France, after the Great Revolution, Bonaparte, and the restored Bourbons, came the July Revolution of 1830, returning the country to the constitutional monarchy and bourgeois dominance of 1789–1791. In Germany the November Revolution of 1918 was followed by the Nazi dictatorship, which yielded in the ashes of defeat to the resurrection of Weimar in the form of the Bonn federal republic. In Spain the struggle of revolution and counterrevolution from 1931 to 1939 and the long Franco era ended with the death of the dictator and the revival of the constitutionalism of the early 1930s. There appears to be a universal phenomenon in all these cases. I term it the "moderate revolutionary revival," representing the final achievement of national stability around the principles and practices of the first, moderate phase of the revolutionary process, but without the passions and polarization that almost always destabilize moderate politics at that point and open the way to violent dictatorship either of the Left or of the Right.

In this perspective, it is clear that Gorbachev represented just such a final turn in the sequence of events set in motion by the Russian Revolution. He totally repudiated the postrevolutionary regime of Stalinism, in its economic policies and structures, its enforced ideological orthodoxy, its Great Russian centralism, and its militaristic approach to national security. Furthermore, he called into question bit by bit the political power structure bequeathed by Lenin. While it still has some distance to traverse to qualify as a real democracy, the USSR no longer suffers under the totalitarianism that distinguishes the modern postrevolutionary dictatorship.

To describe the Gorbachev era as a moderate revolutionary revival, seventy years after the original event, raises a question about the connectedness of these episodes. In the other instances I have cited, the process took only thirty to fifty years to run its course. However, the Russian case would not appear exceptional if one considered the Khrushchev era of reform, forty years after the revolution, as an early, abortive attempt at introducing the moderate revolutionary revival. Then the "era of stagnation" between Khrushchev and Gorbachev becomes comprehensible as an artificial prolongation of the postrevolutionary dictatorship after it had served its purpose of social consolidation, with all the consequences of frustration and demoralization in Soviet society that ensued.

Particular generational circumstances explain the failure of reform in 1956–1964 and its rapid success after 1985. In Khrushchev's time, effective power still lay in that same generation of New Class functionaries promoted by Stalin in the course of the purges; by the time of Gorbachev, they were dead or dying. Khrushchev never attacked the postrevolutionary dictatorship either in its institutional fundamentals or in its maintenance of doctrine; he seems to have been that *rara avis*, a true believer. He clearly did reject the third phase of Stalinism, above all the purges and the personal cult, and he did moderate Stalin's second postrevolutionary phase by taking steps toward a more egalitarian ideal, for example in his educational ideas (an immediate failure) and in his labor and wage policy (to the ultimate detriment of the Soviet economy). Evidently Khrushchev took seriously a foreseeable transition to pure communism, even though the actual authors of his Party Program did not.[24] Gorbachev, by contrast, challenged every phase of Stalinism, a stance symbolized by his rehabilitation of Bukharin. He even rejected the most fanatical period of early revolutionary extremism, though he continued to justify his revisionism by evoking the spirit of an appropriately sanitized Lenin.

Neither Khrushchev nor Gorbachev altered the reality of New Class *egemonia*. What finally began with Gorbachev's moderate revolutionary revival is a distinctive shift of influence among the elements of the dominant stratum, with the partial eclipse of the party bureaucracy and the sons of peasants, and the liberation of the creative intelligentsia.

The concept of the postrevolutionary dictatorship helps answer the question whether the Soviet Union can once again be turned back from reform as it was at the end of the Khrushchev era. It highlights the fundamental historical dynamics that have underlain the Gorbachev era and have made a serious and enduring reaction hard to conceive of. Where postrevolutionary dictatorship responded to national needs for stability and authority as the context for development, the moderate revolutionary revival is a response to a mature society that demands the liberation of its creative forces. Nothing shows this better than the elections to Gorbachev's Congress of People's Deputies. Khrushchev's attempt at reform was ill-conceived and perhaps, for Russia, premature; Gorbachev's has been long overdue, and a conservative reaction against it is bound to be an intolerable anachronism.

None of this argument is intended to suggest that the time of the moderate revolutionary revival is placid and stable. As the other historical instances show, it is a moment of crisis and of struggle over the nation's future. The Left, who want more revolution, and the Right, who want less, will both challenge the choice. But if historical precedents are upheld by the progress of reform in the Soviet Union, Stalinism and the postrevolutionary dictatorship are destined soon to become a closed chapter in history.

Notes

1. M. S. Gorbachev, Speech at a conference of the Khabarovsk Territory Party Organization, *Pravda*, 2 August 1986.

2. Quoted in *The New York Times*, 13 March 1989.

3. Engels to Vera Zasulich, 23 April 1885, Karl Marx and Friedrich Engels, *Selected Correspondence, 1846–1895* (New York: International Publishers, 1942), pp. 437–438. See above, pp. 12–13.

4. G.W.F. Hegel, *Sämtliche Werke*, b. 7, *Grundlinien der Philosophie des Rechts* (4th ed., Stuttgart: Friedrich Frommann Verlag, 1964), preface, p. 37.

5. Crane Brinton, *The Anatomy of Revolution* (rev. ed., New York: Prentice-Hall, 1952). See above, p. 28.

6. Quoted in H. H. Gerth and C. Wright Mills, eds., *From Max Weber: Essays in Sociology* (New York: Oxford University Press, 1958), editors' introduction, p. 54.

7. See below, ch. 11.

8. See, e.g., Stalin, "On the Draft Constitution of the USSR" (speech delivered at the Extraordinary Eighth Congress of Soviets of the USSR, 25 November 1936), in Joseph Stalin, *Problems of Leninism* (Moscow: Foreign Languages Publishing House, 1953), pp. 683–686.

9. On Stalin's conservative shift, see below, ch. 10.

10. See, for example, Robert C. Tucker, "Stalinism as a Revolution from Above," in Robert C. Tucker, ed., *Stalinism: Essays in Historical Interpretation* (New York: Norton, 1977).

11. The First Five-Year Plan was officially adopted by the Congress of Soviets in May 1929, but back-dated to October 1928 to include the annual plan for 1928-29 already in effect under the so-called "control figures." When Stalin declared the Five-Year Plan fulfilled in four years at the end of 1932, it had officially been in effect for only three years and eight months—an example of the ascendancy of irrational propaganda purposes over rational economic calculations.

12. Robert V. Daniels, ed., *The Stalin Revolution: Foundations of the Totalitarian Era* (3rd edition, Lexington, Mass.: D. C. Heath, 1989).

13. See Sheila Fitzpatrick, ed., *Cultural Revolution in Russia, 1928–1931* (Bloomington: Indiana University Press, 1978), esp. editor's introduction, p. 1.

14. See Lynne Viola, *The Best Sons of the Fatherland: Workers in the Vanguard of Soviet Collectivization* (New York: Oxford University Press, 1987).

15. See, e.g., Stephen F. Cohen, *Bukharin and the Bolshevik Revolution: A Political Biography, 1888–1938* (New York: Knopf, 1973), pp. 316, 361.

16. Quoted in "Vnutri pravo-tsentristskogo bloka" (Inside the Right-Centrist Bloc), *Biulleten' Oppozitsii*, July 1929, p. 17.

17. See James R. Millar, "Mass Collectivization and the Contribution of Agriculture to the First Five-Year Plan," *Slavic Review*, XXXIII:4 (December 1974); Holland Hunter, "Soviet Agriculture with and without Collectivization," *Slavic Review*, XLVII:2 (Summer 1988).

18. Stalin, Report on the Work of the Central Committee, to the Seventeenth Congress of the CPSU (B), *Problems of Leninism*, p. 635.

19. See, e.g., Vera Dunham, *In Stalin's Time: Middle-Class Values in Soviet Fiction* (Cambridge, Eng.: Cambridge University Press, 1976).

20. Roy A. Medvedev, *Let History Judge: The Origins and Consequences of Stalinism* (New York: Knopf, 1971), pp. 412–413.

21. On the rules of status in the Communist Party, see above, ch. 6.

22. V. M. Molotov, Report to the Supreme Soviet of the USSR, "O ratifikatsii sovetsko-germanskogo dogovora o nenapadenii," *Pravda*, 1 September 1939.

23. Stalin, "Obrashchenie k narodu" (Address to the People), *Pravda*, 3 September 1945, in Robert H. McNeal, ed., *I. V. Stalin: Sochineniya 1934–1953* (Stanford, Cal.: Hoover Institution, 1967), vol. 2, pp. 212–215.

24. Interview of Dr. A. P. Butenko by the author, 10 April 1984.

10

Soviet Thought in the 1930s: The Cultural Counterrevolution

The Russian enigma is largely a product of the preconceptions into which the outside world has customarily forced the observed facts of Soviet life. Not the least serious among such a priori distortions is the assumption that the affairs of the Soviet government have been guided by a fixed system of ideology. Both the fixity and the guidance are in fact highly questionable. Change of a most fundamental and often unwilled sort distinguishes the history of the Soviet regime, and nowhere is it as clear as in the field of ideological pronouncements and intellectual work—in the realm of thought, if the offhand comments of Soviet leaders and the frenzied exegesis by Agitprop's functionaries can be dignified by the term.

Changes in the various fields of mental activity in Soviet Russia have all been noted abroad, but usually such awareness has been confined to specialists' understanding of particular subjects.[1] A broader view of the evolution in Soviet thought shows striking correspondences between the developments in different fields. This pattern in turn suggests an explanation of how and why these changes came about and what they reveal about the emergent nature of Soviet society.

The Context—Ideology and Politics

During the first two decades after the revolution, Soviet ideology and Soviet policy bearing on a wide range of social institutions and intellectual activities changed profoundly, although the original Marxist terminology was largely retained and the regime continued to describe itself as the true executor of the Marxian scheme. Under Stalin, Soviet society became

This chapter, based on work done at the Russian Research Center, appeared in *Indiana Slavic Studies*, vol. 1 (1956), pp. 97–135.

a stable, even rigid, though internally very tense structure, organized in an all-embracing bureaucratic order. In substance, the original revolutionary goal of a free, equalitarian, noncoercive "communist" society was completely abandoned; for all practical purposes the regime was interested only in maintaining its stability and authority and in building national power. The social policies dictated by this interest were the diametric opposite of the ideals which inspired the revolution: the Stalinist regime undertook to produce the disciplined, compulsive, authoritarian personalities which make the best cogs in a vast military-industrial machine.[2] In the effort to justify the new stabilized order and the social policies that it entailed, and to explain away older expectations about the revolution, a truly sweeping revision of ideology was carried out.

Compelling circumstances pressed for such changes. Russia's isolation and backwardness deprived the revolution of the material basis for the socialist society as it had been envisaged by Marxists. A different sort of order was called for by the problems Russia faced, and "socialism in one country" provided the ideological smoke screen for the transition. Driven by the relentless will of one man with an invincible political machine, a new system with new principles emerged in 1929–1930 to undertake a solution of the basic problems of economic backwardness and national weakness.

The history of Soviet society from that time on proceeded largely outside the compass of Marxian sociology. Rather than determining the basic form and development of society, economic forces became derivatives of the state, which became the prime mover of history; the role of leading personalities became decisive and society developed henceforth through command from above. Ideology was duly revised to adapt to these conditions. Old revolutionary leaders who had supported Stalin but perhaps lacked the cynical flexibility required by these maneuvers were liquidated. Nevertheless, the regime insisted that its new ideology was the only correct interpretation of Marxism and that all others constituted counterrevolutionary treachery.

The General Pattern of Ideological Change

The Situation Before 1929

Until 1929 intellectual life in Soviet Russia enjoyed a remarkable degree of freedom. Many prerevolutionary intellectual figures continued their work. The Party recognized limitations to its competence in areas outside of politics, although it encouraged Marxist thinkers. "I favor . . . a general leadership and the maximum of competition," declared

Bukharin when he was still the party's main theoretical voice.[3] Much contact was maintained with the outside world. Soviet arts and sciences were generally abreast of the rest of the world; modernistic developments similar to those abroad, amid a variety of schools of thought, animated the Russian scene. Party doctrine, dominant though not rigorous in the social sciences, was characterized by thorough-going Marxian economic and environmental determinism, and by mechanistic views of nature, history, and personality—ideas not greatly at variance with intellectual fashion abroad.

In social policy the Party continued to affirm the ideals of the revolution, even if they were toned down in practice. Social reform was limited by an acute awareness of Russian cultural backwardness and by the consolidation of the state and industrial administration on more or less conventionally bureaucratic lines. Particularly in industry, practical considerations militated against revolutionary ideals; workers' control of factories was condemned by 1921, and income inequality grew. Notable efforts continued to be made to sustain certain revolutionary ideals— progressive education, the equality of women, the anti-religious campaign, and the party "maximum," a ceiling on monetary income for party members.

The First Phase of the Change, 1929–1932

Stalin's dictatorship set the political context of the transformation in Soviet intellectual life. All opposition in the Party was crushed, and party doctrine was elevated to the level of an absolute, compulsory, and exclusive creed. On this basis Stalin undertook his revolution from above, with the aim of accomplishing (a) the incorporation of all aspects of society, particularly the peasantry and intellectual activities, under the direct control of the Party; (b) the intensive development of the industrial base of state power; (c) the introduction of measures in social policy which accorded with the effective functioning of this emerging totalitarian political order.

The common theme in the intellectual and social policies instituted in accordance with the new objectives of the regime was the establishment of discipline, controls, and the principle of party supremacy in all aspects of life. *Partiinost*—"party-ness" or party spirit—and service to the Party were imposed on intellectual activity as the supreme criteria of value and truth. A sweeping offensive was directed against non-party people and nonconforming party members, especially people imbued with the traditional Marxian deterministic and mechanistic outlook, who were now identified with the Bukharin opposition. Their works were suppressed; they lost their jobs; and frequently they were arrested as counterrevolutionaries. The Party typically directed this action through its strongmen, party members working in the various fields who put power ahead of intellectual integrity and who, invested with the authority of the Party, proceeded to suppress all dissenting thought. Such were M. N. Pokrovsky in history, A. B. Zalkind in psychology, and L. L. Averbakh in literature (and later on, T. D. Lysenko in biology). All this action was described as the pursuit of the class war "on the ideological front," "on the historical front," etc. In the name of class war, Soviet cultural life was thoroughly militarized.

The intellectual content of the orthodoxies imposed by the party was not entirely uniform. On the one hand there was the extreme, "vulgar" determinist Marxism, which prevailed in history under Pokrovsky. On the other there was the Marxism with voluntarist overtones (rooted in Lenin's prerevolutionary thought) which became the rule in the arts and psychology. In general, the period can be described as one in which extreme Marxism, however interpreted, was imposed in the arts and in the social sciences. (Natural science remained relatively free for the time being.) Immediate utility to the Party, in justifying its policies, discrediting its enemies, and propagandizing the masses, was the standard to which intellectual activity was made to conform.

The Second Phase of the Change, 1932–1937

After the system of party control and supremacy in intellectual activity was established, and as crises developed in each field, the control system was used to compel drastic changes in the substance of ideas and policies. The imposition of extreme Marxism had devastated one field after another. In literature and the arts, little or no worthwhile work was produced; in history, students failed to learn the chronology of events; psychology failed to make the most out of the available human material; no one was taking law schools seriously. As the regime became aware that the "proletarian" thought and policies which it was imposing were not the best for its purposes, the extreme Marxism of the First Five-Year Plan period was successively repudiated in various fields. The people who had espoused and imposed these views in the name of the Party were denounced as anti-Marxist wreckers and in many cases liquidated. Revolutionary intellectual fashions were then replaced by a surprisingly obvious and thorough traditionalism, which was declared to be the sole true application of Marxist principles. The controls put in place during the process of imposing extreme Marxism were retained, but were turned around to operate in the opposite direction. Traditionalism, under the label of "Socialist Realism," "Soviet humanism," "dialectical materialism" as opposed to "vulgar economic materialism," or whatnot, was imposed with all the compulsions at the Party's command. There was a great practical difference, however, compared with the 1929–1932 period: whereas extreme Marxism had broken down, traditionalism in intellectual life, under strict controls, satisfied the needs of the regime.

This transformation took place with surprising consistency in a wide variety of fields. It occurred in literature and in the arts between 1932 and 1934, with the liquidation of RAPP (the Russian Association of Proletarian Writers) and the analogous organizations in other artistic areas, and the instituting of the norm of "Socialist Realism." In history, it was accomplished with the restoration of the traditional kings-and-battles presentation and the rehabilitation of the Russian past, in 1934, and the posthumous repudiation of Pokrovsky as an anti-Marxist, in 1936. Law followed, with the downfall of Ye. B. Pashukanis and the repudiation of the theory of the withering away of law in 1936–1937. In psychology there was a gradual reaction from environmental conditioning toward emphasis on individual will and responsibility, culminating in 1936. Political theory awaited Stalin's pronunciamentos, the clearest of which came in 1939—the state would be the chief instrument for the building of "communist society" as well as for protection against the capitalist encirclement, and it would not wither away as long as these needs existed.

Parallel developments took place in social policy. Finding inadequate for its needs the stimulus of proletarian enthusiasm supplemented by outright force, the regime turned progressively to the building blocks of the traditional social order: glorification of the state and of legality; encouragement of status distinctions; income differentiation as an incentive; traditional authoritarian family and educational policy, to cultivate the self-driving yet compliant qualities needed by the new bureaucratic industrial order; the rehabilitation of patriotism as a potent source of loyalty to the state; even a *de facto* concord with religion, as the Orthodox Church in return for a measure of toleration undertook to encourage political loyalty to the state.

The pattern of change in social and cultural policy is striking in its regularity. It suggests the need for a new conception of the real nature, interests, and motivations of the Stalinist state—the kind of state for which the intellectual and social policies adopted in the thirties were most appropriate.

Completion of the second stage of the transition did not reduce the problem of controls over intellectual activity to the simple negative task of censorship. Much of the "deviation" which continued to occur seems to have been due to the lack of a clear definition of the Party's positive desires. What the Party really wanted was to eradicate the revolutionary tradition and replace it with a conservatism which would make the state and the economy easier to run and would appeal more to the evidently authoritarian proclivities of the Stalinist leadership. This goal could not, of course, be stated explicitly, because the stability of the regime and its support abroad depended on continuity with the revolutionary tradition. Perhaps the leadership itself was not prepared to recognize its real objectives in frank terms. Consequently, the Party felt compelled to continue professing its adherence to Marxism, while the objectionable features of Marxist thought were discarded and pronounced un-Marxist. This reversal of content under the old labels was highly confusing to Soviet intellectuals, steeped for years in all aspects of Marxism. They did not realize what was wanted; they could not be told this directly; and they were unlikely to come to an understanding of it on their own because the regime was to them axiomatically the pure embodiment of Marxism. Consequently, official condemnations of their work came as bolts from the blue, completely incomprehensible. Intellectuals could only try to learn by trial and error—perhaps one should say, error and trial—what work would be condemned and what would be approved.

Literature and the Arts

As in other intellectual fields, there was wide latitude for literary work in the 1920s. Although direct party control of literature was advocated by some extremist literary groups, the Party did not accord its official sanction to any one school. Lenin, Trotsky, and Bukharin all endorsed the position of the moderate Marxist critic Alexander Voronsky, "No literary current, school, or group must come forward in the name of the Party."[4]

In 1929 the Party's effort commenced to mobilize all intellectual activities for its own purposes. In literature this was accomplished simply by giving a free hand to the Averbakh group of extreme Marxists, who, organized in RAPP and armed with the authority of the Party, proceeded to impose on all writers rigid utilitarian standards of propagandistic proletarian writing. Both those who resisted in the name of artistic freedom, and the Marxist group led by V. F. Pereverzev who contended that only proletarians could write proletarian literature, were condemned. The attack on the Pereverzev people for "vulgar economic determinism"[5] illustrates the new voluntarist philosophy with its emphasis on subjective factors such as the enthusiasm of individuals. Political dedication could prevail over "objective conditions" such as class status.

The spirit of the campaign for *partiinost* and against any nonconformity or notion of art for art's sake was belligerently expressed by the playwright V. M. Kirshon at the Sixteenth Party Congress in 1930:

> We must pass over to a decisive offensive, mercilessly liquidating bourgeois ideology. . . . The class enemy on the literary front is becoming active. At a time of sharpened class struggle any liberalism, any respect for aesthetic language, even though it may be directed against us, is direct aid to the class enemy. . . . The whole purpose of our activity and our work lies in the fight for the building of socialism.[6]

Even the celebrated proletarian poet Vladimir Mayakovsky was attacked, and this shock apparently contributed to his suicide in April 1930.[7]

The intensity of politicizing literature under RAPP led to an early crisis. Literature was consequently the field where the second phase of intellectual change began, to compel the restoration of traditional content disguised as Marxism. Under RAPP, literature was simply no good. In 1932, the party leadership became aware of this situation, abolished RAPP, and made its leaders scapegoats for the disastrous policy carried out by them in the name of the Party. Both Averbakh and Kirshon, among others, became victims of the Great Purge. Thus were the extreme "proletarian" policies of 1929–1932 repudiated as anti-Marxist, while the infallibility of the Party was preserved.[8]

The new official line for literature, "Socialist Realism," was soon extended to the other arts. At first it had little definite meaning; only as various artists were criticized for failing to conform did the desires of the regime become clear. By 1936, roughly, Socialist Realism had acquired a practical definition that completely contradicted the revolutionary tradition in culture. One observer recognized this "paradoxical development" in spite of his political sympathy: "It is a fact that new revolutionary political ideas are faced with reactionary stylistic principles in art. The same government that is courageously piloting the ship of state through the uncharted seas of socialistic practice is enjoining its artists to stay behind in safe haven."[9]

The patterns of change in other fields of artistic work were much the same as in literature. All the arts went through the period of proletarian propaganda beginning in 1929. All then experienced a more or less abrupt change from revolutionary content to the traditionalism of Socialist Realism—the theater and film in 1932; music in 1932–1933; architecture around 1935. Even the ballet toed the party line with precision.[10]

Socialist Realism was characterized by impassioned nationalism (corresponding to the revival of nationalist propaganda and historiography), by reverence for the classics (corresponding to the rehabilitation of the Russian past), by an emotional rather than analytic approach, and by catering to the public taste. Any deviation was attacked as "formalism." "Socialist Realism," Gleb Struve has pointed out, was

a reaction against what was described, sweepingly and therefore mean-
inglessly, as "bourgeois Formalism." This phrase was used to include all
experiments with form and technique, and much of earlier Soviet literature
came under this description. . . . Those who were responsible for running
the most "advanced" state in the world suddenly turned conservative and
began to look askance at all revolutionary experiments in art, dubbing
them as "bourgeois Formalism."[11]

Under the terms of Socialist Realism and formalism, good and evil were
starkly counterposed, without any sense of a continuum of values or a
middle ground between them. This structuring of judgment was typical
of Soviet thought after the transformation of the 1930s. It fits the patterns
of thought ascribed by some psychologists to the so-called "authoritarian
personality,"[12] which clearly distinguished the Soviet regime under Stalin.

Such positive philosophy as Socialist Realism had was initially expressed by Maxim Gorky: an optimistic individualism idealizing the
"New Soviet Man."[13] A later formulation called for

monumental works wherein the man of our age, the man of the Stalin
type, the creator of the Plans, will be revealed in his full stature; works
in which will be shown how was forged the will-power of that man, how
his soul was formed and how his consciousness was strengthened, enriched,
and armed by the teaching of Marx, Engels, Lenin, and Stalin.[14]

The parallelism of the new conception of personality in literature,
psychology, and history was perfect.

Under the conditions of a totalitarian state this new individualism
was in practice largely of and for the leaders, who patently *did* "make
history." For the masses, it seems, Socialist Realism in the arts was
designed to reconcile people to the regime, to satisfy vicariously their
aspirations for power and control over their own fates, and to stimulate
eager participation in the projects undertaken by the regime. For the
arts no new development was possible, but since the style to which
they were constrained was an artistically meaningful one with much
vitality in its history, artistic production did manage to go on.

In the immediate postwar years, in literature as in other fields, the
Party took steps to restore controls and reassert the principle of party
supremacy. In content, the prewar traditionalism and nationalism of
Socialist Realism were only strengthened. Some attacks on writers, as
in the celebrated case of Mikhail Zoshchenko and Anna Akhmatova in
1946, recalled the atmosphere of 1929–1930. Again, the targets were
writings that lacked "party spirit," that violated the ideological insulation
of the Soviet peoples against Western or bourgeois influences, or that

expressed philosophical pessimism and threatened to undermine the compulsory optimism of Soviet "humanism."

History

The imposition of "party spirit" and the enforcement of Marxist orthodoxy occurred suddenly and violently in the writing and teaching of history. Pokrovsky, a professional historian but also a long-standing party member, head of the Communist Academy and the Institute of Red Professors and a member of the Central Control Commission of the Party, set up a virtual dictatorship in the field of history, terminating the fairly broad tolerance which had been accorded the activities of non-party historians during the NEP. Between 1929 and 1931 non-Marxist historical science was eradicated, and all important positions were filled with newly trained party men.[15]

The kind of historical thought that Pokrovsky imposed in the name of the Party was distinguished by absolute economic determinism, an acerbic anti-nationalist attitude toward the Russian past, and a highly abstract treatment of history in a rigid framework of class struggle and socioeconomic formations, where the individual was merely the agent of impersonal forces. Of the facts, particularly as worked up by bourgeois historians, Pokrovsky was frankly disdainful.

This attitude, as well as Pokrovsky's uncompromising hostility toward all dissenting trends of historical thought, stemmed from the doctrine of *partiinost* carried to an extreme. "History is present-day politics turned to the past," simply a weapon in the class struggle, Pokrovsky asserted. There was no such thing as objectivity, all science being merely class science, so the scientist could not fail to take sides.

In accordance with the principle of *partiinost*, Pokrovsky revised his own presentation of Russian history. Previously he had argued that Russia had not been behind Europe in development; thus he could show the October Revolution as a natural development, and refute Trotsky's theory of permanent revolution. After 1929, it became desirable to emphasize the backwardness in the Russian past, to contrast it with the progress being made under socialism, and to stress the importance of the subjective factors of mass will and enthusiasm.[16] Voluntarist Marxism superseded determinist Marxism.

After the purge of bourgeois historians was completed, *partiinost* was vigorously applied to the Marxist historians themselves. Waves of criticism and reorganization established and enforced party doctrine as the basic truth for historical science. Stalin himself set the tone for this campaign, denouncing as "rotten liberalism" any failure to accept party principles as "axioms."[17]

Shortly after the change of course in literature and the arts, it became evident that the regime in history which Povrovsky left at his death in 1932 was not compatible with the changing conceptions and new requirements of the party leadership. Corrective action was taken in 1934 by a decree of the Central Committee of the Party and the Council of People's Commissars:

> The teaching of history in schools of the USSR is unsatisfactory. The textbooks and oral instruction are of an abstract schematic character. Instead of the teaching of civic history in an animated and entertaining form with an exposition of the most important events and facts in their chronological sequence and with sketches of historical personages, the pupils are given abstract definitions of social and economic formations, which thus replace the consecutive exposition of history by abstract sociological schemes.[18]

This statement of common sense betrays complete indifference to the Marxian conception of history and Marxian notions of what is important in history. The party leaders simply perceived that the teaching of history was deficient in certain practical results, and they decreed direct action to correct the deficiency. Reference to Marxist doctrine served only to put the old labels on the new line. This device typified the changed relation between ideology and policy under Stalin: ideology ceased to pose the goals for policy, and served only as a means for rationalization after the fact.

The new (i.e., conventional) history called for in 1934 dovetailed with the regime's decision to utilize the force of nationalism and to rehabilitate the Russian past. The cultivation of national pride, in turn, required increased efforts to discredit Pokrovsky's anti-nationalist influence. Marxism continued of course to be verbally adhered to; the Party called for new history texts which would embody its criticisms and hence provide "correct analysis and correct explanation of historical events leading to the Marxist conception of history."[19] However, the concrete wishes of the Party were insufficiently clear, and no satisfactory texts were produced.

In January 1936, in a sweeping decision of the Central Committee and the Council of People's Commissars, the leadership reviewed the difficulties of Soviet historiography during the preceding few years and attributed them all to the insidious influence of the Pokrovsky school of historians.[20] Like RAPP in literature, Pokrovsky's ghost was made a scapegoat for the nonsensical extremes and pedagogical failures of the Party's past policy in history. In substance, Marxism was abandoned, because it had become inexpedient for an authoritarian state to uphold the spirit of the old determinist doctrine. However, this transformation in basic theory was camouflaged by representing the attack on Pokrovsky as a defense of the true Marxist faith against those who had been trying to pervert it.

"Vulgar economic materialism" was the term used to describe Pokrovsky's alleged deviation from the Marxist conception of history. This phrase revealed what the men in control of the Party now thought of the doctrine on which they had been brought up. The subjectivism of Pokrovsky's extreme *partiinost*, his position that the historical record could and should be shaped according to the interests of the party, was likewise repudiated, by the very people who excelled at reshaping of the truth. Drawing their ideas from the "dialectical" philosophers who received the sanction of the Party in 1930, Pokrovsky's critics reaffirmed scientific objectivity—of a sort: "Every theory in a class society has a class bias, and serves as a weapon for one class or another. But from this it does not follow that every theory is false, subjective. Today only Marxism defends absolute truth, i.e., fundamental science."[21]

The new task for historians was stated bluntly: "The historical scheme of Comrade Stalin and the problems posed by it must be worked out in the concrete historical material and made the property of the broadest masses of the toilers."[22] But because it retained the old Marxist terminology, the Party had great difficulty in sifting the influence of the Pokrovsky school out of the work of Soviet historians. The textbook competition of 1936–1937 yielded such unsatisfactory results that no first prize was awarded; only a "second prize" went to the work by A. V. Shestakov, which nevertheless stands as a milestone in the transition back to the traditional style of narrative, nationalistic political history.[23]

The outlines of the new Soviet historiography emerged gradually in the course of the campaign against the Pokrovsky line. Most striking was the new emphasis on the role of the individual in history, and particularly of the great men who by their exceptional understanding of the laws of history provided the proletariat with the farsighted leadership essential for its victory—i.e., Marx, Engels, Lenin, and Stalin. Though material conditions were at least formally taken into account, the main emphasis shifted to subjective factors—consciousness, will, ideology, leadership, and organization. Objective conditions were treated passively; the understanding, critical in Marxism, of the internal dynamics of socioeconomic conditions and systems in the mass was lost or rejected entirely. What kind of Marxism is it, after all, which can conceive of economic and social forces pushing the proletariat to the brink of power and then ceasing to operate when heroic leadership becomes decisive?

Stalin disposed of the Marxian model of society as early as 1934, in emphasizing the critical importance of the Party and the Soviet state:

Precisely because their strength and prestige have grown to an unprecedented degree, it is their work that now determines everything, or nearly
everything. *There can be no justification for references to so-called objective
conditions.* Now that the correctness of the Party's political line has been
confirmed by the experience of a number of years, and that there is no
longer any doubt as to the readiness of the workers and peasants to
support this line, the part played by so-called objective conditions has
been reduced to a minimum; whereas *the part played by our organizations
and their leaders has become decisive*, exceptional. What does this mean?
It means that from now on nine-tenths of the responsibility for the failures
and defects in our work rests, not on 'objective' conditions, but on ourselves
alone.[24]

Law

Nowhere was the doctrinaire determinism of traditional Marxism
carried to such extreme defiance of reality as in the field of legal theory.
According to Pashukanis, who dominated Soviet jurisprudence until his
fall in 1937, law was exclusively a phenomenon of the bourgeois social
order. Like state power, it was to be used by the proletariat as a temporary
measure in the struggle against vestiges of the old order, and then it
would wither away. The most remarkable thing about this theory was
that it was seriously applied: civil law was neglected and law schools
threatened to wither away from lack of interest.[25] The concepts of guilt
and punishment were rejected as implying an un-Marxian notion of
individual responsibility.[26]

In keeping with the shift from determinism to voluntarism in the
First Five-Year Plan period, the dynamic conception of *plan* was formulated
to contrast with law. Pashukanis had to adapt to the new subjectivism
by emphasizing himself the role of the state and the plan in building
socialism.[27]

In 1936, with the introduction of the new constitution, the entire
revolutionary conception of law was suddenly repudiated. Stalin demanded "stability of laws." The notion of the withering away of law
was denounced as wrecking, and Pashukanis, vainly recanting, was
disgraced early in 1937. His place at the head of the Soviet legal
profession was taken by his erstwhile assistant Andrei Vyshinsky. Instead
of the subordination of law to political expediency, "revolutionary legality"
was redefined as strict observance of the law (with the tacit exception
of political opposition). Conventional law codes and prerevolutionary
law professors were restored to their places.[28] "Crime," "punishment,"
and the concept of individual guilt were restored. The standards for
determining the responsibility of psychopaths and minors were drastically
narrowed.[29]

As long as the Soviet leadership was still interested in revolutionary change, it viewed law as an obstacle to the supreme authority of the Party and its policies. When stability became the prime concern of the leadership, law in its most traditional forms (under the "socialist" label, to be sure) was restored to buttress the authority of the state and help enforce a sense of individual responsibility. In this respect there is a close correspondence of law with political theory, psychology, family policy, and education.

Political Theory

Changes in the field of political theory, closely paralleling the shift in law, illustrate further the transformation in the official Soviet mentality. From the original view of the proletarian state as a necessary evil destined to wither away after the revolutionary transformation, party doctrine shifted around 180 degrees, to extol the state as the highest form of social organization and a great creative force.[30]

Until 1929, Marxian political theory was still upheld in more or less its original form. The Soviet one-party state was described as the revolutionary dictatorship of the proletariat, required during the transition period to suppress the resistance of the former property-owning classes. Like the legal system, it was supposed to wither away once this essentially negative task had been accomplished and the realization of socialism completed.

Stalin introduced two potentially significant innovations in political theory during his rise to power in the 1920s. One was the doctrine of socialism in one country, which set the stage for later arguments on the necessity of the state, even under "communism," for national defense. Stalin's other idea was an extension of the familiar Leninist doctrine of the inspirational and guiding role of the Party, applying it not only to the preparation and execution of the revolution, but to the organization of the postrevolutionary socialist order. "The proletariat needs the Party," Stalin asserted, "not only to achieve the dictatorship; it needs it still more to maintain the dictatorship, to consolidate and expand it in order to achieve the complete victory of socialism."[31] For Stalin, even at this early date, it was not underlying economic development which should be relied upon for "preparing the conditions for the inauguration of socialist production," but rather the indoctrination of the masses by the Party.[32]

During the period of the First Five-Year Plan and collectivization, as social and intellectual life were being subjected to all-embracing party and state controls, Stalin began to give the positive functions of the Soviet state a more explicit and less transitory place in the corpus of

Marxian doctrine. Perhaps the irony of his "dialectical" twist escaped him when he explained his position to the Sixteenth Party Congress in June, 1930:

> We are in favor of the state dying out, and at the same time we stand for the strengthening of the dictatorship of the proletariat, which represents the most powerful and mighty authority of all forms of state which have existed up to the present day. The highest possible development of the power of the state, with the object of preparing the conditions for the dying out of the state: this is the Marxist formula. Is it "contradictory"? Yes, it is "contradictory." But this contradiction is a living thing, and completely reflects Marxist dialectics.[33]

By 1934 Stalin had arrived at a definite rationale for this "strengthening of the dictatorship of the proletariat":

> It goes without saying that a classless society cannot come of itself, spontaneously, as it were. It has to be achieved and built by the efforts of all the working people, by strengthening the organs of the dictatorship of the proletariat, by intensifying the class struggle, by abolishing classes, by eliminating the remnants of the capitalist classes, and in battles with enemies both internal and external.[34]

This remark illustrates graphically how Stalin's political needs led him to a fundamental revision of the Marxian theory of the state and the role of political factors in history, asserting their transcendence over "objective conditions." It is not mere coincidence that conventional history was rehabilitated at the expense of Pokrovsky's sociologism in the same year.

With the promulgation of the Stalin Constitution in 1936 class exploitation was officially declared to be at an end.[35] Nevertheless, no grounds were to be found for diminishing the rigors of the dictatorship of the proletariat—in complete disregard of the most elementary Marxian notions about the responsibility of class antagonisms for social conflict. Beginning with the purges, political opposition was described and explained more in moralistic than in social terms—"dregs of humanity," "Whiteguard insects," "traitorous hirelings of foreign intelligence services," "Trotsky-Bukharin fiends"—rotten apples, in short, corrupted by something approaching original sin.[36] This change of attitude ties in closely with the shift from sociological explanations of human behavior to emphasis on individual will and responsibility in history and in criminal law.

In 1939, in his speech to the Eighteenth Party Congress, Stalin addressed further the need to bring the official theory of the state into accord with the obvious permanence of the Soviet state machinery. "The leader and teacher of the Party, the leader of world Communism," declared *Pravda*, "has pointed out the path of our historical development and has given us a complete program of struggle for the construction of the fully communist society. Comrade Stalin has worked out and posed in a new way the question of the state in the epoch of the transition from socialism to communism."[37] This acclaim was an understatement: Stalin departed altogether from his Marxist heritage by making the state a star player in the historical drama. He declared that the new social order had been realized through "economic and organizational work and cultural and educational work performed by our state bodies with the purpose of developing the young shoots of the new, socialist economic system and re-educating the people in the spirit of socialism."[38] He noted the continuing necessity of police repression, though he left unmentioned the social roots of crime under socialism: "In place of this function of suppression the state acquired the function of protecting socialist property from thieves and pilferers of the property of the people."[39] Above all the state had to carry out the responsibilities of national defense. Would the state "wither away" once the stage of "communism" were attained? Marx and Engels to the contrary, it would not, if the "capitalist encirclement" continued. "Engels' general formula about the destiny of the socialist state in general cannot be extended to the particular and specific case of the victory of socialism in one separate country," Stalin explained.[40]

On occasions such as this Stalin sometimes found it opportune to make direct criticism of inadequacies in the thinking of the masters, particularly where his theory of socialism in one country was involved. Back in 1926, in reply to criticism of the theory by the Left Opposition, Stalin maintained, "Engels . . . would welcome our revolution, and say: To hell with all old formulas! Long live the victorious revolution in the Soviet Union."[41] In truth, it was not the capitalist encirclement that would necessitate retention of the state even under the phase of "communism," but the reverse: the continued existence of the Stalinist state necessitated retaining the fear of the capitalist encirclement. Here is one key to the ideological function of international hostility for Soviet Russia following World War II.

Education

Before 1931 there was much diversity in Soviet educational thought. Educational practice, however, was dominated by a single problem: the lack of resources for meeting the vast unsatisfied educational needs of the country. Universal compulsory primary education was not achieved until around 1937.[42] Lenin nevertheless recognized education as an important weapon of the proletarian dictatorship in extending the influence of the working class and in preparing the population, particularly the backward peasantry, for socialism.[43] This political aspect distinguished Soviet education ever after, whatever the changes in the direction of the political line.

Though he refered to the goal of "self-activity of children in the school,"[44] Lenin was relatively conservative in comparison with many Soviet educational specialists. Lunacharsky, commissar of education until 1929, was a promoter of the progressive education methods then becoming popular in the West.[45] The head of the Marx-Engels Institute for Pedagogy, V. N. Shulgin, was the chief exponent of the theory of "unorganized" or "spontaneous" education, according to which organized education was only a temporary measure to be supplanted by the "socialist environment" as the school withered away along with the state.[46] This doctrine was closely related to the mechanistic and determinist interpretation of Marxism that prevailed until 1929–1930. It was, however, opposed by many Soviet educational leaders, including Krupskaya, as too anarchistic.[47] Generally held assumptions in Soviet education in this period were the innate goodness of man and the spontaneous development of personality. "Learning by doing" was the ideal method, and formal instruction and discipline were to be held to a minimum.[48]

Under the impact of the First Five-Year Plan and the rejection of the mechanistic philosophy, drastic change was bound to occur. An alternative educational doctrine had already been formulated, positing the state as a "purposive organization" which deliberately utilized organized education to manipulate unorganized educational influences on the child and eventually to supplant them.[49] Concerned with fitting education to the immediate needs of economic development, the party leadership took action in the fall of 1931. In a series of decrees, it attacked "Left opportunists" for the doctrine of the withering away of the school; abolished Shulgin's pedagogical institute; criticized progressive methods; re-established the separate teaching of traditional subjects, at the expense of craft and technical training; and restored old-fashioned discipline and grading.[50] Progressive educational theory was rejected on the same grounds as the mechanistic philosophy, for running counter to the regime's demand for a great organized and purposeful effort to transform the nation.

The new attitude of the regime in education was closely related to the officially encouraged changes in Soviet psychology, where again in the years 1930–1931 the mechanistic and deterministic orientation was being replaced with a more purposive and voluntaristic, less biological approach.[51] Together with the theory of consciousness and will went the restoration of authority in educational practice. The state now relied on organization and authority to accomplish its purposes in spite of inadequate material conditions, as Stalin himself had emphasized. Practical results in the inculcation of knowledge, as well as in the molding of personalities to make them more amenable to social discipline, became the norm for the educational process in the USSR.

The trend back to formal, disciplined education continued during 1932–1934, and expanded to higher education, while the ideas of the "leftist deviation" continued to be attacked.[52] Two major steps completed the transition. The first was the decree of July 1936 abolishing the science of "pedology" (developmental child psychology) because it stressed "fatalistic conditioning" by hereditary and environmental factors and neglected the allegedly vast potentialities of education in directly molding personalities.[53] The final measure was taken in 1937 with the abolition of polytechnical training in the schools and the return of the entire formal educational effort to traditional subjects.[54] This change in educational policy reflected growing acceptance of the increasing social differentiation between the intelligentsia and the masses, and marked the abandonment in practice of an ideal still verbally adhered to, the elimination of the distinction between mental and manual labor.

In its eventual form after 1936–1937, the educational system evidently satisfied the regime. It has remained fairly stable ever since, with only minor tightening up and shifts in emphasis. The political aspects of education were re-emphasized after 1945 as "a weapon for the communist transformation of society," and vigorous attacks were made on ideological weaknesses and "formalism" (here as elsewhere a vague term for unsatisfactory results).[55] The stern, disciplinary nature of the new Soviet educational ideal was highlighted by postwar criticism of the educational measures of 1918 for "serious errors" including "idealization of the nature of the child."[56]

Social Mores

During the revolution the family as an institution fell within the sweep of the Bolsheviks' hostility to what they considered the authoritarian legacy of the past. Among its early acts the Soviet regime secularized marriage, affirmed the complete equality of women, curtailed parental authority, legalized abortion, and made divorces available automatically at the request of one party. There was much explicit advocacy of free love (exemplified by Alexandra Kollontai), although Lenin was critical of it. In general, the family was expected to "wither away" except as an entirely informal association. In conformance with this theory the legal code of 1927 made *de facto* or non-registered marriages legally equal to registered ones.

The attack on traditional family ties was intensified during the First Five-Year Plan. Compulsory labor assignments sometimes split families, with no redress. Buildings were even designed for completely communal living.[57] Revolutionary repudiation of the bourgeois amenities sometimes gave rise to a sort of Communist asceticism, making virtues out of unkemptness and abstention from social pleasures.[58]

A change in official social values occurred very suddenly in 1935 and 1936, as the regime shifted from one extreme to the other.[59] The precipitating cause of this shift was no doubt the social pathology generated by intensive industrialization and collectivization, including a declining birthrate, a high divorce rate, and serious juvenile delinquency. But the regime used these problems, paralleling the damage done by extreme revolutionary notions in fields such as literature, history and law, as the excuse to repudiate, explicitly and as a matter of principle, the earlier libertarian family policy. Instead, the family was extolled as a pillar of socialist society: "So-called 'free love' and all disorderly sex life are bourgeois through and through."[60] The Victorian attitude toward female chastity was affirmed. A decisive step was the law of June 27, 1936, which prohibited non-therapeutic abortions, made divorce possible only through legal procedure and with the payment of a fee, and established special allowances for large families.

These changes were accompanied by a burst of official commentary justifying the new policies and denouncing earlier ideas about the informality of family relationships:

> Assertions that socialism brings the withering away of the family are profoundly erroneous and harmful. They play into the hands of bearers of the survivals of capitalism in people's consciousness, who are trying to conceal their exploitative behavior with empty-sounding 'leftist phrases.' The family under socialism does not wither away, but is strengthened. Comrade Stalin, the Party, and the government are giving much attention to questions of strengthening the Soviet family.[61]

Another theorist affirmed a hyper-traditional conception of the family:

> The state cannot exist without the family. Marriage is a positive value for the socialist Soviet state only if the partners see in it a lifelong union. So-called free love is a bourgeois invention and has nothing in common with the principles of conduct of a Soviet citizen. Moreover, marriage receives its full value for the state only if there is progeny, and the consorts experience the highest happiness of parenthood.[62]

Also reversed was the attitude toward parental authority: "Young people should respect their elders, especially their parents," declared *Komsomolskaya Pravda*.[63]

The parallel between these statements and the concurrently developing doctrine on the nature of the socialist state is striking. In both cases the regime's interest was in justifying the retention or restoration of institutions of authority. Trotsky commented from exile,

> Instead of openly saying, "We have proven still too poor and ignorant for the creation of socialist relations among men, our children and grandchildren will realize this aim," the leaders are forcing people to glue together again the shell of the broken family, and not only that, but to consider it, under threat of extreme penalties, the sacred nucleus of triumphant socialism. It is hard to measure with the eye the scope of this retreat.[64]

The change in family policy was accompanied by a sweeping alteration in the officially approved standards for social conduct. All of the ordinary bourgeois amusements, even dancing and fashionable dress, returned, to the evident gratification of the population.[65] These developments reflected the increasing social stratification that the repudiation of equalitarianism facilitated, and the emergent material desires among the newly privileged bureaucratic strata.

The trend away from the revolutionary conception of the family continued during World War II, with curtailment of the freedom of children and strengthening of parental authority. Children under sixteen were excluded from evening theater performances in 1934,[66] and the inheritance law of March 1945 gave more freedom in the disposition of estates. Co-education in secondary schools was abolished in 1943, allegedly to facilitate military training for boys and domestic training for girls.[67] (It was restored in 1954.)

A far-reaching step, second only to the law of 27 June 1936, was the decree of 8 July 1944. With this measure, the retrogression of the USSR in family policy clearly put it behind most democratic countries, and nearly on a par with the fascist regimes. Divorce was made subject to a rigorous judicial procedure and high fees. Unregistered or *de facto* marriages ceased to be recognized as legal. Paternity suits and the right of illegitimate children to inheritance from the father were discontinued; a state subsidy was instituted instead. In the words of one observer, "There is still no legal stigma of illegitimacy, but the likelihood of effective social stigmatization is increased by the fact that the child now takes the name of the mother."[68] Most striking in its implications was the provision that instituted titles and medals for motherhood, capped by the award "Heroine Mother of the Soviet Union" for the bearers of ten children or more. On the material side, incentives were provided by extended child subsidies to families with three children or more, coupled with a special tax on smaller families and single persons.

The changes in Soviet family policy are difficult to account for fully. Nicholas Timasheff believes that the regime merely sacrificed an unpopular element of the revolution, "one of the most unpleasant, almost intolerable aspects of the Communist Experiment. . . . Obviously, this was one of the concessions which the government could grant wholeheartedly, since actually it conceded nothing and gained very much."[69] For Trotsky it was an aspect of the Thermidorean betrayal of revolutionary humanism. Rudolph Schlesinger sees the change as the natural result of postrevolutionary stabilization, and Alex Inkeles believes that "the development of Soviet policy on the family constitutes a striking affirmation of the importance of that institution as a central element in the effective functioning of the type of social system which is broadly characteristic of Western civilization."[70] Left unaccounted for, however, is why, instead of leaving the family alone, the regime turned firmly in the opposite direction (still in the name of socialism, of course). The Soviet government aimed not simply at the stabilization of social relationships but at encouraging a family of a certain type, to serve a particular kind of state; besides, the leadership, authoritarians themselves, found the public embrace of authoritarian family relationships, mores, and personality patterns more congenial to the authoritarian political structure.

Religion

Regarding religion, Soviet policy changed neither so soon nor so much as in other fields. The substance of the original revolutionary attitude toward religion as an evil continued to be asserted. The regime did not declare that religion was good and also in accordance with Marxism, as would follow by analogy with its shifting attitude, for example, on the all-powerful state. In practice, however, the authorities shifted significantly toward conciliation with the Orthodox Church.

Active suppression of religious activities was carried on from the revolution through the period of the collectivization and the First Five-Year Plan, with some relaxation during the NEP. During the period of the imposition of extreme Marxist doctrine, from 1929 to 1932, anti-religious propaganda was intensified under the direction of the Society of Militant Atheists. By 1936 there was a distinct relaxation, marked by certain symbolic concessions such as curtailment of anti-religious demonstrations and the restoration of Sunday as the day of rest. Civil disabilities were removed from the clergy by the Stalin Constitution.[71]

A measure of the resiliency of religion was the official estimate of 1937 indicating that half the population were still believers.[72] In keeping with the traditionalist trend in social policy the regime came to see more clearly the potential of the Orthodox Church as an instrument for strengthening popular loyalty and discipline.

Spectacular developments occurred during World War II. In 1941 the Orthodox leadership declared its firm support of the war effort, and anti-religious activity by the regime was suspended altogether. The *rapprochement* was capped in 1943 when the regime permitted the restoration of the Patriarchate, with its own journal. Soon afterward, monasteries and the Orthodox Theological Institute were reopened. Governmental supervision over the Church continued, however, through the Council for Russian Orthodox Affairs.[73] To this extent, state-church relations fit the pattern of cultivation or toleration of traditionalist values, under strict political control.

At the same time, the Party retained its official anti-religious policy. It took the stand that anti-religious propaganda and education were necessary to prepare for the transition to communism, but that no coercion or violence should be allowed. The Party seemed content to hold its own and maintain ideological discipline among its own membership.

Social Stratification

The ideal of egalitarianism was firmly rooted in the revolutionary tradition, both Western and Russian, although Marx and Engels had cautioned that this goal could not be attained immediately and that the abolition of private property in the means of production was a fundamental prerequisite. In *State and Revolution* Lenin subscribed wholeheartedly to Marx's dictum on keeping officials' salaries to the level of workers' wages, and invited the masses to take over administrative functions and eliminate the need for bureaucrats standing above the populace.[74]

Soon after the Bolsheviks came to power, the party leadership woke up to the need for trained administrative experts, in the government, in industry, and in the army. Accordingly, over the protests of the idealist left-wing opposition in the Party, they began to resort to "bourgeois specialists" (*spetsy*), including former tsarist officers and officials, who were well paid in accordance with their skills. In administrative methods, the leadership found the anarcho-syndicalist notions current among the Party and its proletarian supporters in 1917–1918 to be a grave weakness, and progressively reinstituted the conventional bureaucratic system of individual authority. Nevertheless, by 1920 a nearly complete egalitarianism was reached, more by necessity than design, as inflation and shortages reduced the urban population to a common level of rationed consumption. The range in real factory wages from lowest to highest was negligible.[75]

During the NEP, the bureaucratic aspect of Soviet economic life was modestly curtailed, as authority was decentralized. Party and trade union representatives shared in industrial management. However, wage differentiation returned to provide incentives, and reached capitalistic proportions by 1928. In the Party and in political life, developments took the opposite direction: bureaucratic authority was systematically tightened, while the personal income of party members remained limited by the "party maximum."[76] The ideal of equality was still an effective restraint on further income differentiation.

With the onset of intensive industrialization the egalitarian ideal was frankly discarded. The trade-union leadership was purged and replaced with firm supporters of the view that the unions should represent primarily the interests of the state rather than the workers. At the start of the First Five-Year Plan, the regime relied heavily on propaganda and the new wave of revolutionary fervor for the "building of socialism" However, monetary incentives soon had to be extended to replace flagging enthusiasm.

In 1931 Stalin sounded the new keynote, as he criticized "the 'Leftist' practice of wage equalization" and emphasized the necessity for monetary incentives to cultivate skills and improve productivity. He warned a meeting of industrial administrators, "Whoever draws up wage scales on the 'principle' of wage equalization, without taking into account the difference between skilled labor and unskilled labor, breaks with Marxism, breaks with Leninism."[77] This new theme would soon become familiar—denouncing former revolutionary notions as "petty-bourgeois" and "anti-Marxist," and hailing the newly re-discovered principles of the traditional social order as the eternal Marxian verity. Particularly significant in the evolution of the Party from a political movement to an association of the socially privileged was the relaxation of the party maximum in 1929 and its subsequent unannounced lapse.[78]

By 1934, Stalin made a virtue of necessity and disposed of the embarrassment of Marxian egalitarianism by redefinition. "Every Leninist knows," he said, "(that is, if he is a real Leninist) that equality in the sphere of requirements and individual life is a piece of reactionary petty-bourgeois absurdity worthy of a primitive sect of ascetics, but not of a socialist society organized on Marxian lines." He made the slogan "to each according to his needs" require inequality because people's needs were different; no doubt those of the ordinary worker and the high official diverged widely. With his slogan "cadres decide everything," Stalin directed the emphasis of the government to well-trained and well-rewarded administrators.[79] Wage differentials and incentives were extended and enshrouded with a mystical halo by the Stakhanovite movement, begun in 1935. De-rationing and official sanction for the material amenities of life, commencing in 1934–1935, lent added force to income differentiation as an incentive for maximum effort and efficiency. Status differences and bureaucratic authority intensified; individual management with broad powers along with heavy responsibility became the rule in industry. Overt trappings of authority, often reminiscent of prerevolutionary Russia, began to return.

Developments in the army were particularly noteworthy in this regard. In 1935, conventional rank designations for officers (except generals) were restored and the new title of marshal was created; generals came back later, in 1939. Discipline and subordination to higher authority were increasingly stressed as ends in themselves.[80] Pursuant to the revival of patriotism and national tradition after 1934, tsarist military figures became heroic models, and medals were even named after them. By the end of World War II, epaulets, the subordination of political officers to military commanders after several false starts, the institution of Guards units, and finally changing the name "Red Army" to "Soviet Army," completed the refurbishing of the military on traditionalist lines.

The general 1930s trend of income and status differentiation was accompanied by two noteworthy developments: the end of social and political discrimination against the intelligentsia as such, and a growing cleavage between the class of administrative and technical specialists and the masses of workers and peasants. Reconciliation with members of the old intelligentsia was, like so many other policy changes in this period, touched off directly by Stalin (in 1931), as the fervent class struggle of the First Five-Year Plan period gave way to more pragmatic considerations of social organization.[81] From this time on, ability and skills (together with political loyalty) displaced class considerations as the basis for the selection of responsible personnel. Educational preference on class grounds was ended in 1934.[82]

In 1936, as the new constitution was about to be promulgated, the attainment of "socialism," defined now as the elimination of class antagonisms, was officially proclaimed. Soviet society was thenceforth conceived of as comprising three "strata" or "non-antagonistic classes," the workers, the peasantry, and the Soviet intelligentsia.[83] At the same time, the new constitution eliminated all political disabilities based on former membership in the old ruling classes. Thus, by 1936, the theoretical route was paved for the recovery of social leadership by the class of educated specialists, including both those remaining from the old regime

and those trained under Soviet rule. "Bolsheviks without party cards,"
Stalin termed them.[84] Party recognition came shortly afterwards; the
negative attitude toward members of the intelligentsia was eliminated
in the Komsomol in 1936 and in the Party itself in 1939, with the end
of the traditional preference for proletarians.[85] At the Eighteenth Party
Conference in February 1941 Georgi Malenkov pointedly attacked the
consideration of social background at the expense of technical and
personal qualifications in the appointment of responsible party and state
officials.[86]

While the educated class was coming into its own in political status
and economic position, the lines between the intelligentsia and the
masses became sharper and stiffer. By 1941 academic education had
become the prime consideration for social advancement; for example,
the technical school rather than experience as a skilled worker became
the main avenue to work in industrial management.[87] The "unity of
mental and physical labor" had long been a point in the Communist
program, fitfully reflected in efforts to combine regular education with
training in manual skills, but the ideal was virtually abandoned in
practice. Industrial training was completely separated from academic
education in 1937.[88]

A potentially serious curtailment of social mobility was the introduction
in 1940 of fees for secondary and higher education, and the institution
of the draft for industrial training in the newly created State Labor
Reserves. These measures had a substantial effect in channeling the
careers of youth to the levels of their families, in spite of the system
of educational stipends—which itself was so arranged as to give an
advantage to the well-to-do in non-technical lines.[89]

Why did the Soviet regime deliberately cultivate social stratification,
at the expense of its ideological commitments and possible popular
resentment? Like other policy changes under Stalin, the shift to social
inequality reflected practical conditions which, at least in Russia, made
the old socialist ideal inoperable. Moreover, the regime faced general
problems of industrialism that had never been sufficiently considered
in socialist thought. In consequence, the Communist system became
something very different from the order envisaged by prerevolutionary
theorists. What it became was never spelled out verbally but only implied
in practice, and one aspect of this practice was the development of a
rigorously organized system of social inequality.

The cultivation of a privileged stratum of qualified and reliable
executives was no doubt essential to the success and stability of the
regime under the given conditions.[90] The Soviet intelligentsia approached
the position of a ruling class, in the sense that relying on it, the regime

had to adapt itself to the interests of this group in order to keep it functioning satisfactorily.

Wartime and Postwar Developments

The new equilibrium in Soviet intellectual life suffered a temporary disturbance during World War II. Under the stress of war the regime sought to broaden its support by further traditionalist steps, especially regarding patriotism, Great-Russian nationalism, concessions to the Church, the symbolic trappings of authority, and the glorification of martial exploits. These symbolic changes had perhaps been delayed by the need to incorporate them into doctrinal reinterpretations, but in the war emergency this consideration fell away, and a direct appeal could be made to nationalist and traditionalist sentiment. Insofar as intellectual work headed in this general direction, ideological strictures upon it could be relaxed, and thanks to the natural primacy of patriotism at a time of foreign invasion, virtually all intellectual work proceeded freely to the satisfaction of the regime. During the war, generally speaking, ideology was superseded by direct sentiments of patriotic fervor as the mental cement binding the activities of the population to the purposes of the regime. This was fortunate for the regime—indeed, it was crucial for its survival, for under the extreme stress of war it could not have compelled allegiance as it did before or afterwards.[91]

Victory was bound to lead to changes. The nature of the Soviet political system required the firm reimposition of ideological controls in all aspects of life, to replace the spontaneous discipline that had bolstered the regime during the war. Through a series of purges, involving reprimands, demotions, denunciations, recantations, and in a few extreme cases, liquidation, the principle of party supremacy and the authority of the party line were re-established in virtually all fields of intellectual activity.

The campaign against ideological laxity was launched in the summer of 1946 with a devastating attack on two literary journals, followed by similar criticism of the theater and films. The common theme of the attacks was the dangerous penetration of bourgeois cultural influences, of "works which cultivate a non-Soviet spirit of servility before the contemporary bourgeois culture of the West,"[92] described by Andrei Zhdanov as "putrid and baneful in its moral foundations."[93] Efforts to reinstill militant party spirit in other fields followed in quick succession, notably in philosophy, music, history, and law. Later, in 1949, the focus of the Party's re-educational efforts was shifted back to literature, in the campaign against "cosmopolitanism" and Jewish cultural figures.

In the meantime, the natural sciences, comparatively free of direct party interference before the war, began to feel the strictures of the party's demand for militant participation in the struggle against all forms of bourgeois ideology. Serious trouble came in biology, where the field of genetics under Trofim Lysenko was subjected to the kind of party controls and extreme Marxist doctrine which had been experienced in most fields during the first phase of the great ideological changes of the 1930s. This was not the only instance where the Party was slow in asserting its primacy; the doctrines of A. Y. Marr in linguistics were likewise enforced rigorously only after the war. Later on, when the Marrists' imposition of their extreme Marxist (and linguistically ridiculous) theories threatened practical damage to linguistic work, their doctrine was repudiated and replaced with essentially traditional linguistic principles.[94] Lysenko likewise fell when his detrimental effect on Soviet biology became evident.[95]

In general, in its criticisms of postwar intellectual work the Party reinforced its pseudo-Marxist rationalization of the continuing traditionalist trend. Struggle with "bourgeois ideology" and Western influence was the dominant theme, with renewed efforts to check modernist and esoteric trends and the notion of art and science as ends in themselves. To maintain its political supremacy and to obtain the desired conservative content in Marxist forms, the Party had to exert continuous pressure in cultural life.

The Role of Stalinist Ideology

The reimposition of rigorous ideological strictures after World War II brings into focus the basic question of the role of ideology in the Soviet political system under Stalin. Having thoroughly transformed the programmatic basis of the social order, why did the regime persist in claiming to represent the revolution? Why did it continue to enforce a body of doctrine which for its maintenance required comprehensive control of thought and expression, with the consequences of intellectual stagnation and widespread disaffection? There are roughly five facets to the explanation.

1. The retention of orthodox belief by the top leadership is a question impossible to decide. It is unimportant from the standpoint of analyzing Soviet policy, for invariably practical considerations prevailed and ideology was reinterpreted as much as was necessary to justify any policy. Perhaps the Soviet leaders really believed that they were leading humanity on the road to the great goal of communism, despite the zig-zags of the path and the necessity of

silencing doubters. Such a belief would account for their insistence on faith in the Soviet regime as the embodiment of the proletarian revolution. To be sure, the ultimate faith would not be allowed to interfere with the regime's short-term interests in power and stability. Even if the Stalinist leadership had ceased to take doctrine seriously, it would be inconceivable for them to admit—by declaring socialism to be nonsense, for example, and allowing free expression of any ideas short of sedition—that they had for a long time been wrong or cynical.

2. Some political support accrued to the regime on the basis of the revolutionary ideology. Ideology gave it a sense of moral justification for the stern exercise of power, supporting the conviction that what the government was doing *must* be correct. At times, much support was derived from ideologically motivated enthusiasm.[96] By contradicting unpleasant realities ideology disoriented potential opponents of the regime.[97] Finally, ideology seems to have played a part in the driving motivation of the fanatic personality which figured importantly in the party control apparatus.[98]

3. Postwar retightening underscored the role of ideology in controlling the educational impact of cultural activity. The Stalinist system required a rigid and authoritative form for stating the purposes of the state, to guide the molding of citizens' minds. The official ideology, as amended and reinterpreted, served as such a guide and standard.

4. The foreign support enjoyed by the Stalinist state came largely from people who identified the Soviet regime with their own revolutionary aspirations. This ideologically based support was extremely important in the postwar international power position of the Soviet Union and could not be dispensed with, although it involved serious complications and weaknesses. Soviet reality had to be concealed above all from Soviet sympathizers, by keeping contact between the Soviet Union and the outside world to a minimum. Changes in ideology or policy, if introduced too suddenly, could cause embarrassment abroad, since foreign Communist parties not in power were not insulated from divergent points of view. This vulnerability contributed to the high rates of defection and turnover among the membership of some foreign Communist parties.

5. Stalinism needed an external enemy. The functions served by postulating threatening foreign forces included: (a) justification of the economic privation and rigorous controls which had to be imposed in the interest of building national power; (b) a partial outlet for the hostility generated by the rigors of the regime; (c)

a stimulus to evoke patriotic feeling in support of the regime; (d) explaining internal deviants as agents of foreign powers or as traitorous allies of the international enemy, taking advantage of "survivals of bourgeois ideology in people's consciousness." Attacking bourgeois ideology was the basis of the entire campaign for discipline and enthusiasm in the service of the state. International hostility furthermore provided justification and reinforcement for the policy of keeping contact with the West at a minimum, which in turn was necessary to curb disaffection and to prevent the free circulation of ideas which might challenge the official ideology. Finally, the conflict situation fits well the military state of mind which prevailed in Soviet politics.

The Stalinist regime—and it is far from alone in this—could not conceive of politics except as a struggle against an enemy. In this respect Marxist-Leninist ideology defined the enemy and provoked the sense of enmity on both sides. Without ideology, there would be little material basis for East-West conflict. Thus we have the paradoxical situation where an ideology far removed from Soviet reality was asserted with great effort to create the artificial sense of conflict and foreign danger which the Stalinist regime required for its internal stability.

*   *   *

One fact should be quite clear from this survey of official Soviet thought during the 1930s: that the Soviet regime changed in its *essence* since the revolution. The pattern of changes within the core of the official ideology, the official purpose-system, cannot convincingly be written off as a series of mere tactical ruses or strategic zig-zags. The Stalinist regime could express no higher articulation of social purpose than its Marxist-Leninist ideology, but that ideology had been reduced to rationalization after the fact. It lost all long-run directing power, no matter what the direction. There was no fixed star for the Stalinists to steer by; they had no ultimate pattern which was not thus subject to reshaping over the years. Regardless of its labels, the Stalinist regime no longer represented the same movement that took power in 1917. This should be a basic premise for anyone who undertakes to establish just what kind of regime it actually was.

Notes

1. There are works which are noteworthy exceptions in their broader grasp of the picture: see Nicholas S. Timasheff, *The Great Retreat: The Growth and Decline of Communism in Russia* (New York: Dutton, 1946); Harold J. Berman,

Justice in Russia (Cambridge, Mass.: Harvard University Press, 1950); Raymond A. Bauer, *The New Man in Soviet Psychology* (Cambridge, Mass.: Harvard University Press, 1952); Klaus Mehnert, *Stalin vs. Marx* (London: Allen and Unwin, 1952).

2. For suggestions relevant to the psychological functions of Soviet social policy, see Bauer, *The New Man*; T. W. Adorno and others, *The Authoritarian Personality* (New York: Harper, 1950); Erich Fromm, *Escape from Freedom* (New York: Farrar and Rinehart, 1941); Wilhelm Reich, *The Mass Psychology of Fascism* (New York: Orgone Institute Press, 1946).

3. Quoted in Harriet Borland, *Soviet Literary Theory and Practice During the First Five-Year Plan, 1928–1932* (New York: King's Crown Press, 1950), p. 13.

4. Quoted, ibid., p. 14. For a general discussion of the arts in the 1920s and early 1930s, see Max Eastman, *Artists in Uniform* (New York: Knopf, 1934).

5. John C. Fiske, "Dostoevsky and the Soviet Critics, 1947–1948," *American Slavic and East European Review*, IX:1 (February 1950), p. 45.

6. Quoted in Borland, *Literary Theory*, pp. 33–34.

7. See Gleb Struve, *Soviet Russian Literature, 1917–50* (Norman, Okla.: University of Oklahoma Press, 1951), p. 172.

8. Edward J. Brown, *The Proletarian Episode in Russian Literature, 1928–1932* (New York: Columbia University Press, 1953), contends that RAPP was abolished because the party found its control work inadequate. However, in the context of the present paper, it appears that a substantive rejection of its line was involved.

9. Kurt London, *The Seven Soviet Arts* (New Haven: Yale University Press, 1938), p. 61.

10. Ibid.

11. Struve, *Soviet Russian Literature*, p. 242.

12. See Adorno et al., *Authoritarian Personality*.

13. See Maxim Gorky, speech to the Soviet Writers' Congress, 1934, *Problems of Soviet Literature* (New York: International Publishers [1935]), p. 65.

14. *Literaturnaia Gazeta*, 23 March 1946.

15. Paul Aron, "The Impact of the First Five-Year Plan on Soviet Historiography" (unpublished seminar paper, Russian Research Center, Harvard University); E. Maksimovich, "Istoricheskaia nauka v SSSR i Marksizm-Leninizm" (Historical Science in the USSR and Marxism-Leninism), *Sovremennyia Zapiski* (Paris), vol. XXXII (1936).

16. Aron, "Impact."

17. Stalin, "Some Questions Concerning the History of Bolshevism" (a Letter to the Editors of *Proletarskaya revoliutsiya*), *Problems of Leninism* (Moscow: Foreign Languages Publishing House, 1953), pp. 484, 494.

18. *Izvestiya*, 16 May 1934; translated in the *Slavonic and East European Review*, July 1934, pp. 204–205.

19. Ibid.

20. Text of the decree in *Istorik Marksist*, 1936, no. 1, pp. 3–5.

21. M. Kammari, "Teoreticheski korni oshibochnykh vzgliadov M. N. Pokrovskogo v istorii" (The Theoretical Roots of the Erroneous Views of M. N. Pokrovsky in History), *Pod Znamenem Marksizma*, 1936, no. 4, p. 7.

22. P. Drozhdov, "Reshenie partii i pravitel'stva ob uchebnikakh po istorii i zadachi sovetskikh istorikov" (The Decision of the Party and the Government on Textbooks in History and the Tasks of Soviet Historians), *Istorik Marksist*, 1936, no. 1, p. 22.

23. P. Miliukov, "Velichestvo i padenie M. N. Pokrovskogo" (The Majesty and Downfall of M. N. Pokrovsky), *Sovremennyia Zapiski*, 1937, p. 384. Shestakov's book appeared in English as *A Short History of the USSR* (Moscow: Co-operative Publishing House of Foreign Workers in the USSR, 1938).

24. Stalin, Political Report of the Central Committee to the Seventeenth Congress of the CPSU (B), *Problems of Leninism*, p. 644. Italics mine.

25. See Berman, *Justice*, pp. 35–37.

26. See Harold J. Berman and Donald H. Hunt, "Criminal Law and Psychiatry: The Soviet Solution," *Stanford Law Review*, XII:6 (July 1950), p. 635.

27. Berman, *Justice*, pp. 30–33.

28. Ibid., pp. 43–50.

29. Ibid., p. 47; Berman and Hunt, "Criminal Law," p. 635.

30. For a more extensive discussion of developments in Communist political theory both before and after the revolution, see Robert V. Daniels, "The State and Revolution: A Case Study in the Genesis and Transformation of Communist Idology," *The American Slavic and East European Review*, XII:1 (February 1953).

31. Stalin, "The Foundations of Leninism" (1924), *Problems of Leninism*, p. 105.

32. Ibid, p. 106.

33. Stalin, Political Report of the Central Committee to the Sixteenth Party Congress, Stalin, *Leninism* (New York: International Publishers, 1933), vol. II, p. 402.

34. Stalin, Report to the Seventeenth Party Congress, *Problems of Leninism*, p. 631.

35. See Stalin, "On the Draft Constitution of the USSR," Report delivered at the Extraordinary Eighth Congress of Soviets of the USSR, 25 November 1936, ibid., p. 683.

36. See *History of the CPSU (B): Short Course* (New York: International Publishers, 1939), pp. 346–348.

37. "Dokument vsemirnogo znacheniya" (A Document of World-Wide Significance), *Pravda*, 12 March 1939.

38. Stalin, Political Report of the Central Committee to the Eighteenth Congress of the CPSU (B), *Problems of Leninism*, p. 796.

39. Ibid., p. 797.

40. Ibid., pp. 793–794.

41. Stalin, Concluding Remarks at the Fifteenth Party Conference, November 1926, *International Press Correspondence*, no. 78, 25 November 1926, p. 1350.

42. M. J. Shore, *Soviet Education* (New York: Philosophical Library, 1947), p. 189.

43. Ibid., pp. 138–141; Lenin, "Pages from a Diary" (January 1923), *Selected Works* (Moscow: Foreign Languages Publishing House, 1952), vol. II, book 2, pp. 709–714.

44. Lenin, draft of a party program, 1919, cited in Shore, p. 144.

45. See Trotsky, *The Revolution Betrayed* (New York: Doubleday Doran, 1937), pp. 180–181.

46. Shore, *Soviet Education*, p. 155.

47. Ibid., p. 156.

48. Bauer, *New Man*, p. 43.

49. Shore, *Soviet Education*, pp. 156–161.

50. Ibid., pp. 172–174, 191–192; Timasheff, *Great Retreat*, pp. 213–214; Bauer, *New Man*, p. 45.

51. Ibid., pp. 94–96.

52. Timasheff, *Great Retreat*, pp. 214–218.

53. Bauer, *New Man*, p. 124; Shore, *Soviet Education*, pp. 176–179.

54. Ibid., pp. 193–195.

55. Ibid., pp. 220–247.

56. Bauer, *New Man*, pp. 43–44.

57. Timasheff, *Great Retreat*, p. 195.

58. Ibid., p. 315.

59. For the texts of laws and for much interesting Soviet commentary, see Rudolph Schlesinger, ed., *Changing Attitudes in Soviet Russia: The Family in the USSR* (London: Routledge & Kegan Paul, 1949), a collection of source materials which vividly documents the changes in official attitudes and policies.

60. *Pravda*, May 28, 1936, cited in Schlesinger, *Family*, p. 252.

61. S. Vol'fson, "Sotsializm i sem'ia" (Socialism and the Family), *Pod Znamenem Marksizma*, 1936, no. 6, p. 64.

62. *Sotsialisticheskaya Zakonnost'*, 1939, no. 2, cited in Timasheff, *Great Retreat*, p. 198.

63. *Komsomolskaya Pravda*, 4 June 1935, cited ibid, p. 202.

64. Trotsky, *Revolution Betrayed*, pp. 151–152.

65. Ibid., pp. 317–318.

66. Ibid., p. 203.

67. Shore, *Soviet Education*, pp. 215–216.

68. Alex Inkeles, "Family and Church in the Postwar USSR," *Annals of the American Academy of Political and Social Science*, May 1949, p. 34.

69. Timasheff, *Great Retreat*, p. 317.

70. Schlesinger, *Changing Attitudes*, editor's introduction, p. 22; Inkeles, "Family and Church," p. 38.

71. See Timasheff, *Great Retreat*, pp. 228–229.

72. Nicholas S. Timasheff, *Religion in Soviet Russia* (London: Sheed & Ward, 1943), p. 65.

73. Timasheff, *Great Retreat*, pp. 231–234.

74. Lenin, *State and Revolution* (New York: International Publishers, 1932), pp. 91–92.

75. See Barrington Moore, *Soviet Politics, The Dilemma of Power* (Cambridge, Mass.: Harvard University Press, 1950), p. 183.

76. Ibid., pp. 184–186.

77. Stalin, "New Conditions, New Tasks in Economic Construction," speech delivered at a conference of business executives, 23 June 1931, *Problems of Leninism*, p. 464.

78. Moore, *Soviet Politics*, pp. 185, 445n99.

79. Stalin, "Address to the Graduates from the Red Army Academies," 4 May 1935, *Problems of Leninism*, p. 662; Moore, *Soviet Politics*, pp. 238–239.

80. See Rudolph Schlesinger, *The Spirit of Post-War Russia* (London: Dobson, 1947), pp. 123–124, for an apologist's admissions.

81. See Stalin, "New Conditions, New Tasks," *Problems of Leninism*, pp. 471–476.

82. See Schlesinger, *Spirit*, p. 40.

83. Stalin, "On the Draft Constitution," *Problems of Leninism*, pp. 683–686.

84. Schlesinger, *Spirit*, p. 40.

85. Merle Fainsod, *How Russia Is Ruled* (Cambridge, Mass.: Harvard University Press, 1953), pp. 226, 246.

86. G. F. Malenkov, Report to the Eighteenth Party Conference, "O zadachakh partiinykh organizatsii v oblasti promyshlennosti i transporta" (On the Tasks of Party Organizations in the Field of Industry and Transportation), *Pravda*, 16 February 1941.

87. Alex Inkeles, "Social Stratification and Mobility in the Soviet Union," *American Sociological Review*, XV:4 (August 1950), p. 477.

88. Shore, *Soviet Education*, pp. 193–195.

89. Inkeles, "Social Stratification," pp. 473–476.

90. Ibid., p. 479; Moore, *Soviet Politics*, passim.

91. Cf. Timasheff, *Great Retreat*, pp. 279–281 and passim.

92. Resolution of the Central Committee of the CPSU, August 14, 1946, quoted in George S. Counts and Nucia Lodge, *The Country of the Blind—The Soviet System of Mind Control* (Boston, Mass.: Houghton-Mifflin, 1949), p. 80. (This work provides an extensive and well-documented treatment of the postwar intellectual disciplining.)

93. Andrei Zhdanov, speech to the First All-Union Congress of Soviet Writers, 21 August 1946, quoted ibid., p. 95 (condensed text in Zhdanov, *Essays on Literature, Philosophy, and Music,* New York: International Publishers, 1950).

94. See *The Soviet Linguistic Controversy* (New York: King's Crown Press, 1951).

95. The foregoing was written before Nikita Khrushchev briefly attempted to rehabilitate Lysenko.

96. See Merle Fainsod, "The Komsomols—A Study of Youth Under Dictatorship," *American Political Science Review*, XLV:1 (March 1951).

97. See F. Beck (pseud.) and W. Godin (pseud.), *Russian Purge and the Extraction of Confession* (New York: Viking, 1951).

98. Ibid.; cf. Henry Dicks, "Observations on Contemporary Russian Behavior," *Human Relations*, V:2 (1952), pp. 130–131.

11

Stalinist Ideology as False Consciousness

Until recently it has been customary among both the adherents and the enemies of Marxism to regard it as the inspiration and the plan that have guided the development of Soviet-style socialism ever since the Revolution of 1917. This is the central myth of Stalinism. Now the presumption of ideological guidance is the basis on which, with the manifest abandonment of old orthodoxies in the Soviet Union and Eastern Europe, Marxism is adjudged a failure—a proposition in which many Soviet intellectuals concur.

This conclusion suffers from the fallacy in its major premise. It was not Marxism that failed under Brezhnev. In the genuine and meaningful sense of the term Marxism has not guided the Soviet Union for more than half a century. It was not Gorbachev but Stalin who put an end to its sway, first by imposing a cynical political manipulation upon the formulation and understanding of Marxian notions, and then by physically liquidating anyone of stature who took the theory seriously. Only the rigid shell of obligatory public dogma remained, a new state religion using the language of Marxism to confer legitimacy upon a reincarnation of Old Russian despotism and to exploit the loyalties of any within the country or outside who remained faithful to the words of the doctrine. What Gorbachev and the promoters of perestroika represent, in ideological terms, is not the rejection of Marxism but the shedding of the withered skin of dogma that Marxism had become at the hands of Stalin and the neo-Stalinist apparatchiki.

That this fate could befall the Marxian revolutionary dream in the land where it had seemingly conquered as the shining banner of the future raises profound questions, not only about the character of the

Reprinted with permission from Marcell Flores and Francesca Gori, eds., *Il mito dell'Urss: La cultura occidentale e l'Unione Sovietica* (Milan: Franco Angeli, 1990), pp. 225–244.

regime that made such perverse use of Marxist doctrine, but about the validity of the doctrine itself as a picture of the driving forces of modern history. Classical Marxism was above all an analysis of early industrial capitalism. Some of its propositions have stood the test of time, others have not. As Marx himself acknowledged, the theory was not capable of forecasting the future of countries such as Russia that were not already committed to a capitalist path of economic development. Marx and Engels avoided making predictions about the specific character of the postrevolutionary socialist society, even though it was this vision that most excited and attracted their followers and successors. But, contrary to what Marx thought, the theory also failed to offer an adequate understanding of the revolution itself, either as to the circumstances generating it or the process through which it naturally unfolded.

Marx and the Bolsheviks alike were fascinated by the Great French Revolution and the inspiration as well as the warnings which it offered later revolutionaries. But they failed to appreciate its main lesson: as the embodiment of the finest principles of Rousseauean democracy, the revolution was a failure. The fall of Robespierre, the corruption of the Directory, and the advent of Bonaparte's dictatorship were as natural to the process as the escalation of revolutionary fervor from Mirabeau's constitutionalism to the Jacobins' fanaticism, once the authority of the Ancien Regime had collapsed in the violence of the Bastille and the Great Fear.

What, then, was the likely course and outcome of socialist revolution, apart from countries where (as Marx acknowledged in his Amsterdam address of 1872) the revolution could come as a democratic transition, thanks to their constitutional traditions already established by past revolutions?[1] The question was never faced. Moderate Social Democrats in one country after another, as Engels observed in his 1894 introduction to *The Civil War in France*, discovered that the path to socialism by ballots rather than bullets could apply to them.[2] Only in countries of unregenerate autocracy—above all in Russia—did a significant element of the Marxist movement remain committed in deed as well as in word to genuine, violent revolution.

Yet even such a serious revolutionary commitment is not enough to bring about revolution, unless the existing political system is so rigid as to preclude the cooptation of new social forces and the gradual response of government to new political and economic demands. As futile terrorist movements have shown in recent decades all over the world, ardent revolutionary action in the absence of a true revolutionary situation will alienate most members of society and in the worst case drive them to fascism. But Russia early in this century was different; it did in fact present a genuine revolutionary situation compounded of rapid economic and social change confronting a government that clung to the prerogatives of traditional monarchy until it was too late.

This was a situation which Marxists avidly seized upon, though not with much analytic clarity. They remained intellectually confined by the artificial Marxian distinction between a "bourgeois" and a "proletarian" revolution; Trotsky alone of the Russian Marxist leaders endeavored to formulate a more dynamic process theory in his conception of the continuous (or permanent) revolution where a moderate—"bourgeois" and democratic—phase would lead quickly into an extreme—"proletarian" and socialist—phase of the same event.

Trotsky's vision, as we know, was borne out with remarkable accuracy in the events of 1917, and became for a time Bolshevik orthodoxy, though it left the survival of Russian socialism theoretically dependent upon an international revolution that failed to materialize. Bolshevik rule thus lacked from the beginning the social foundation that Marxian determinism judged necessary to sustain it. As such, it was like any revolution in the extremist phase that outruns its base of support; it must retreat and adapt or succumb to counterrevolution. This is the context for Thermidorean reaction and Bonapartist dictatorship, a trend that set in clearly in Russia with the NEP in 1921.

Given these circumstances, how is one to account for the attractiveness of Marxian theory in Russia prior to the revolution and its persistence afterwards? It was not out of intellectual appropriateness to Russia's circumstances; Russian Populism would have fit the revolutionary movement much better, with its premises of the direct transition of a peasant society to socialism, and the guidance of the process by a dedicated intellectual elite. Yet by the first decade of this century Marxism had manifested an extraordinary intellectual pull in Russia, as it has more recently in developing countries all over the world. It enjoyed this appeal not because it fit those circumstances—the working class in these situations was weak or nearly absent—but because its aura of scientific inevitability leading to a utopian future answered the emotional needs of *déraciné* elements at all levels of a society in transition, alienated both from their traditional culture and from the power centers of Western capitalism.

Marxism in its inevitabilistic reading, carried to power by its Russian devotees, thus became the legitimizing belief of an extremist revolutionary regime lacking most of the conditions that would have made the propositions of the doctrine minimally realistic. It did not provide a program for the conscious legislative enactment of socialism, and therefore cannot be judged by any empirical test of success or failure. At every step, Lenin and his lieutenants and successors improvised their concrete policies, with the criteria of political survival or factional victory uppermost in their minds. All that Marxism did was to cast a veil of sanctity and self-justification around these pragmatic steps. Of necessity, official representations of the theory became more defensively dogmatic as expedient practice carried the Soviet regime ever further from the prerevolutionary spirit of its official faith.

*   *   *

This was the state of ideological affairs in the CPSU by the mid-1920s, when Stalin was consolidating his personal control over the party organization and preparing his bid for supreme power over the country. He proved adept at manipulating ideological verities for factional advantage, above all in the socialism in one country controversy of 1924–1925.[3]

This episode is of utmost importance for understanding the ideological mechanisms of Stalinism. It established the ability of the party leadership to advance reinterpretations or even patent misrepresentations of Marxist theory and to impose these new versions of the truth in all public discourse, by virtue of the monopoly of power in the hands of the party apparatus backed up by the secret police. What is more, the new versions of theory were represented to be what Marxism had always meant from the beginning in the minds of its undeviating adherents. The "official ideology," as Giuseppe Boffa has observed, had to be upheld in the name of "ideological purity" against any sort of "revisionism." Ultimately all this was codified in the *History of the CPSU: Short Course* (English version, New York: International Publishers, 1939), which became the obligatory textbook for Communists all over the world. "Any independent research was considered out of place," Boffa continues. "The essential task of the scholar was in practice the exegesis and correct commentary on Stalin's works."[4]

The effect of such dogmatic claims was to suppress any public acknowledgment of the distance between original Marxist propositions and current interpretations thereof, and any possibility of correcting the latter by reference to the former. And because interpretation was the province of political authority, original Marxist propositions lost all force for that authority even as ultimate guides to action There was no way to call the leadership to account ideologically. Marxism, in short, became whatever Stalin said it was at the moment. As such, Marxist ideology became the most sensitive and most tightly guarded area of discussion in all of Soviet life. Paradoxically, the function of Marxist ideology as a vehicle of political control and intellectual discipline grew all the more prominent as the substantive meaning and guiding role of the doctrine were being suppressed. This was a source of profound confusion for outside observers. Until very recent times the Soviet Union was permeated verbally with Marxist ideology in every aspect of life, yet the system embodied institutional forms and social values that had nothing in common with Marxism except in the most superficial sense.

After the defeat of the Left Opposition and the affirmation of socialism in one country, the principle of political control over the meaning of ideology was reinforced in two more important steps. The first, extending ideological authority and orthodoxy into all fields of inquiry, was a conference of "Marxist-Leninist Scientific Research Institutions," in April 1929, coinciding with Stalin's victory over the Bukharin wing of the party and the launching of his industrialization and collectivization drive. A resolution adopted at the conference called for an intensified effort "in instilling the methodology of Marx, Engels, and Lenin in the various fields of specialized knowledge," and warned against "ideological tendencies openly inimical to Marxism-Leninism, as well as various revisionist deviations from it," that "sometimes array themselves in Marxist dress and come forth under the flag of specialized knowledge, or . . . distort Marx, Engels and Lenin, and conceal themselves with incorrectly explained citations from their works."[5] In other words, the authority of the political leadership to define doctrinal truth was now to be extended to all fields of intellectual and cultural life.

The second step in asserting political control of ideology came with Stalin's letter to the journal *Proletarskaya Revoliutsiya* in 1931, when he put received doctrine ahead of historical inquiry: "The question as to whether Lenin *was* or *was not* a real Bolshevik cannot be made the subject of discussion."[6] This stricture meant that matters of historical and scientific fact would be subject to the test of political orthodoxy. From this time on the ideological line might change, as it often did, but the principle was firmly established that *ex cathedra* pronouncements by the leader in the name of the Party would be the last word in any field of thought or endeavor.

The most salient emendations of Marxism introduced by Stalin are familiar enough to any student of Soviet history.[7] He rejected the goal of economic equality, exalted the role of the state instead of anticipating its withering away, and revived the nation and nationalism both as positive historical categories and as ends of current policy. He repudiated most aspects of post-1900 modernistic culture and most notions of social experiment, all on the alleged grounds that they were "anti-Marxist." To justify his purges, Stalin proposed the infamous doctrine that the class struggle intensifies as the bourgeoisie approaches annihilation. Simultaneously he abandoned policies, notably in education and party recruitment, that until the mid-1930s had still favored the proletariat as a class. On the other hand he clearly did retain a form of socialism in the sense of publicly owned enterprise, carried in fact to the extreme of bureaucratic statism in the Russian tradition. This was a model of economic organization that many outsiders and even some commentators now in the Soviet Union itself have judged incompatible with socialism in any sense.

*   *   *

If Stalinism was not in reality an embodiment of the dictatorship of the proletariat, guided by Marxism into the historic channels predicted by its prophets, what kind of social system did it in fact represent, and what was the function of the Marxist ideology to which it clung so ferociously? These are questions that have perplexed generations of commentators and polemicists. Much Western analysis has proceeded from the rather simplistic, institutional judgments of the "totalitarianism" school: the entire system is purely an organization for the maintenance and extension of despotic power. But this begs the question as to what social elements serve that power and are served by it. More fruitful is the neo-Marxist attempt, originating with Trotsky and Rakovsky, to reassess Stalinist society in class terms, as a socio-economic formation dominated by the class of officials serving the state—in other words, the bureaucracy or, in the formulation that Milovan Djilas popularized, the "New Class."[8]

The prospect of a "new class" rising to dominance over the proletariat is an idea with old roots, going back to Bakunin's warning about "the new privileged scientific-political class."[9] Marx himself, citing the French experience under Napoleon III, warned repeatedly against the danger of the bureaucratic apparatus of the state making itself an independent power over the workers.[10] Jan Machajski warned long before the Russian Revolution of a "dictatorship of the intellectuals."[11] Worker resentment of intellectuals and bureaucrats in the early Soviet years fueled the series of ultra-left opposition movements of that era, though ironically these movements, including "Proletcult," were themselves for the most part led by intellectuals.[12] The role of experts and "bourgeois specialists" continued to be a subject of ideological agonizing for the Communists until the early 1930s, though their services were indispensable just to run the Soviet economy, let alone modernize it. Suspicion of the experts culminated in the trumped-up trials of engineers and other specialists staged by Stalin between 1928 and 1931 to disarm opposition to his radical program of those years.

But it was also Stalin who finally made a virtue of necessity, by reversing a whole range of policies affecting the experts—in educational philosophy and access, in salary differentials, in the whole atmosphere of class struggle. He provided ideological cover for all of these policy shifts by his simultaneous proclamations (in the Constitution of 1936) that "socialism" had been achieved and that the exploiting classes had ceased to exist. This of course did not deter him from asserting at the same time that the class struggle was intensifying, or from purging hundreds of thousands of experts and intellectuals along with the party bureaucracy. However, the Yezhovshchina, despite its magnitude and terror, was not directed against a system but only against individuals, or rather a generation—the generation (distinguished by the number of Westernized intellectuals in it) who had made the revolution, or compromised with it enough to serve it. To be sure, the purges opened up wide avenues for social advancement to sons of the proletariat and peasantry, the *vydvizhentsy* ("promotees") who were prepared through quick courses in engineering and political agitation to assume the vacant posts and privileges of the purge victims. But this process did not make the proletariat as such the ruling class—it only enabled selected individuals to rise out of the proletariat (or the peasantry) and enter the bureaucratic ruling class. It was a classic example of Pareto's "circulation of the elites," where circulation may renovate and alter the ruling class but does not put an end to the fact that a ruling class still rules.[13]

To be sure, the concept of the bureaucracy or the "New Class" as a ruling class presents a number of difficulties. The most immediate one, to a Marxist, is that it is not based on private property but rather on public function. This discrepancy has given rise to numerous contrived efforts to argue that the Soviet bureaucracy under Stalinism really controlled state property in its private interest and exploited the masses for its personal benefit.[14]

A more serious problem is that the New Class cannot be reduced to one homogeneous social group. Is it the intelligentsia? The bureaucracy in general? The *nomenklatura* of the party? Or all educated non-manual workers, "*sluzhashchie*," the "Soviet intelligentsia"? In fact these are all elements of a complex social system, where, just as under modern capitalism, it is impossible to draw sharp lines between classes and analyze society into two clearly opposed camps of exploiters and exploited. I have suggested elsewhere the long-standing historic distinction, particularly in Russia, between the creative intelligentsia and the technical intelligentsia, along with a "quasi-intelligentsia" that is characteristic of developing countries.[15] The latter type, more intellectual in pretension than in substance, is the principal contributor to revolutionary activity.

In Russia the quasi-intelligentsia was the main source of the Bolshevik mentality that combined a futuristic faith in modernity with a primitive dogmatism. Its spirit became the reigning spirit of the nomenklatura. The creative intelligentsia was ambivalent about the revolution, and has been the prime basis for such critical sentiments as the circumstances of the party dictatorship have permitted to emerge. Influential in the early years of Soviet rule, it was heavily victimized by the purges, and revived only after the death of Stalin, ultimately to become the most enthusiastic source of support for reform under Gorbachev. The technical intelligentsia, indifferent or hostile to the revolution, has been its most favored beneficiary in class terms. Vastly expanded by postrevolutionary programs of education, shading down into the millions of vocationally trained technicians and white collar workers, and offering until the end of the Stalin era a wide avenue of social mobility to ambitious men from the masses, the technical intelligentsia became the backbone of modern Soviet society.

But where, in this hierarchical maze of social elements, is the ruling class? Here it is useful to invoke the distinction made by Svetozar Stojanović (and hinted at by Antonio Gramsci), between the "ruling class" and the "dominant class."[16] The dominant class is that sector of society whose function, interests and outlook contribute most to the general character of the system; the ruling class is the sector where power actually resides even though its effective exercise must respect the interests of the dominant class. In this analysis the dominant class in the Soviet Union is the intelligentsia, creative and technical taken together, and the ruling class is obviously the nomenklatura, in its precise sense as the party apparatus plus the party members holding responsible positions in the civil government, the military, and all other organized social institutions.

*   *   *

The great paradox of the Stalinist system is the persistence of the ideology of the classless society at the same time that a new social hierarchy was settling into place. There is ample historical precedent for revolution yielding to Thermidorean reaction as the class brought to dominance by the upheaval consolidates its gains, but there was no precedent, prior to the Russian Revolution, for the continuity of the revolutionary party and the revolutionary ideology into the postrevolutionary stages of Thermidor and Bonapartism. This was Lenin's unique achievement, to adapt the party to the circumstances of an ebbing revolutionary wave, and to hold power in the name of the revolution after the revolution was over. This maneuver gave his successors an indispensable stake in clinging to the verbal forms of the ideology as well as to the dictatorship of the party. Thus, the fact that the state of the New Class was saddled with the doctrine of Marxism as its point of reference for ideological legitimation was essentially a historical accident.

This accident created a situation of considerable political and intellectual difficulty for the ruling class of Communist officials who stayed in power artificially, and who needed, in order to maintain their ideological self-justification, to bridge the ever-widening gap between Soviet reality and the doctrinal baseline of Marxism. Stalin had no choice among ideologies to legitimize his dictatorship: Marxism was a given which he was obliged to use as his point of departure, even though it was much more at variance with the actual Soviet situation than were either fascist or liberal ideologies in relation to their respective societies. It must be conceded that Stalin and his entourage made very clever use of the Marxian doctrine without in the least permitting it to circumscribe what they adjudged to be their real interests. Certainly, since the time Stalin tightened his political grip on the country, no one in a position of influence in the Soviet Union, neither the dominant intelligentsia nor the ruling nomenklatura, has had any interest in the classless society. Not since the 1920s has the classless society been an operational goal of the regime. Assertions that it has in fact been achieved have only served to smother any concern about actually pursuing it.

If this position represented the interests of the ruling and dominant classes, how and why was the revolutionary ideology, so far at variance with reality, actually sustained? Here the Marxian model of society does become relevant, specifically in Marx's theory of the ideological super-structure. While ideological systems of law, philosophy, and religion, according to Marx, reflect and justify the class structure of society and the interests of the ruling class, they are not necessarily direct and accurate expressions of social reality. On the contrary, ideological systems may lag behind reality or may even be imposed by political authority in terms that contradict reality. In either case they are functional in the given socioeconomic formation as a whole, as sources of legitimation and self-satisfaction for the ruling and dominant orders of the social structure.

Who among all the diverse elements of the Soviet New Class actually benefitted from the imposition of Marxist ideology as a false public consciousness on society at large? Certainly not the creative intelligentsia, which has been the most injured victim of the system of ideological control. Obviously, the nomenklatura, exercising its power and enjoying its privileges in the name of the dictatorship of the proletariat. In a secondary and less direct way, the technical intelligentsia and white-collar class broadly speaking, at least to the extent that membership in these categories meant education, social status, and urban residence, if not always better pay than industrial workers. In general, the elements who had risen to fill the social vacuum created by the revolution. Marxism as false consciousness thus served until the end of the Stalin era and beyond to support the position and interests of the ruling class and a portion of the dominant class, leaving the other part of the dominant class—the creative intelligentsia—in a state of demoralized but potentially dynamic opposition. The strength of the creative intelligentsia and the durability of its traditions of independence and devotion to true "consciousness" were attested by the leading role that it quickly assumed in the reforms of the era of perestroika.

*   *   *

The concept of ideology as false consciousness is frequently cited but infrequently explored or applied in the Soviet instance. Karl Mannheim traced the history of the idea back to classical antiquity and ancient theology.[17] The Emperor Napoleon popularized "ideology" in its pejorative sense by dismissing the liberal French thinkers, Destutt de Tracy and his school of "idéologues"—really psychological philosophers—as impractical dreamers.[18] Hegel felt that human consciousness was fated to remain "false" or "imperfect" because people cannot understand their actual role in history until they can look back at it retrospectively.[19]

Marx of course made the concept of ideology an important element in his social model of historical materialism, asserting as early as *The German Ideology* of 1846 that the social reality of classes and the class struggle governs the formulation and influence of ideas:

> The ideas of the ruling class are in every epoch the ruling ideas. . . .
> Each new class which puts itself in the place of one ruling before it, is
> compelled, merely in order to carry through its aim, to represent its interest
> as the common interest of all the members of society, put in an ideal
> form; it will give its ideas the form of universality, and represent them
> as the only rationally, universally valid ones.[20]

However, Marx never quite formulated his approach to ideology in the crisp term "false consciousness." That, as Melvin Rader has pointed out, was the contribution of Engels, and only in a late letter: "Ideology is a process accomplished by the so-called thinker, consciously, indeed, but with a false consciousness," Engels wrote to the German Social-Democratic scholar Franz Mehring. "The real motives impelling him remain unknown to him, otherwise it would not be an ideological process at all"—an intriguing anticipation of the Freudian unconscious. Engels then focussed this insight on "the bourgeois illusion of the eternity and the finality of capitalist production"; the great error was to regard the laissez-faire philosophy of the eighteenth-century physiocrats and Adam Smith "not as the reflection in thought of changed economic facts but as the finally achieved correct understanding of actual conditions subsisting always and everywhere."[21] No one yet imagined that socialism, in its turn, could convert its own ideology into a false consciousness that would express the momentary interests of the ruling elite as universal and eternal truths.

While subsequent Marxist thought devoted much attention to the relation between the socioeconomic base of society and its ideological superstructure, little effort seems to have been made until well after the Russian Revolution to work out the implications of false consciousness. Plekhanov, addressing the frequent discrepancy between conscious understanding and the state of the forces of production, did allude to the triumph of capitalist inequality in the French Revolution under the banner of universal principles of freedom and equality.[22] Eduard Bernstein noted how the Social Democrats often acted contrary to their theory, though he underestimated the staying power of verbal formulas: "A theory or declaration of principle which does not allow attention being paid at every stage of development to the actual interests of the working classes, will always be set aside. . . ."[23] Alexander Bogdanov, without doubt the most original of Russian Marxists, took an extreme relativist position that foreshadowed what Gramsci was to say about Marxist ideology a quarter of a century later: "Any given ideological form," positive though its role might be, "can have only a historically transitory meaning, not an objectively supra-historical meaning. . . . Marxism includes the denial of the unconditional objectivity of any truth whatsoever," no exception being made for Marxism itself.[24] But no one before 1917 grasped the possibility of a systematic attachment to a false or deceptive image of reality to justify a postbourgeois social order.

A very early critique of the Soviet regime from a Marxist standpoint came from Karl Kautsky. He argued as early as 1919 that the Bolshevik experiment was headed toward Caesarism and de facto counterrevolution, thanks to the one-party dictatorship and the immaturity of the Russian proletariat.[25] Otto Bauer anticipated the same tendency almost as early; he wrote in 1921 of "a sort of technocracy, the hegemony of the engineers, of the economic managers and the state bureaucracy."[26] By 1930, when Stalin's new revolution was in full swing, Kautsky adjudged the Soviet system to be a new sort of feudal hierarchy, headed by the Communist Party bureaucracy as a "new class"—the first application of that term to the Soviet system—that ruled through its control of state property.[27] But the Stalinist system was still not linked to the "ideological" use of Marxism.

György Lukács used the term "false consciousness," but only to describe the limited outlook of the individual worker who could not rise to a clear view of the whole social situation.[28] His highly voluntarist reading of Marxism-Leninism, with its emphasis on the role of force and the instrumental function of historical materialism in the class struggle, came close to anticipating how Stalin would actually operate—

and perhaps that explains why the Soviets condemned his *Geschichte und Klassenbewusstsein* so emphatically: it was not a sufficiently false version of the ideology to serve their purposes. Meanwhile, Lukács had a direct influence on Karl Mannheim's formulation of the more general theory of ideology; as the connection has been described by Morris Watnick,

> It was Lukács' highly instrumental Marxism . . . which suggested to Mannheim that *all* social and political doctrines which pass for knowledge might better be regarded as "existentially determined" doctrines, i.e., as elaborate rationalisations of group interests—mainly the interests of classes— which must 'distort' the actualities of social life if they are to serve those interests effectively.[29]

For the first direct application of the theory of ideology to the Soviet system we have to turn to Gramsci. In his critical comments on Bukharin's *Historical Materialism* that appear early in the *Prison Notebooks*, Gramsci observed, "The meaning which the term 'ideology' has assumed in Marxist philosophy implicitly contains a negative value judgment," reaching in its extreme form "the assertion that every ideology is 'pure' appearance, useless, stupid, etc."[30] (This understanding of ideology, incidentally, approaches the prevailing view of ideology in the United States, which prides itself on being a very unideological society though in fact an ideological false consciousness—in this case the myth of competitive capitalism according to Adam Smith—is deeply embedded in the national mentality. Far from arriving at the "end of ideology," the United States is so ideological that it is not even aware of the fact.)

Gramsci went on to distinguish the two different meanings that "ideology" had for him: it could be either "the necessary superstructure of a particular structure," or "the arbitrary lucubrations of particular individuals." Then he made a comment that is extraordinary for that date: "If the philosophy of praxis [Marxism] affirms theoretically that every 'truth' believed to be eternal and absolute has had practical origins and has represented a 'provisional' value . . . , it is still very difficult to make people grasp 'practically' that such an interpretation is valid also for the philosophy of praxis itself." Gramsci was addressing Bukharinism, but unknowingly anticipating Stalinism: "As a result, even the philosophy of praxis tends to become an ideology in the worst sense of the word, that is to say a dogmatic system of eternal and absolute truths."[31]

Trotsky's postexile critique of Stalinism was more trenchant than Gramsci's in concrete social terms, though less so in the theoretical respect. "Stalinist Bonapartism" was "a contradictory society halfway between capitalism and socialism," in which "under a socialist banner . . . the bureaucracy . . . painstakingly conceals the real relations both in town and country with abstractions from the socialist dictionary."[32] Bruno Rizzi took Trotsky's critique further towards its logical conclusion by frankly stating that the Soviet Union was "neither bourgeois nor proletarian" but had fallen under the domination of the bureaucracy as a class, exploiting the masses through the collectivized property that it controlled.[33] The American Trotskyist James Burnham broke with the Marxist schema altogether, to assert that the USSR represented "a new structure of society—managerial society, a new order of power and privilege which is not capitalist and not socialist." It was only one case in an international trend legitimized by various different ideologies— "Leninism-Stalinism; fascism-nazism; and at a more primitive level, by New Dealism." Here Burnham clearly grasped the notion of false consciousness: "Leninism-Stalinism ('Bolshevism') is not a scientific hypothesis but a great social ideology rationalizing the social interests of the new rulers and making them acceptable to the minds of the masses."[34]

Milovan Djilas, echoing in *The New Class* (1957) what we might term the neo-Trotskyist theory of bureaucratic class rule, gave it international renown. He made the function of ideology even clearer: "The so-called socialist ownership is a disguise for the real ownership by the political bureaucracy. . . . The promise of an ideal world increased the faith in the ranks of the new class and sowed illusions among the masses." False consciousness, Djilas suggested, was a weakness of human nature— "Every ideology, every opinion, tries to represent itself as the only true and complete one"—and then he turned the proposition against the verities intolerantly pronounced by Marx and Engels themselves.[35] The Hungarian dissidents György Konrad and Ivan Szelenyi go so far as to direct "false consciousness" against the intellectuals as a class: "The intellectuals of every age have described themselves ideologically in accordance with their particular interests . . . , to represent their particular interests in each context as the general interests of mankind." Their aim is clear: "to maintain their monopoly of their role."[36]

The most coherent development of the concept of Stalinist false consciousness has been the work of the Yugoslav social theorists in and around the "Praxis" group, following implicitly in the wake of Trotsky and Djilas. Veljko Korać, proceeding from the familiar Yugoslav critique of Soviet bureaucratism and "étatism," wrote in 1964 of Stalinism and the "ascendency of the technobureaucracy" as the outcome of attempting socialism in a backward country. "This led to an absolutizing of politics and to its conversion into a specific mythology and theology. . . . In the name of Marxism, Stalin distorted Marx's ideas into a closed system of dogmas making of himself the sole and absolute interpreter of those dogmas."[37] The more official theorist Najdan Pašić called Stalinist ideology "a pragmatic-bureaucratic revision and dogmatization of Marxism carried to the extreme."[38] Stojanović, in his work *Between Ideals and Reality* of 1969, elaborates the point: "In the degeneration of the October Revolution there developed a new class system—étatism—which is still being successfully legitimized ideologically as socialism. True Marxists," he adds, "have the duty of breaking through that curtain of myth to the statist reality. Its paradigm is Stalinist society."[39] In another connection Stojanović writes, "The world is governed ideologically by those who possess the power to assign names to social phenomena."[40] Branko Horvat refers to a "theological socialism . . . masquerading as science," again the consequence of attempting to achieve socialism in a backward country. "Scientific ideology provides a justification for, and so an efficient defense of, established interests,"[41] i.e., of the counterrevolution of étatism. Zagorka Golubović concludes even more directly, "A special place and role belong to Stalinist ideology, which is a necessary, integral part of the Stalinist order, because it preserves its legitimacy, through ideology as a justification of the position of the ruling class."[42]

Italian Eurocommunist thinking has closely paralleled the Yugoslav view. Boffa concludes in his history, "Ideological orthodoxy . . . actually represented the consciousness—or if you prefer, the 'false consciousness'—of the whole directing stratum of Soviet society."[43] This means, he contends in a later work, that "Marxist theory was in practice for Stalin . . . an instrument of power, manipulated by him casually at the moment of any changeable demand of policy. Theoretical concerns were manifested by Stalin only to the extent that they served to justify practice."[44]

Soviet critics in the Marxist tradition have been inclined along with the Yugoslavs to explain Stalinist ideology in religious terms. Roy Medvedev, recognizing how Stalin had been "masking his power in ultrarevolutionary phrases," suggests in *Let History Judge* that with "the deification of Stalin . . . the social consciousness of the people took on elements of religious psychology. Perceptions of reality were distorted." The petty bourgeoisie and the degenerated bureaucracy "prefer dogmatism, which frees them from the need to think."[45] In a later context Medvedev laments the "dogmatization of Marxism," and asserts, "The USSR is the last great religious state on earth."[46] The religious analogy has been echoed in a variety of Western discussions, though this line of argument leads away from the recognition of Stalinism as class ideology.[47] Under perestroika the theme has even been stated publically in the Soviet Union and Eastern Europe: a Soviet author, V. Chubinsky, introducing the first publication of Arthur Koestler's *Darkness at Noon* in the USSR, referred to the "idolatrous mode of thought" of Stalinism,[48] and a Polish writer, Zbigniew Safjan, has remarked on its "magic, liturgical language. . . . In Stalinist times, there was a magic code for reality that had nothing in common with reality. It was spoken, and therefore it must be."[49]

* * *

The description of Stalinism as ideological false consciousness invites some refinement. Mannheim distinguishes two senses of "ideology," the "particular" and the "total." Ideology in the "total" sense denotes "the characteristics and composition of the total structure of the mind of this epoch or this group." In the "particular" sense it refers to ideas "regarded as more or less conscious disguises of a situation. . . . These distortions range all the way from conscious lies to half-conscious and unwitting disguises; from calculated attempts to dupe others to self-deception."[50] This distinction is virtually identical with the one drawn independently and almost simultaneously by Gramsci between the "necessary super-structure" and "arbitrary lucubrations."

Martin Seliger has more recently elaborated the point as a contrast between the "restrictive conception" of ideology (including the Marxist view) as denoting "specific . . . , extremist belief systems and parties," and the "inclusive conception" that extends it to "all political belief systems . . . , sets of ideas by which men posit, explain, and justify ends and means of organized social action, and specifically political action, irrespective of whether such action aims to preserve, amend, uproot or rebuild a given order."[51] In the broader sense, ideology thus extends far enough to embrace the familiar notions of culture in an-thropology and frame of reference in psychology, insofar as either concept impinges on the political realm.[52]

Both senses of ideology apply to the Soviet situation under Stalin. On the one hand, as the manipulative contrivance of an individual or clique, Stalinist ideology corresponded to the "particular" or "arbitrary" or "restrictive" conception of ideology, formed with a greater or lesser degree of self-deception to provide political cover and self-satisfaction for the regime. On the other hand, when Stalinized Marxism was imposed on society as a whole to the exclusion of any independent forms of political thought, even Marxist, it assumed the "inclusive" role of "total ideology" or "necessary superstructure," even if it was Ersatz. Thus, Stalinism extended the arbitrary false consciousness of ideology from the sphere of individual thinking to the mental life of the whole society. As Rudolf Bahro has noted in his treatise on bureaucratic Communism, "The party organization of today is a structure that *actively produces false consciousness on a massive scale.*"[53]

The ideological desert of the Stalin and Brezhnev eras has been well described by Lukács, who finally awoke to the real nature of Stalinist ideology after the Twentieth Party Congress: "In the conditions of intellectual centralization which he created it was impossible for any theory to be firmly established unless it was at least authorized by him. . . . Stalin's unscrupulousness in this matter reached the point of altering the theory itself if necessary." Lukács was among the first to grasp the totally instrumental place of ideology in Stalinist behavior:

> Principles were simplified and vulgarized according to the exigencies (often purely notional) of practice. . . . Because Stalin wanted to maintain at any cost a continuity 'in quotation marks' with Lenin's work, not only facts but Leninist texts were distorted. . . . For him, in the name of *partiinost,* agitation is primary. Its needs determine . . . what science must say and how it must say it.[54]

This situation has not escaped the attention of Soviet observers who were set free by perestroika to draw the ultimate conclusions. Tatiana Zaslavskaya has spoken of "a false public consciousness," that "continued to reflect the revolution's lofty aims and fed the masses' enthusiasm," while "the forms" of "a complex tangle of social relations" have "more often than not . . . been at variance with their content," i.e. "indirect exploitation by the *nomenklatura* stratum of the remaining mass of the population."[55]

As a result of the long history of single-minded efforts to indoctrinate the Soviet public, the arbitrary ideological assertions of Stalinism, *faute de mieux,* were genuinely absorbed by large numbers of the Soviet political class as their world view, to the exclusion of any overt exercise of their own critical faculties. This Stalinist false consciousness was not the spontaneous product of the class structure, as the Marxian classics suggested, but rather a forcible imposition by the party-state that was accepted by the officialdom with a varying mixture of cynicism and self-deception. Its real implantation in the minds of that group is testified to by the strength of conservative resistance to the "new thinking" of perestroika.

Historically speaking, the ideological superstructure of a society is not entirely and automatically a matter of false consciousness. The reality is far more complex. Theorists up to Stalin's time, when they addressed false consciousness at all, always saw it as a more or less natural development within a given socioeconomic formation. This is often true, but the gap between ideology and reality can vary widely. Under Stalin, as a counterrevolutionary leader committed to a revolutionary ideology and armed with the power to command any form of belief he chose, the relationship was different. In this case the state imposed false consciousness—in other words, official lies—and inculcated it so effectively that it remains part of the mental equipment of a large part of articulate Soviet society.

Notes

1. Karl Marx, "Speech on The Hague Congress," Amsterdam, 8 September 1872, in Marx, *Political Writings*, vol. III, *The First International and After* (New York: Vintage Books, 1974), p. 324.

2. Friedrich Engels, 1895 introduction to Marx, *The Class Struggles in France, 1848–1850*, in Marx, *Selected Works* (New York: International Publishers, n.d.), vol. II, pp. 188–189.

3. On Stalin's early use of ideology, see above, ch. 3.

4. Giuseppe Boffa, *Storia dell'Unione Sovietica* (Milan: Mondadori, 1976), vol. I, p. 613.

5. Resolution of the Second All-Union Conference of Marxist-Leninist Research Institutions, April 1929, "O sovremennykh voprosakh filosofii marksizma-leninizma" (On Contemporary Problems of the Philosophy of Marxism-Leninism), *Pod Znamenem Marksizma*, no. 5, 1929, pp. 7–8.

6. Stalin, "Some Questions Concerning the History of Bolshevism," Stalin, *Problems of Leninism* (Moscow: Foreign Languages Publishing House, 1953), pp. 483–484.

7. On Stalin's revision of Marxism, see above, ch. 10.

8. Milovan Djilas, *The New Class* (New York: Praeger, 1957). On Rakovsky, see above, pp. 178–179.

9. G. P. Maximoff, ed., *The Political Philosophy of Bakunin: Scientific Anarchism* (Glencoe, Ill.: Free Press, 1953), p. 288.

10. See, e.g., Marx, *The Eighteenth Brumaire of Louis Bonaparte* (New York: International Publishers, 1926), pp. 130–131, and *The Civil War in France* (Chicago: Kerr, n.d.), p. 42.

11. "A. Volskii" [pseudonym], *Umstvennyi rabochii* (Geneva: [s.n.], 1905).

12. See Sheila Fitzpatrick, "The Bolsheviks' Dilemma: Class, Culture, and Politics in the Early Soviet Years," *The Slavic Review*, XLVII:4 (winter 1988).

13. See Vilfredo Pareto, *The Mind and Society* (4 vols., New York: Harcourt, Brace, 1935), vol. III, pp. 1421–1432.

14. Anton Pannekoek (*De Arbeidersraden*, Amsterdam: Van Gennep/DeVlam, 1946) and Bruno Rizzi (*La Bureaucratisation du monde*, Paris: Hachette, 1939) were among the first writers to advance this argument. For a more recent version, see Michael Voslensky, *Nomenklatura: The Soviet Ruling Class* (Garden City, N.Y.: Doubleday, 1984), pp. 112–118.

15. Robert V. Daniels, "Intellectuals and the Russian Revolution," *American Slavic and East European Review*, XXII:2 (April 1961).

16. Svetozar Stojanović, "Marxism and Democracy: The Ruling Class or the Dominant Class?" *Praxis International*, VI:2 (July 1981); Antonio Gramsci, "Notes on Italian History," in *Selections from the Prison Notebooks of Antonio Gramsci,*

ed. Quentin Hoare and G. N. Smith (New York: International Publishers, 1971), pp. 104–105. Pareto anticipated the distinction when he wrote of "governing elites and non-governing elites." *The Mind and Society,* vol. III, p. 1423.

17. Karl Mannheim, *Ideology and Utopia: An Introduction to the Sociology of Knowledge* (Bonn, 1929, New York: Harcourt, Brace, 1936), pp. 70–71.

18. Ibid., pp. 71–72.

19. See George Lichtheim, *The Concept of Ideology and Other Essays* (New York: Random House, 1967), p. 15.

20. Marx and Engels, *The German Ideology* (New York: International Publishers, 1947), pp. 39–41.

21. Engels to Franz Mehring, 14 July 1893, Marx and Engels, *Selected Correspondence, 1846–1895* (New York: International Publishers, 1942), pp. 511–512; Melvin Rader, *Marx's Interpretation of History* (New York: Oxford University Press, 1979), p. 42.

22. Georgi Plekhanov, *The Materialist Conception of History* (New York: International Publishers, 1940), p. 34.

23. Eduard Bernstein, *Evolutionary Socialism* (New York: Schocken Books, 1961), p. 205.

24. Aleksandr Bogdanov, *Empiriomonizm* (St. Petersburg: Dorovatovsky & Charushnikov, 1905), book 1, pp. 40–41. Cf. Zenovia Sochor, *Revolution and Culture: The Bogdanov-Lenin Controversy* (Ithaca, N.Y.: Cornell University Press, 1988), pp. 68–72.

25. See Massimo L. Salvadori, *Karl Kautsky and the Socialist Revolution, 1880–1938* (London: New Left Books, 1979), p. 261ff.

26. Otto Bauer, *Kapitalismus und Sozialismus nach dem Weltkrieg* (Vienna, 1921), p. 154, quoted in Christine Buci-Glucksman, "L'Austro-marxisme," Lily Marcou, ed., *L'Urss vue de gauche* (Paris: Presses Universitaires de France, 1982), p. 90.

27. Salvadori, *Karl Kautsky,* pp. 288–292; Kautsky, *Der Bolschewismus in der Sackgasse* (Berlin: Dietz, 1930), pp. 65–69, and "Die Aussichten des Sozialismus in Sowjet-Russland" (The Prospects for Socialism in Soviet Russia), *Die Gesellschaft,* VIII:2 (1931), pp. 437–438.

28. See Tom Bottomore, "Class Structure and Social Consciousness," in Istvan Meszaros, ed., *Aspects of History and Class Consciousness* (London: Routledge & Kegan Paul, 1971), p. 52.

29. Morris Watnick, "Georg Lukács: An Intellectual Biography," *Soviet Survey,* July–September 1958, p. 63.

30. Gramsci, "Problems of Philosophy and History," *Prison Notebooks,* p. 376.

31. Gramsci, "Some Problems in the Study of the Philosophy of Praxis," *Ibid.,* pp. 406–407.

32. Leon Trotsky, *The Revolution Betrayed: What is the Soviet Union and Where is it Going?* (New York: Doubleday, Doran, 1937), pp. 238, 244–245, 255.

33. Rizzi, *La Bureaucratisation du monde,* pp. 29–35.

34. James Burnham, The Managerial Revolution (New York: John Day, 1941), pp. 65, 185.

35. Djilas, *New Class,* pp. 47, 124.

36. George Konrad and Ivan Szelenyi, *The Intellectuals on the Road to Class Power* (New York: Harcourt Brace Jovanovich, 1979), p. 14.

37. Veljko Korać, "Socialism in Underdeveloped Countries," *Praxis*, no. 2–3, 1964, p. 301.

38. Najdan Pašić, "Suština i smisao borbe jugoslovenskih komunista protiv staljinizma" (The Essence and Meaning of the Struggle of the Yugoslav Communists Against Stalinism), *Socijalizam*, XII:5 (May 1969), p. 634.

39. Svetozar Stojanović, *Izmedju ideala i stvarnosti* (Belgrade: Prosveta, 1969), p. 13.

40. Stojanović, "Marxism and Democracy," p. 106.

41. Branko Horvat, *The Political Economy of Socialism: A Marxist Social Theory* (Armonk, N.Y.: M. E. Sharpe, 1982), pp. 28–29, 43–46.

42. Zagorka Golubović, *Staljinizam i Socijalizam* (Belgrade: Philosophical Society of Serbia, 1982), p. 283.

43. Boffa, *Storia dell'Unione Sovietica*, vol. II, p. 595.

44. Boffa, *Il fenomeno Stalin nella storia del XX secolo: Le interpretazioni dello Stalinismo* (Rome–Bari: Laterza, 1982), pp. 259–260.

45. Medvedev, *Let History Judge: The Origins and Consequences of Stalinism* (New York: Knopf, 1971), pp. 362, 363, 375, 418.

46. Medvedev, *On Soviet Dissent: Interviews with Piero Ostellino* (New York: Columbia University Press, 1980), pp. 88, 146.

47. See, e.g., Bruce Mazlish, *The Meaning of Karl Marx* (New York: Oxford University Press, 1984); Lorenzo Infantino, "Marx e il regno di Dio—senza Dio" (Marx and the Kingdom of God—Without God), *Mondoperaio*, November 1985.

48. *Neva*, no. 7, July 1988.

49. *The New York Times*, 15 July 1988, reporting on Mikhail Gorbachev's meeting with Polish intellectuals.

50. Mannheim, *Ideology and Utopia*, pp. 55–56.

51. Martin Seliger, *Ideology and Politics* (New York: Free Press, 1976), p. 14.

52. See Paul Ricoeur, *Lectures on Ideology and Utopia* (New York: Columbia University Press, 1986), esp. pp. 119–120, 254–258.

53. Rudolf Bahro, *The Alternative in Eastern Europe* (New York: Schocken Books, 1978), p. 247.

54. Georg Lukács, "Reflections on the Cult of Stalin," in E. San Juan, ed., *Marxism and Human Liberation: Essays on History, Culture, and Revolution by Georg Lukács* (New York: Dell, 1973), pp. 66–69.

55. Tatiana Zaslavskaya, "Tochka zreniya: Perestroika kak sotsial'naya revoliutsiya" (Viewpoint: Restructuring as a Social Revolution), *Izvestia*, 24 December 1988 (*Current Digest of the Soviet Press*, vol. 40, no. 51, 18 January 1989, pp. 2–3).

About the Book and Author

As attempts to reform the Soviet system under the banner of perestroika are clouded by mounting uncertainty, there has been a resurgence of interest within the Soviet Union and around the globe in the forces, ideas, and circumstances that contributed to the Stalinist inheritance. The investigation of possible historical alternatives to that system and the early debates over the meaning of "socialism" and its variants have become vital concerns in the Soviet Union today. These issues have been central to the work of Robert V. Daniels. In this book he offers a selection of his writings—mostly unpublished or unavailable in English—on the formative period of the Soviet political and economic system. The focus of his essays is on the two commanding personalities that dominated the Soviet scene after Lenin: Trotsky, the flamboyant theorist, and Stalin, the vindictive pragmatist.

Robert V. Daniels is professor emeritus of history at the University of Vermont, where he taught for over thirty years and served as department chairman. He was elected vice president of the American Association for the Advancement of Slavic Studies for 1991 and president for 1992.

Index